DATE DUE

JUL 09 2008			

BALDNESS
A Social History

by

KERRY SEGRAVE

McFarland & Company, Inc., Publishers
Jefferson, North Carolina, and London

The present work is a reprint of the library bound edition of Baldness: A Social History, *first published in 1996 by McFarland.*

LIBRARY OF CONGRESS CATALOGUING-IN-PUBLICATION DATA

Segrave, Kerry, 1944–
    Baldness : a social history / by Kerry Segrave.
        p.   cm.
    Includes bibliographical references and index.

    ISBN 978-0-7864-4079-5
    softcover : 50# alkaline paper

    1. Baldness—History.   I. Title.
RL155.S44   2009
616.5'46—dc20   95-47375

British Library cataloguing data are available

Cover photograph ©2008 Shutterstock

Manufactured in the United States of America

McFarland & Company, Inc., Publishers
    Box 611, Jefferson, North Carolina 28640
    www.mcfarlandpub.com

CONTENTS

PREFACE

This book is about male pattern baldness (MPB), often referred to as alopecia in the past. Something on the order of 90 percent plus of all baldness falls into that category and is the result of heredity and hormones culminating in hair loss in men at the front of the scalp or crown of the head, with a fringe remaining on the sides and back.

In my research, which was done at the UCLA library system and the Los Angeles Public Library, I have looked at the social history of baldness primarily for the last one hundred and twenty years. I have considered theories of the causes of baldness, cures of hair loss from the medical establishment, various kinds of quackery and attitudes toward rugs, plugs, and drugs.

Chapter 1 is a brief summary of baldness in ancient times as well as a summary of current opinion on the prevalence of baldness in men and how it occurs. Chapters 2 and 3 look at a variety of theories advanced by credible medical personnel about the causes of baldness that range from widely held, long-lived theories such as the idea that hats cause baldness to eccentric theories held by few, such as the idea that certain kinds of breathing cause baldness. Cures advanced by medical science are the focus of Chapter 4, while Chapter 5 is given over to quackery. The following three chapters deal with wigs, weaves, implants, transplants, and flaps. Chapter 9 covers hair loss among celebrities and politicians, Chapter 10 covers attitudes and psychology about baldness in general. Finally, Chapter 11 is about the most publicized hair loss treatment in history—Rogaine.

1

BALD FACTS
AND FICTIONS

A bald-headed man is seldom found in an insane asylum.
Literary Digest, February 4, 1928

To see a bald-headed man denotes that sharpers are to make
a deal adverse to your interests, but by keeping wide awake,
you will outwit them.
Gustavus Hindman Miller,
10,000 Dreams Interpreted

One of the earliest overreactions by a baldie concerned the prophet Elisha. In the second book of Kings, Chapter 2, it is recorded; "And he went up from thence unto Bethel: and as he was going up by the way, there came forth little children out of the city, and mocked him, and said unto him, Go up, thou bald head; go up, thou bald head. And he turned back, and looked on them, and cursed them in the name of the Lord. And there came forth two she bears out of the wood, and tare forty and two children of them."[1]

Dr. Condict Cutler reported that the annoyed Elisha immediately sought relief for his condition by applying bear grease to his head. In Cutler's view the grease must have been effective in restoring Elisha's hair because there were no more references to his bald head. Bear grease remained a popular remedy for baldness over time. It was reportedly very popular in the 1500s. Its appeal lay in the fact that bears were very hairy creatures.[2]

The first known written medical record is the Ebers Papyrus, penned around 1500 B.C. One of its recipes to be applied to the bald area was a mixture containing the fat of a lion, a hippopotamus, a crocodile, a cat, and a serpent. A second recipe from the eleven given for baldness advised the sufferer to apply a mixture of burned prickles of a hedgehog immersed in oil, fingernail scrappings, and a potpourri of honey, alabaster, and red ocher, all with appropriate incantations.[3]

Julius Caesar was very sensitive about his baldness, fearing he was losing his powers along with his hair. Desperately he attempted to regain his hair by the use of massages and tonics. One popular remedy in his day was to rub berries of myrrh into the scalp. Roman coins showed that Caesar vainly tried to minimize his baldness. Thus he became one of the earliest baldies to resort to what much later came to be known as "illusion styling" of the hair. Roman biographer Suetonius reported in his *Lives of the Caesars* that Caesar's "baldness was a disfigurement which troubled him greatly…. Because of it he used to comb forward his scanty locks from the crown of his head, and of all the honors voted him by the Senate and the people, there was none which he received or made use of more gladly than the privilege of wearing a laurel wreath at all times." Suetonius observed that Romans who failed to grow hair with potions generally bought wigs. While Caesar worried about his powers receding with his hair, the groundwork for a contradictory image was also being fostered— that of baldies being more virile sexually than the hairy. When Julius Caesar entered Rome in triumph, it was the polite custom to carol, "Romans, guard your wives: the bald adulterer comes!"[4]

The Roman poet Ovid was no fan of the aesthetics of baldness, for he wrote, "A field without grass is an eyesore, so is a tree without leaves, so is a head without hair." More stoic about the condition was Roman poet Martial, who said, "Be content to seem what you really are and let the barber shave off the rest of your hair." Along the same lines, he added, "There is nothing more shocking than a bald man with a wig on." Martial even had something to say on the very early use of illusion styling. Admonishing a friend, he said: "You collect your straggling hairs on either side, Marinius, endeavoring to conceal the vast expanse of your shining bald pate by the locks which still grow on your temples. Why not confess yourself an old man? There is nothing more contemptible than a bald man who pretends to have hair."[5]

Other notable baldies from the past were Socrates, Napoleon, St. Paul, many other saints, Hippocrates, Aesculapius, and the mummy of Pharaoh Rameses II of Egypt, which showed crown and frontal baldness. The physician Hippocrates believed the answer to baldness was to be found in a mixture of opium and essence of roses blended into an ointment with wine, oil of acacia juice, or unripe olives. He was the first person to describe the pattern male baldness commonly took, but he had no idea what caused the hair loss. Aristotle, however, thought sexual intercourse caused baldness. He was bald and hated it. Hippocrates also applied sheep's urine to his bald spot, to no avail. Keeping to an excrement theme, early Romans plastered their scalps with chicken dung. Napoleon started to go bald at 23. Once he met with Czar Alexander of Russia to discuss the future of Europe, but the two leaders instead ended up talking about the latest cures for baldness. One ancient remedy featured dogs' paws, dates, and asses' hooves as the main ingredients. A first-century physician suggested the cure could be found in boiling snakes alive and then rubbing the broth into the bald areas. At a fifteenth-century symposium called De Capelli e Peli that concerned the scalp and hair, the blame for baldness was placed on "miasmi pestiferi"—air pollution.[5]

Wigs and toupees were common at least as far back as the days of the Ebers Papyrus because baldness was considered a sign of servitude or immorality by all ancient nations. From time to time, there was a backlash against that attitude with artificial baldness, the shaved head, becoming a fashionable mark of rank or religion. Even in that era, headgear was sometimes blamed for causing baldness. Heavy metal helmets were blamed for causing baldness among Egyptian and Roman soldiers. A number of kings retained bald jesters, the better to tease them.

During one ancient Greek battle, the Lycians were defeated. Their conqueror Mausoleus directed all the vanquished men to shave their heads, an extremely humiliating punishment. Keenly aware of their ridiculous appearance, the Lycians were able to bribe a general to allow them to import wigs. The modern day military organizations of most countries routinely shave the heads of all recruits. The basis for this practice may lie in hygiene—it is easier to control for lice, for example—but it also symbolizes the recruits' lack of power and their passive submission.

Monks have shaved the crowns of their heads in the familiar tonsure shape for centuries as a symbol of their devotion, submission, and humility. The bald spot was supposed to indicate where God reached down from the heavens and touched the monk with his vocation. In the tenth century, a monk named Hucbaldi of St. Armand wrote a poem called "In Praise of Baldness." Samson's strength was linked to his hair. When Delilah shaved his head, his strength vanished and he was captured by the Philistines. Only when his hair had grown back was he strong enough to tear down the temple, destroying the Philistines and himself.

The scalping of a slain enemy did not originate with the North American Indian. Ancient groups such as the Scythians and Visigoths took the topknot in battle because he who took the hair of a slain enemy took onto himself all the strength and courage of that enemy. Prisoners and traitors have also had their heads shaved across time to announce their utter dreghood. In medieval England the life span of an individual was estimated by the hair on his forehead. If the hair grew low on the forehead and receded above the temples, it was believed to indicate a long life.[7]

Samuel Johnson got his shot in at baldies in 1778. He argued they were stupid, saying, "The cause of baldness in man is dryness of the brain, and its shrinking from the skull." It was bad enough that baldies were mocked, but worse still that they had to endure some of the "cures" for the condition. Earlier that same century, animal remedies were recommended in Scotland: "(1) Ashes of little frogs burnt applied suddenly cureth the Fall of the Hair. (2) The burnt ashes of Bees with Oyl anointed on the bald Place. (3) Wash the Head with a Dog's urine, and you shall not be bald. (4) Burnt ashes of Goat's-dung anointed with Oyl multiplieth Hair." Writing in 1716, John Moncrief recommended washing the head often with the middle bark of an elm tree, which he said, "causeth to make the Hair grow effectually."[8]

Other items used to treat baldness over time included watercress, onions, cholesterol, cortisone, and creosote. John Wesley offered this cure in 1814: "Rub the part morning and evening with onions till it be red; and rub it afterwards with honey, or wash it with a decoction of box-wood." Wesley claimed to have used this remedy himself. In Rouen, France, the mystic number three was combined with a plant remedy: baldies were advised to walk three times against the sun around an elder bush to cure the condition. An elaborate 1849 remedy advised the afflicted to take snails out of their gardens and pound them with horse leeches, bees, wasps and salt. This mixture was to be buried for eight days in a hot bed and then applied to the bald spots.[9]

Occupational and class distinctions often were part of theories about who went bald. An English statistician who studied the influence of music on hair at the close of the last century came to some unusual conclusions. For the "liberal professions" generally, he concluded the proportion of bald men to be 11 percent. Musical composers, with 12 percent baldness, were almost right on the average. In the case of instrumental players, those who played the violin or piano had good heads of hair. This statistician stated, "The piano and the violin, especially the piano, have an undoubted preserving influence" on hair. Instruments such as the harp and double bass had lesser amounts of preserving ability, with the clarinet and flute exerting only a "feeble effect" as hair preservers, "not more than a fiftieth as strong" as the piano. Working in the other direction were the brass instruments, whose results were "deplorable." Coronets, trombones, and French horns had a notably "fatal" influence on hair. Players of these instruments were bald in a proportion much higher than average. So prevalent was baldness among members of regimental bands that the condition was called "trumpet baldness." It was also noted that in the professions physicians had the highest rate of baldness—30 percent.[10]

A physician in London, England, would have agreed with that assessment. In a letter to a friend, he lamented that despite all of his hard work he was a failure as a doctor because he lacked the necessary items for success in his field—money and a bald head. "I have no money and my hair is inconveniently thick," he explained. "Incipient baldness gives the appearance of a high and dome-like forehead and inspires the ladies with confidence. The fortunate possessor of this beautiful feature is pronounced very clever, which settles the matter. Besides, it is almost indispensable for a good bedside manner. All my medical friends who are getting on well have either money or bald heads; most of them have both." This complaining doctor fixed the commercial value of baldness at an extra £500 a year in income.[11]

The idea that baldness was more prevalent among the overclass was a common one. It both led to and reinforced theories that lack of hair was caused by mental activity or high intelligence. A writer for the *Medical Record* estimated in 1886 that at least half of all American-born men over 30 living in cities and engaged in business or the professions were bald. Cited as evidence was the view of the floor of the New York Stock Exchange from the visitors' gallery, which disclosed "a mob of shining pates belonging, as a rule, to rather young men."[12]

Writer Virgil Eaton thought along the same class lines. Over many years he made a personal study of churches, museums, and other institutions in all large Eastern cities as well as Chicago, St. Louis, and points west. Eaton visited all these places expressly to count heads. He found bald ones to be most plentiful in New York City, followed in decreasing order by Boston, Philadelphia, and Washington. When he attended Boston's Trinity Church, Eaton counted 71 bald men and 46 going that way in a group of 243 men. At King's Chapel in that city, he counted 38 bald men and 14 with some baldness in a group of 86 men. Sixty-three men turned out for a performance of the "Mikado"; 27 were bald, 10 had a tendency toward baldness. On two nights in a Boston theater, there were 46 percent and 42 percent bald heads among the men. For a performance of "Fra Diavolo" 38 percent were bald; 46 percent of the attendees at a Matthew Arnold lecture were missing some hair.

Contrasted with this were Eaton's observations at dime museums and cheap variety performances, where the underclass hung out. Of 30 men at the World's Museum, 8 were bald and 5 had a tendency toward baldness. Less than 25 percent had no hair or thin hair at the Windsor Theatre. Eaton noted that only 12 percent of the men at a boxing exhibition given by John L. Sullivan were bald. From his hundreds of observations over the years, Eaton concluded, "I have found that the higher the price of admission, and presumably the more refining nature of the performance, the larger the per cent of bald heads."[13]

Just before World War I, French physician Dr. Guelpa observed that peasants and workmen became bald less often and less rapidly than members of the leisure classes and hairdressers and barbers themselves. "Doctors who specialize in affections of the scalp are precisely those who generally lose their hair most quickly." A generation later, *Time* magazine stated: "Wiry, energetic men are apt to be shaggy. Dumpy, cunning men are apt to be bald."[14]

Class was still being discussed as a factor in baldness into the late 1970s. College professor George De Leon observed that in his youth derelicts in his Brooklyn neighborhood didn't seem to go bald. To test this theory, he and some of his students questioned a number of Bowery derelicts, some random men walking into or out of Bloomingdale's or along Fifth Avenue, and a group of college professors. All subjects were rated as either hairy, receding, bald pate, or totally bald. De Leon found that 71 percent of the professors fell into one of the three hair loss groups, as did 53 percent of the Fifth Avenue men and 36 percent of the derelicts. Factors such as race and ethnicity made no difference. In the 26 to 40 age range, the percentages of the groups who fell into one of the hair loss categories were as follows: professors 40 percent, Fifth Avenue 35 percent, derelicts 33 percent. For the 41 to 55 age group, the percentages were, respectively, 82, 84, and 44 percent. De Leon speculated that the difference must be the result of "alcohol and some resulting biochemical activity."[15]

Where you lived also made a difference. Dr. R.E.G. Armattoe of the Lomeshie Research Center in Londonderry, Ireland, reported to the American Association of Physical Anthropologists in 1948 that there were more bald young men in Sweden than in France. While he found Swedish baldness more common among educated men, he didn't attribute the cause to excessive brain work. The need to study baldness from the perspective of geography and occupation was self-evident to Armattoe. Researchers in the 1980s claimed that northern Europeans had a higher incidence of baldness than dark-haired residents of the Mediterranean area.[16]

Anyone worried about the state of his own hair could have turned to Dr. Alfred Copley of New York University for a scientific assessment. In 1948, Copley invented a machine which he christened a "pilometer." A hair on the head was attached to the machine, and a crank was then turned until the hair was pulled out of the head. A needle moved along a scale to indicate how much pressure was needed to pull out a hair—the firmness of attachment, as Copley called it. He speculated it would be possible to prove that hair on the heads of men going bald was less firmly attached to their scalps. Copley further reasoned that by measuring firmness of attachment before and after the application of some baldness cures, fake remedies could be singled out. If the firmness of attachment was greater after the treatment, it could be argued that the treatment was responsible. When Copley tested baldies, he found that hairs came out much more easily from their heads than from hairy heads. Because of a theory that baldness is much less common in Orientals, Copley tested subjects with his pilometer and found hair to be more firmly attached to Oriental scalps than to Caucasian ones. He also found hair on female heads to be more firmly attached than hair on male heads.[17]

Apparently baldness could also sweep through an area almost like an epidemic. Physicians at a Kittanning, Pennsylvania, meeting in 1926 announced they had received over 300 applications for baldness treatment from men between 19 and 30 years of age in just two weeks. Noted a report, "A strange malady ... is rapidly denuding the heads of the town's young men of hair." Doctors, having ruled out causes such as "barber's itch," were unable to explain the epidemic. They were baffled.[18]

Even Uncle Sam could not be depended on to provide safety from the condition. During World War II, an unidentified man was arrested in New York City for draft violations. He told authorities that he thought he couldn't trust the Army to stop his hair from thinning; therefore he didn't report for induction.[19]

Some writers looked beyond the sea of shining domes to place baldness within a larger framework. Back in 1886 a physician speculated in a medical journal that "The probabilities point to a race of hairless Americans, for baldness is extremely liable to be propagated in the male line, and to appear a little earlier in each generation." Increasing mental and physical strain found in the American way of life was supposedly to blame. In an equally gloomy statement in the popular press that same year, Virgil Eaton predicted, "If the present state of things continued, [men] will be bald-headed and toothless." Eaton claimed this would happen because men lived indoors, wore hats, and cut their hair too short, unlike their ancestors. Disuse would cause the hair and teeth to go the way of the dinosaur. Eaton's article generated a stir in its day. One medical journal used it to confirm the view that the future man would be a bald man and that "the percent of baldness is in direct proportion to amount of education and cultivation which a community receives." For that scribe, mundane reasons such as living indoors or wearing hats were unimportant. The major factor was our relentlessly increasing intelligence.[20]

A physician by the name of Dr. Gottheil also noted that "savages" in tropical climates who wore little or no headgear usually all had abundant crops of hair. He concluded: "Baldness is without doubt a disease of civilization and is one of the penalties attached to being an inhabitant of a progressive and cultural country. Perhaps the more civilized the country the more prevalent will baldness be, for extreme civilization infers a mode of life furthest removed from that of nature. Indeed, a lack of hair is almost synonymous with the acme of civilization and is one of the most annoying of the white man's burdens."[21]

In the 1920s, Greenpoint Hospital chief dermatologist Charles F. Pabst thought that while baldness was a modern phenomenon it was the result of very ancient race habits handed down through the ages. He thought heredity was involved, but only in the sense it was heritage from our ancestors centuries ago, who first discarded the habits and customs of the cave man. "Man is undergoing a gradual transformation…. The hair on our body is but the vestige of a former shaggy coat," he wrote. Because Pabst was convinced that baldness was due to nature's decree and was caused by the habits of our ancestors from centuries ago, he believed that men of his time could not correct baldness by not wearing a hat or by undergoing "unusual exposure." Pabst believed, "He would have had to start with his ancestors ages and ages ago and prevented them from wearing hats and adopting costumes which result in premature baldness to-day."[22]

Evolutionary gloominess on the topic persisted into the 1950s. Veronica L. Conley, assistant secretary of the American Medical Association Committee on Cosmetics, believed scientists were generally optimistic about an eventual solution to baldness, except for one factor, "In the course of evolution there has been a marked reduction in the amount of hair covering the human body. The loss of scalp hair may be part of an evolutionary trend. If this is true, future centuries will bring not a cure but the appearance of more and more bald men."[23]

When Chicago doctors Hans Elias and Adolph Brown studied the tissues of cadavers, they found a thick layer of fat under the skin of those with hair. Under the bald scalp, the fatty layer was absent. Theorizing that the fatty layer provided support for the follicles, they concluded, "The hair-bearing human is the fat head." The doctors believed the fat layer disappeared "because of an evolutionary trend toward higher skull dome in relation to the amount of face." It all caused a journalist to remark: "Persons who are bald may thus be a step ahead of the others on the evolutionary road that many predict will some day lead to complete baldness in all humans."[24]

A variation on the evolution theory was to be found in the *New York Times* in 1959. Gerald Walker noted the evolutionary theory that the ape man was superseded by the less shaggy primitive man, who gave way to the still less hairy modern man. He said one explanation for that theory was that ages ago the most hairy fellow was also the one with the most vermin. Those vermin may have killed off all but the least hairy by Darwinian natural selection.[25]

There were also those who tried to fit females into the evolutionary baldness landscape. One writer, E. Andrews, wrote in 1893 that there would be no chance of women falling victim to Eaton's bald and toothless future. Men had a "practical monopoly on baldness" despite the fact females often treated their hair badly and wore constricting hats. Elaborating, Andrews stated: "Women, as a general thing, enjoy much less vigorous health than men, eat less nourishing food—pickles and candy often constituting a large part of their diet—are more frequently sufferers from headaches, deficient circulation, general debility and yet, with all this, the sorriest specimens of the sex, physically, often luxuriate in the most abundant suits of hair." It was a seeming paradox easily explained under the Darwinian concept of sexual selection. Women, said Andrews, "will, as a general thing, marry anybody they think likely to give them a support, regardless of personal defects or attractions, men are more fastidious, and it goes without saying that a bald-headed woman would stand little chance, to use Mr. Darwin's argument, of bearing offspring to inherit her deficiencies." Thus bald men married as often as hair-bearers, passing on the trait, while men, finding bald women unattractive, "would not impregnate one even if they found one. Hence the trait is not passed on." Andrews was a female writer, incidentally.[26]

Others such as Dr. Woods Hutchinson agreed with that idea. Baldness did not hinder a man's success in life nor his ability to find a mate; thus the trait continued. One writer twisted Andrews's theory a little: Andrews argued baldies and hair-bearers competed equally, while the variation proponent argued that beards and baldness in men and beauty of face and hair in females were their respective attractions. He concluded, "Men may be bald because women admire and marry bald men." Within this framework baldies had at least a slight advantage competing for mates against the hair-bearers.[27]

In the 1980s, physiologist Michel Cabanac offered his evolutionary take for why men were bald. He hypothesized that male pattern baldness developed in the human species as a compensation for the growth of a beard in order to achieve heat loss. As the brain grew it produced more heat. While the beard—presumably a sexual signal—would have insulated the face in cold climates, it would have limited heat loss from the head during heat production. In order to compensate, men began to go bald to achieve better heat loss. Attempting to prove his hypothesis, Cabanac took measurements that indicated that the bald area on the head was proportional to the area of the beard, that a bald area sweat more than a hairy scalp, and that a bearded chin sweat less than a hairless chin. Describing these positive correlations to be "coherent measures," Cabanac concluded that his results "support the hypothesis that common baldness, far from being a disease, has developed as a compensation for the growth of a beard."[28]

What happened eons ago, though Cabanac, was that when very early humans left the warm countries of their origins to move to colder areas, they had to limit their heat loss by putting clothes on their bodies, which had been mostly naked. By doing that, they covered up their anatomical sexual signals. The beard may then have been positively selected as a sexual signal of mature men, easily recognizable by observers at a distance. Because the beard also limited heat loss from the head, Cabanac believed baldness may have developed in a parallel fashion, "thus increasing the heat loss capacity of the head."[29]

Today it is believed that the average head contains around 120,000 hairs; blonds average 150,000, brunettes 100,000 and redheads 90,000. Blond hairs are less coarse than the other two kinds but fall out more easily. In specialized cells such as hair follicles, cell division creates new cells which form along the periphery, crowding the older ones toward the center of the follicle. These flatten, attenuate, and turn into filaments of protein called keratin. It is this keratin which is the hair. Hair is strongly resistant to attack by almost all chemical and physical agents. Next to the skeleton, hair is the last part of the body to pass into oblivion. It is a nonliving structure, without nerves, composed mainly of a form of keratin, a horny type of tissue which is the main constituent of skin, nails, and the organic matrix of tooth enamel. Each hair on the head grows for three to five years and then enters a resting phase of around six months during which that hair remains attached but does not grow. When a new hair starts to grow, it pushes the old hair out. Researcher Julio Barman determined the percentage of hair in the resting phase ranged from 13 percent to 23 percent in the 16 to 48 year olds he studied, increasing with age. The average growth rate for hair is 3.44 mm in ten days, 0.344 mm per day. Another researcher stated that hair thinning (called shrinkage) averaged 10 percent per decade between the ages of 20 to 40 and then 20 percent per decade thereafter. This shrinkage was part of the normal aging process and had nothing to do with male pattern behavior.[30]

Looking at the percentage of men who were bald, one 1930 account stated that at least 50 percent of men under 30 showed distinct evidence of beginning baldness. A late 1950s account reported that common baldness afflicted 43 percent of American men and about 8 percent of women. A more thorough study estimated that for Caucasian males 47 percent of those in the third to fifth decade were defined as bald, and the number rose to 80 percent of those in the seventh and eighth decades. Overall the rate was 43 percent, and the rate for men between 35 and 44 was 34 percent. Researcher Muller admitted that a confusion between thinning and balding made baldness figures difficult to determine, particularly among older groups. Women had a baldness rate he also estimated to be 8 percent. Muller noted baldness was only around 15 percent in Chinese men and 25 percent in blacks. While he had no figures available for Eskimos or American Indians, he said, "There is general agreement that these racial groups have the lowest occurrence of common baldness."[31]

In the late 1970s, the *New York Times* wrote that cosmetically significant hair loss occurred in 12 percent of men who were 25, 37 percent of those who were 35, 45 percent of those who were 45; and 65 percent of those who were 65. Dr. Norman Orentreich estimated one-third of men in America were at least partly bald by 30, half by 50, and two-thirds by 60. Reporter Dan Carlinsky put the number of American men who suffered hair loss at 40 to 80 percent. One in five started balding rapidly in his 20s, one in five kept his hair forever, and the other three went bald at varying, slower rates. Edwin Kiester estimated that four out of five men in their 50s and 60s showed evidence of hair loss. Another article noted that one man in four was balding by 25, 50 percent by age 50, and 75 percent by age 75.

In baldness there is a progressive shrinkage of the follicles which produce an ever diminishing amount of hair. The growing phase is progressively shortened, resulting in shorter hairs, while the percentage of hairs in the resting phase increases. Eventually the hair produced by the declining follicle is a fragile, downy filament not unlike that of the lanugo of the newborn. Ultimately, the follicle becomes essentially abolished. Maturation and maintenance of scalp hairs are not dependent on androgens, unlike beard and pubic hair.[33]

The growth phase of a hair is called the anagen phase and lasts three to five years. The second phase, catagen, is a transitional one lasting ten days and leading quickly to the resting phase, telogen, which lasts four to six months. Hair literally thins as one ages; the diameter of the shaft decreases. Both men's and women's hair loses a little more than 5 percent of its thickness from age 20 to 50 and another 15 percent from age 50 to 70, according to one account. At puberty the gonads and adrenals secrete androgens in both male and females; the bulk is produced in the gonads. In most women baldness is held in check by female hormones which overpower the androgens they also have in their bodies. Some women find their hair thins rapidly after menopause when the production of female hormone drops. Eunuchs do not go bald. If they were adult and balding when castrated, the baldness is immediately arrested. If they later receive testosterone therapy, the balding process begins anew.[34]

It has always been a mystery to science how testosterone is necessary to maintain growth of beard hair yet not only is not necessary to support scalp hair growth but actually kills it. The latest theory comes from 1980s research which indicates that hair follicles, predestined by heredity to die, are able to metabolize testosterone into dihydrotestosterone (DHT), the male hormone that destroys the follicle. According to this theory, the conversion of testosterone occurs only if a catalytic enzyme called 5-alpha-reductase is present in the body. Some hair follicles have genetically programmed receptor sites for DHT that bind the hormone and ultimately die. Thus male pattern baldness in this theory has nothing to do with testosterone per se—only with its derivative DHT.[35]

2

HATS, IVORY DOMES, RAZORS, AND DANGEROUS BARBERS

Grass doesn't grow on a busy street.
Literary Digest, February 4, 1928

What He hath scanted men in hair, He hath given them in wit.
Shakespeare

The idea that hats caused baldness was one of the more popular, long-lived theories. At a very superficial level, it did appeal to common sense because hair loss was usually contained within the area covered by the hat. However, members of both sexes wore hats during the first half of this century and before. Men of the lower classes invariably wore soft hats or caps; it was only members of the upper classes who wore the stiff, hard top hat. No matter what type of hat was worn, it was removed immediately upon entry into a building. Finally, it was rare for the bald area to extend down to the point where the hat made contact with the head. Some proponents of the hat theory tried to argue around these inconsistencies; some simply ignored them.

Writing in a medical journal back in 1868, Dr. A.F.A. King argued hats were guilty because they compressed the circulation system, thus reducing nourishment to the hair. He thought baldness occurred in different places on men's heads due to differences in the shape of the head. In a wide-shaped head, balding might start at the crown; in a narrow shaped head, it might start at the front of the head. King even had an explanation for the little tuft of hair so often a feature on an otherwise bare scalp. The tuft remained because it was nourished by two arteries which escaped pressure since they passed under the forehead in an area of slight concavity. He argued that men went bald while women didn't because the latter didn't wear tight fitting hats and men wore their headgear longer since they spent more time outdoors. As a prophylactic

14

measure, King recommended hats be made to contact the head at points where "no considerable vessel would be compressed, or hats made to order for each individual might be arranged with a notch or semi-circular concavity in the rim over the spot of skin under which the artery passed."[1]

Virgil Eaton created a minor flap in 1886. At first he wrote that baldness should "yield to the laws of heredity as much as curly heads." Ignoring his own statement, Eaton then asserted the cause of baldness "to be no other than wearing tightly fitting head-coverings, living in-doors, and the lately developed habit of keeping the hair closely cropped." As evidence, he cited the "savage races" who lived outdoors most of the time, went bareheaded, and were never bald. Eaton believed hair was a protection for these people. When headgear came along, it took the place of this natural shield. No longer having a function to perform, hair began to fall away. If hair was to make a comeback, men "must stop making close crops, and must go bare-headed," insisted Eaton. Women were rarely bald, he believed, because they didn't "shingle" their hair in the fashion of the "sterner sex." He worried the recent fashion of "banging" and "frizzing" women's hair could lead to as many bald women as men. Because farmers did not engage in any fashionable hair care, said Eaton, they had "comparative freedom from baldness," but he cited no supporting evidence to show farmers were hairier than the general population. Using similar logic and analysis, Eaton argued teeth would fall away due to disease. As to man's future, he grimly predicted, "If the present state of things continues, he will be bald-headed and toothless."[2]

W. C. Gouinlock refuted some of Eaton's contentions a few months later in the same popular magazine. He dismissed heredity on the basis that women were entirely exempt from baldness even though they were subject to the same laws of heredity as men. Headgear per se couldn't be the cause because the custom of wearing warm coverings on the head had been common for a long time, as, for example, in European armies, where many men with close cropped hair wore heavy, warm headgear for a longer period of time than modern city dwellers, without the same tendency to baldness. Indoor life couldn't be a factor as women spent more time indoors than men. Close cropping of the hair also could not be a factor, thought Gouinlock, since the back and sides of the head didn't go bald even though those areas were more likely to be cut close. For this writer, baldness was due entirely to the "kind of hat that is worn, principally to the high hat and the hard felt hat but also to any other head-covering that constricts the blood-vessels which nourish the hair-bulbs."[3]

As evidence for the hard hat theory, Gouinlock pointed out that baldness started at the top of the head, where circulation was the weakest, and gradually descended to the hat band, where it stopped. "Mark this point, it never goes below the rim of the hat," he said. Although he admitted the line of denudation didn't correspond exactly with the hat band, he thought this occurred because differing head shapes afforded a cushion from pressure in some points. He asserted confidently: "I have never seen a person whose habitual head-covering was soft and yielding suffer from baldness.... I think it will be noticed that the most rapid cases are among city men with close cut hair who wear the high hat." In this theory, short hair might play an indirect role by providing less of a cushion against hat pressure than would long hair. Gouinlock agreed with Eaton's contention that farmers rarely went bald, but he thought it was because they wore loose headgear, while Eaton thought it was due to lack of hair styling. Singled out for blame was the hatter's instrument which marked on paper the outline of a customer's head so that the band could be molded to press uniformly all around. This practice was "more destructive of the natural head-coverings than ever were the scalping-knives of the North American Indians," thought Gouinlock. Although he scorned the high hat as ugly and unnatural, he agreed it was popular with men. Still, he cautioned, "let him remember, as he takes his after-dinner repose, that his favorite hat will certainly and inevitably extend the pasture-lands of the domestic fly."[4]

Stepping in to referee this scientific tussle was a *New York Times* editorialist, who dismissed Eaton's opinion and declared Gouinlock had set forth "the real cause of baldness."[5]

At a meeting of the New York County Medical Society in 1887, physician George Thomas Jackson read a paper in which he cited several factors in baldness. He argued, for example, that stiff hats caused baldness due to compression. Women didn't go bald because they didn't wear hats as often as men. When they did, the hats were not so tight-fitting and were made of permeable material. Women also had greater cushioning because "they preserve the cushion of fat under the scalp longer than men do."[6]

That medical society meeting erupted into a rancorous debate when Dr. George Henry Fox offered the thought that no hats of any type had anything to do with baldness. The society's president took indignant exception to that opinion, stating unequivocally and firmly that the wearing of stiff hats had a great deal to do with baldness. Fox retaliated that baldness was no more common than it was before stiff hats were worn. For inscrutable reasons, Jackson joined the debate to side with Fox and to point out that the English had always worn stiff hats, but it had not been shown they were the particular subjects of baldness. All of this bickering took place after Jackson delivered his paper condemning stiff hats.[7]

Around the same time, Pittsburgh doctor Chevalier Jackson agreed that hats were responsible for many cases of baldness. He cited as evidence the fact that baldness was not only limited to the head but to that portion of it covered by the hat. In addition, the hat excluded the beneficial effects of sunlight, and the portion of the head covered by the hat was "deprived of the beneficial effects of the reactionary congestion following exposure to cold air." Agreeing that bald women were rare, Jackson contended they were common in England and France back when it was fashionable for women to wear wigs and build up mountains of false hair. After studying 31 baldies, he concluded that confining the head in a close and unventilated hat would cause the "disease" in cases where a predisposition existed and in certain cases baldness would be produced in the absence of any predisposition. Cited as predispositions were "heredity, poor general health, mental exertion, worry, loss of sleep, etc." Jackson did not think that one or more of these factors were sufficient to produce baldness in the absence of headgear, for if such were the case the baldness "ought not to be confined solely to the portion of the scalp which is covered by the head-gear."[8]

Unventilated hats were blamed by one medical writer, who called them one of the greatest sources of failure of the hair to receive adequate nutrition. He reasoned the beard never failed to grow because it got plenty of exposure to air and sunlight, while women had more adequately ventilated scalps due to the wearing of a different type of headgear. "Young Americans who do not wish to lose their hair before they are forty must begin to look after their scalps before they are twenty," he admonished. Another medical practitioner argued that hats worn by men stimulated perspiration while preventing evaporation. Kept unnaturally warm and moist, the hair on the scalp weakened and died.[9]

Articles in several medical journals in the 1890s continued to condemn hats. One offered a remedy: "A head covering should never be worn indoors, in trains, or in closed carriages." Straw was recommended as the best hat material for summer and windless weather as it was light and permeable. For winter, unlined and well-ventilated light felt was recommended. "The ordinary tall hat, and the thick, heavy unventilated top hat, cannot be too strongly condemned," noted this *Lancet* writer.[10]

When Dr. J. O. Cobb offered his opinion in 1909, he was a surgeon with the U.S. Public Health and Marine Hospital Service. Reviewing baldness in the ancient past Cobb named examples such as Socrates, Caesar, Hippocrates, and Elisha and also noted that many saints such as St. Paul were so afflicted. In spite of the fact that none of those named was ever seen in a stiff top hat, that headgear was what Cobb chose to blame. "Among semicivilized peoples it is nearly unknown, and especially is this true of the dark races. Old Indians and old negroes seldom are bald, unless they have adopted the white man's stiff hat…. Among certain European rural classes, whose headdress is distinctive, baldness is very rare, but when they come to America and begin to wear stiff hats, the usual percentage became bald," said Cobb. He went on to assert that baldness "is a condition brought about almost solely by the tight hatband and the heavy hat." Parasites could not be a factor, he reasoned, or baldness would be general over the entire head. Heredity could not be a factor since women, subject to the same laws as men, did not go bald.[11]

Admitting that some men who wore tight, heavy hats escaped the affliction, Cobb put the reason down to the shape of the head, stating that a man with a "low brow, and thick, heavy hair rarely is bald," regardless of hat. Of all the stiff, rigid hats "universally worn," he thought the straw hat was the worst offender because it was harder to keep it from blowing away and as a result the wearer would force it down on his head that much tighter. "The derby hat, and the silk hat, are great hair destroyers, and not far behind them in destructiveness are the automobile caps, which are being pulled down on the head very tightly," he said. Cobb recommended all stiff hats be light in weight and purchased one size too large to allow the insertion of felt strips which would have a cushioning effect. "Some one ought to invent a hat which will prevent baldness, though the idea will probably not become popular because there is more money in hair tonics, and hair restorers, and fake electric massage apparatus, than in some new kind of a hat which will prevent the disease," moaned the surgeon. Given that no appropriately constructed hat was on the horizon, Cobb urged men to exercise the greatest precaution in wearing headgear. "Every few minutes, when outside, the hat should be lifted from the head and gently replaced," he advised. To get some idea of what happened to the head when wearing a hat, Cobb suggested one should tie a string lightly around one's finger and observe the effect on the circulation in the end of that finger. Enough was thought of Cobb's ideas that the *New York Times* summarized them in an editorial.[12]

Former Chicago commissioner of health Dr. Arthur Reynolds stated, "The hats that men wear ... are the cause of their baldness." Explaining why some men who wore hats were not bald, Reynolds remarked: "Some heads are so free from corners and protuberances and are so round that a hat fits tightly down all around quite like one length of stovepipe over its mate. Heads so shaped become bald earliest and most completely." Inheriting a certain head shape could predispose a man to baldness, but that was the only part heredity played in the process, argued Reynolds. As further evidence of the role of headgear, he noted: "It's well known that hatless Indians are not bald.... There is no account of baldness among other savage races.... The hat wearing American negro becomes bald quite frequently." Reynolds regarded his theory as self-evident. He did suggest that the common sense solution was to do away with hats altogether but failing that, "it would be wise for some enterprising hatter to make a scientific study and learn to fit non-destructive hats to the heads that need them, and so constructed that the pressure will rest only upon the corners of the forehead and on the center of the back of the head." Declining to blame hat makers or hat retailers, Reynolds believed they were just selling what the public wanted to buy.[13]

During 1913 a flurry of letters to the editor were published in the *New York Times* on the subject of baldness. While many causes were cited by the correspondents, several stuck with the hat theory, as was typified by one letter writer, who said, "I thought it was a well-known fact that men who wear stiff hats that prevent circulation of the blood to the roots of the hair become bald."[14]

The topic surfaced again 12 years later in the same newspaper with letters to the editor, followed by an editorial. In the latter the *Times* admitted that evidence on hats as a cause of baldness was confusing and conflicting but concluded it was more prudent to "wear more sensible hats, not to go without them altogether."[15]

Physician Benjamin Dorsey of Los Angeles published *Baldness, Its Causes and Prevention* in 1939. It was a book which kept the hat theory alive and kicking. He determined that temporal arteries in the heads of baldies were almost completely shut down. Thus he concluded that baldness was associated with the region of the head dependent on the temporal arteries for nourishment and that seldom, if ever, was baldness associated with the parts of the head which were not exclusively dependent upon those blood vessels. Dorsey asserted that those arteries "are not only connected with the production of simple permanent baldness, but solely responsible for it." Over the years Dorsey confirmed his findings when he performed autopsies on baldies. This activity led him to formulate his theory that "the basic cause of common baldness is the prolonged constriction or even deformation of the temporal blood vessels at a point just above and in front of the ears. This condition is invariably brought about by the wearing of tight fitting hats." Regarding the question of why some men who constantly wore tight hats did not go bald, he stated, "The reason for this seeming immunity is due entirely to the shape of their heads." Heads that were long and flat at the sides did not go bald, while oval-shaped skulls broadest just above and in front of the ears invariably did. Heredity was a predisposing factor only in the sense that a person inherited a head-shape type.[16]

Looking back in time at baldness among the ancients, whom he said were "thought of as hatless," the doctor explained the contradiction by claiming infectious diseases were more common in ancient times and that it was once a custom to wear hair long and hold it back by means of head bands placed where the modern hat band rested. Finally, Dorsey argued that ancient military helmets were worse than modern hats as producers of baldness. Believing hat manufacturers would not make a product that relieved the pressure points from the sides of the heads, he offered a remedy of his own. It was the Dr. Dorsey Scalp Protector, which fit inside the hatband on each side. A set of two could be ordered from a company whose address Dorsey conveniently provided in his book.[17]

For those men already bald, Dorsey bluntly offered no hope at all, giving each one "our sympathy and regrets, and advice to go home and examine the shapes of their sons' heads. For though he may be able to do nothing for himself, he certainly can save the hair of his boys." Prevention, he thought, should begin in the public schools with an examination of each boy's head to determine whether he was a potential victim of baldness. Those boys whose heads were widest at the sides would receive a note to take home to their parents informing them of the necessity of protecting their child from "the usual type of hats." Dorsey's last word was *No boy should be permitted to arrive at maturity with a physical handicap that modern science has found a method of preventing* (emphasis in original).

In Dorsey's world, females didn't go bald because they didn't wear tight fitting hats. Nowhere in his book did the doctor make the most obvious recommendation—that men go hatless. All that was left, it seemed, was to order a set of his scalp protectors. In the book's afterword, Dr. Albert Hunt lavishly praised the author by saying, in regard to the hat theory, "The man who developed and indisputably proved his theory by 30 years of patient investigation and observation is a Los Angeles physician, B. L. Dorsey, M.D., and millions of men and mothers will bless his name for his discoveries."[18]

By the end of World War II, the genetic and hormonal basis of baldness had been established, causing the hat theory to fade away. The *New York Times* announced in 1946 that tight hat bands and changes in blood supply to scalp areas had "nothing to do with baldness."[19]

Not everybody abandoned the hat theory, however. In his 1960 book, *New Hope for Your Hair*, Dr. Irwin Lubowe still subscribed to the idea that skull shape and compressed circulation from tight hats were factors in baldness. He discussed the hat theory at length, even though this theory had long been shown to be false. In addition, 1960s America was a society in which almost nobody wore hats anyway.[20]

Many medical men blamed the scalp or skull; there were muscle heads, fat heads, and the dreaded ivory domes. Usually the problem was seen as resulting from a reduction of blood supply to the scalp caused by internal factors instead of outside pressure, as in the hat theories.

Appearing before 5,000 dentists at a dental convention in 1937, a Columbia University Medical School associate professor of clinical surgery, Dr. Gustave Aufricht, delivered a paper on a topic unrelated to baldness. Halfway through his presentation, he surprised the group by devoting the last half of his remarks to baldness. As far back as 1900, he said, physicians had noted that tight scalps usually meant scant hair. Skin tension closed tiny blood vessels which shut off the food supply to follicles. Confirmation for that idea came from the observation of cows. Bovines with full udders usually had little hair on their milk sacs, while cows with "scrawny" udders had lots of hair. Because of this evidence Aufricht went to work to find a means of loosening the scalp and tried using surgery on the scalp muscles to relax their "drumhead pull." With tension thus lessened, he believed hair would grow satisfactorily. However, as he performed his procedure just one week before the convention, he had no results to report. Nothing more was heard from Aufricht and drumhead easement.[21]

Ten years later Howard University professor Dr. M. Wharton Young offered further evidence that a tight scalp caused baldness. At an annual meeting of the American Association of Anatomists, he announced that baldness was a matter of anatomy. The top of the head, he explained, didn't have as rich a blood supply as the sides of the head. Tension zones in the scalp cut down the blood supply to the top, which meant the start of baldness. These tension zones, he said, "may result from contraction of the muscles, from continued growth of the skull, or from external pressure." Young claimed to have produced permanent baldness in monkeys, similar to male pattern baldness, by cutting out curved slices of their scalp and sewing the edges together. That artificially produced a tight scalp, which set up tension areas; baldness followed.[22]

In 1957, Young surfaced again. With not so much as a word about tight scalps, he declared this time that if you had muscle in your head, your chances of avoiding baldness were good. Anatomist Young applied electrodes to the hairy and hairless parts of the scalps of bald volunteers and connected them to a machine that recorded the electrical response of contracting muscle. Then his subjects were instructed to move their scalps and wiggle their ears. Responses typical of muscle were found under the hairy areas, while the bald spots registered no activity. Since previous studies indicated muscles under the scalp had a rich supply of blood vessels to nourish the follicles, Young concluded that muscle heads did not get bald.[23]

Also in the 1950s, Chicago Drs. Hans Elias and Adolph Brown reached a somewhat similar conclusion. After studying the tissues of 35 cadavers with bald heads, they concluded there was a thick layer of fat under the skin in normal scalps that offered support for the hair follicles. In the bald scalp, the fatty layer was absent, they stated, adding that "Growing hair under such circumstances is impossible. No amount of massage or tonic will help." A journalist was moved to comment, "The hair-bearing human is the fat head."[24]

At the end of the 1950s, New York Memorial Hospital plastic surgeon Philip Corso claimed he had disproved the theory that baldness was caused by a reduction in the amount of blood circulated through the arteries of the scalp. Corso injected a plastic material called methyl methacrylate into the veins and arteries of the heads of nine male cadavers. While that experiment convinced him arteries played no role in baldness, he thought a reduction in the circulation of blood through the veins in the scalp was involved. In this theory a fibrous layer of tissue which stretched tightly under the skin of the scalp made it difficult for blood to pass through the veins in the area. Corso suggested that surgery to relieve tension in this fibrous layer of the skull might improve venous circulation and possibly arrest hair loss.[25]

One of the oddest and most whimsical of these theories came from Dr. Frederick Hoelzel of Chicago. It was published in 1942 in the prestigious *Journal of the American Medical Association*. Hoelzel's theory on baldness was based on observations he made in 1916–17 while he served as a technician in gross anatomy at the College of Medicine of the University of Illinois. During that time he removed the brains of around 80 cadavers and noticed a seemingly obvious relation between the blood vessel supply to the scalp and the quantity of hair. Why the doctor ruminated on these observations for a quarter of a century before announcing his theory went unreported. "Baldness occurred in persons in whom calcification of the skull bones apparently had not only firmly knitted the cranial sutures but also closed or narrowed various small foramens through which blood vessels pass," explained Hoelzel. He thought this explained why men went bald and women didn't "since bone growth or calcification is generally greater in males than in females." Also obvious was the fact that hair tonics or vitamins couldn't restore blood circulation through a skull that had practically become "solid ivory." A worried Hoelzel fretted, "one wonders whether the promotion of a higher calcium intake among adults may not eventually increase the incidence of baldness and the sales of its vaunted remedies." This ivory dome theory was popular enough to be picked up in several outlets of the popular press.[26]

During the 1960s, Dr. Lars Engstrand of Stockholm, Sweden, agreed that baldness was caused by an insufficient blood supply to the scalp, which was caused in turn by a thickened membrane of the scalp, the galea. That thickened galea pressured and reduced the blood supply still further as it enlarged. Reasoning that if the galea could be reduced to normal thickness the baldness would be stopped and new hair would grow, Engstrand developed "The Radical Scalp Operation" to correct the galea surgically. According to one report, by 1964 the doctor had performed over 1,000 successful operations, with 70 to 80 percent of the patients experiencing hair regrowth within six months to a year after the operation. Even in cases of complete baldness, there was supposedly new hair growth in 40 to 50 percent of the cases. New age guru Paavo Airola spoke enthusiastically of Engstrand's method, but then he also recommended massaging the scalp with electric vibrators and standing on one's head.[27]

Some drew connections between facial hair or length of hair and baldness. One of the earliest was Charles Dickens, who in an article titled "Why Shave" advanced the idea that shaving the beard increased the thickness of hair on the chin, taking hair away from the top of the head. *Science Digest* reported in 1948 that even then some still believed the idea.[28]

More "scientific" evidence for the theory that shaving caused baldness was provided by Dr. J. Blaine, professor of dermatology at Gross Medical College and dermatologist at St. Anthony's Hospital. Writing in the *Journal of the American Medical Association* in 1899, he dismissed heredity as a factor, asserting that a young man inherited not his father's bald head but a good supply of healthy hair, which he lost after a few years due to carelessness. Blaine claimed that tracing our progenitors back a few centuries yielded people with hair in abundance. He then concluded, "The bald head can only be found among enlightened nations, and it must therefore be caused by following the arts and customs of civilization." There was no baldness to be found among "uncivilized" tribes and nations, according to Blaine. What was notable was that while some of those people had no beards, some has sparse beards, and some had full beards, none of them shaved. "We are brought then, to the conclusion, that , in most cases, idiopathic alopecia prematura is caused by the too frequent use of the razor on the face." Blaine believed it to be a well-known fact barely worth repeating that frequent use of the razor stimulated the growth of the beard to its "utmost limit." The constant drain necessary to supply that rapid growth caused a weakness in the scalp. Shaving acted as a counter-irritant causing hyperemia of the face, which reduced nourishment of the scalp.[29]

Since baldness started between 25 and 35 years of age, Blaine recommended men allow their beards to grow during that time, stating, "If all men allowed their beards to grow during this period there would be no baldness prior to the senile period." As further evidence he cited women and North American Indians, who didn't shave because they had no beards and were never bald. There were also the "semi-bearded" Chinese who were never bald, thought Blaine. Curiously, he never argued that shaving made all men bald, nor did he attempt to explain why it did not. In his conclusion Blaine offered some hope by writing: "I have not observed a single case where I have succeeded in persuading that patient to stop shaving but what resulted in arresting the retrograde process. However, it will not reverse damage; once hair is gone, it's gone."[30]

When the *New York Times* published its letters to the editor on the subject on baldness in 1913, a few believed it was obvious that the more heavily bearded a man was, the more likely it was he would become bald. Which, of course, explained why there were no bald women.[31]

It was a natural step, and a more popular one, to consider that the cutting of the hair on the head was a factor in baldness. One medical man asserted in 1893 that short hair grew faster than long hair but didn't have the same vitality. Nor did short hair give the same protection to the scalp. He advocated hair should not be cut too short, and he dismissed as a fallacy the "common belief" that frequent cutting of the hair would prevent baldness.[32]

A decade later Dr. J. Cobb also warned against the belief that when hair started to fall it should be cut short. In fact, he said, "close clipping is the most harmful thing that can be done to any head of hair. Then, of all times, the hair should be worn long."[33]

French physician Dr. Guelpa agreed, suggesting that the length of a man's hair was important. He believed it should be worn long to enhance the vitality of the hair, which "is systematically destroyed by the cutting of the hair too short and too frequently."[34]

Taking the opposite line was Dr. Menahem Hodara of Constantinople, who reported excellent results in treating baldness in a number of cases by shaving the head. Hodara shaved the heads once or twice a week for a total of five to ten times. The journalist reporting this in a 1900 medical publication felt obliged to note that the time-honored practice of shaving heads to stop baldness had lately lost favor among medical men.[35]

During a 1920s meeting of medical men about baldness, one physician remarked mysteriously: "Have your hair cut only during the first quarter of the moon. Skeptics will smile at this. However, 'fools deride, philosophers investigate.'" In the 1940s, Charles Nessler, a self-styled scalp specialist reported to be the inventor of the permanent wave machine, warned women not to adopt male-type haircuts as "Baldness would not occur if the hair were not continually cut short or kept short in youth, that habit forming period."[36]

Paralleling theories about cutting or not cutting facial and head hair was a movement damning barbers as a major factor in baldness. Blame came their way after several researchers established the "fact" that baldness was caused by a microbe, or bacillus. The theory that baldness might not be a natural event or the result of poor hygiene or improper attire but might instead be a disease caused by bacteria had always had its adherents. One of these theories given a degree of credence at the time was that announced by M. Sebouraud of France to the Dermatological Society of Paris in 1897. An eminent physiologist, Sebouraud was considered an expert on ringworm. He had once been a pupil of Louis Pasteur. After several years of research on skin diseases Sebouraud announced to the world he had discovered the cause of baldness: it was a microbe. This finding clearly moved baldness into the category of disease instead of condition.

No doubt existed for this investigator, who asserted the malady was "one of the most purely microbial I have ever seen." The microbe was a minute colorless body, pointed at both ends, that increased in number by constant division into two. Since the divisions did not immediately break off, long chains frequently formed, each link in the chain being a distinct microbe. Enormous colonies of these microbes congregated in the hair follicles, from which point they secreted a toxin which slowly killed the root of the hair. Attack by these microbes always began at the vertex or temples and expanded from there. Sebouraud was silent on why these bugs stopped short, leaving the fringe of hair on the side of the head which most bald men had. One writer commenting on this new theory thought it might help to make a clearing around an infected spot by shaving off a margin of hair, like a clearing around a prairie fire, to perhaps prevent the microbe from spreading.

Sebouraud had discovered no case of baldness in which the microbe was absent. Although he was satisfied in his own mind that it was the cause of baldness, he knew he did not yet have scientific proof. Baldness and the microbe could both be the result of a third, unknown factor. He would have to

produce baldness with his microbe. As no human volunteered, he had to set-
tle for animals. First Sebouraud had to isolate and culture the bug. Of course,
there never was such a microbe, but that didn't stop the Frenchman, eminent
scientist that he was. He "isolated the microbe" and then grew it in his lab in
an appropriate medium. Taking this substance, he injected it into the bloodstream of a rabbit, a sheep, and a guinea pig. In every case the creature lost
all its fur, becoming completely bald in five to six weeks of treatments. Thus
Sebouraud thought he had proved causality. One reporter was obviously awed,
for he wrote, "the poison is so acute and individual that, even when inocu-
lated into the general system of an animal, it flies at once to the hairs, and acts
solely upon them." According to Sebouraud, the microbe had already caused
so much structural damage in the heads of bald men that a cure was an
"impossibility." Other writers were optimistic, however, believing that because
the cause had been discovered perhaps somebody would come up with an anti-
toxin.[37]

In 1899, Dr. Saymonne isolated a bacillus which he said caused baldness.
Naming it bacillus crinivorax (Sebouraud called his bug bacillus Sebouraudii),
he reported the bug invaded the hair follicles, causing the hair to break off at
the skin. Then it attacked the roots, killing them. If the microbes were treated
early enough, hairs could be saved, but after a certain point structural damage was irreversible. Saymonne's treatment consisted of once a week vigorously rubbing into the scalp a mixture containing ten parts crude cod-liver
oil, ten parts onion juice, and five parts mucilage or egg yolk. Insisting this
treatment would restore hair if the roots were not damaged, Saymonne admitted, "the application of the remedy must be very distressing to the patient's
friends and neighbors."[38]

By the turn of the century, medical personnel began to believe that baldness was caused by seborrhea. The skin contained glands to secrete perspiration. Glands termed sebaceous emitted the oily material designed to lubricate
the skin. An excessive secretion of that oily substance was a dermatological
condition known as seborrhea—oily skin and hair. Examination of the secretion under a microscope showed "millions of small bacilli," one journal noted.
"The transmission of bacilli and the resulting contagion are produced by a
thousand hazards, perhaps more than one thinks, by barber shops, where the
brushes and combs pass a hundred times from one head to the other without
the least real cleaning." The microbe developed, multiplied, and gained the
"orifice of a gland where it establishes itself as victor in a vanquished city."
Seborrhea was created rapidly, according to this theory, and in its wake came
baldness.[39]

New York City dermatologist Dr. L. Duncan Buckley agreed seborrhea
was an important factor in causing baldness, which he thought was much
more common in recent years. "It is distinctly a barber's disease and has
spread as a consequence of the universal recourse to these in later generations,"

he said. While Buckley didn't know the nature of the seborrhea-causing parasite, he declared it differed from such parasitic diseases as barber's itch and favus.[40]

Dr. A. Ohmann-Dumesnil, wasn't sure if baldness was caused by parasites or by neurotic behavior. He thought evidence for all baldness stemming from parasites was less than convincing and noted that the claims that applying antiseptics tended to promote growth of hair did not prove the result was due to destruction of parasites. The growth could be due solely to stimulating properties of the chemicals. As for those researchers who "found" the microbes under a microscope, he thought they might be simply saprophytes which could be obtained from healthy, hairy scalps. In some cases of neurotic baldness, however, no treatment was effective until strong parasiticides were applied. That led Ohmann-Dumesnil to say that an impartial conclusion would have to be that it was of parasitic origin in those cases. He did agree with those who argued baldness was due to either parasites or nervous influences, or a combination. When baldness was due to parasites, the "disease may be traced to the barber's brush, infection from caps, hats, etc., worn by other individuals suffering from the same trouble," he concluded.[41]

German physician Oscar Lasser concluded from experiments and observations that baldness was a disease due to microorganisms. He stated in the 1880s that it was a contagious disease spread by barbers because they used combs and brushes on customers one after the other without cleaning those items after each use. To prove his point, Lasser collected hair clippings from bald men from barber shops. Then he mixed them with Vaseline into an ointment which he applied to the fur of mice and rabbits. Baldness was rapidly produced in the treated areas. Within a few years, Lasser had an American disciple by the name of Dr. R. W. Bishop, who read a paper touting Lasser's theory in 1886 at a meeting of the Chicago Medical Society. The pair worked together busily denuding creatures with their concoction. As a cure, the duo advised the head first be washed with tar soap, following which a warm water "douche" was applied, with the water steadily getting colder. After being dried, the head was treated with a solution of corrosive sublimate, then with a solution of lithol, and finally with a 1½ percent solution of carbolic acid, which was applied very slowly. If that treatment was started early enough and repeated daily for at least eight weeks, the result was, said Bishop, "a fine growth of new hair."[42]

American physician Dr. George T. Jackson also believed seborrhea "causes dandruff and baldness." He stated that there were two forms of seborrhea, oily and dry. It was the dry form which caused first dandruff on the scalp and then baldness. Discussing the theory that microbes caused the seborrhea, Jackson observed, "There is enough merit in this view, also, to justify the person who does not wish to get bald prematurely in having his own brush and combs at the barber's." Sulfur was the treatment of choice; it was suspended in oil or Vaseline and rubbed into the scalp nightly for one week. Then the hair was washed, and the treatment was applied every other night during the second week. Frequency of application was decreased over time until only one treatment was applied in a week. "By this time the disease will be cured," a confident Jackson predicted.[43]

Dandruff soon came to be viewed as the form of seborrhea that was most harmful to the hair. Dr. Condict Cutler argued there were several forms of seborrhea which could result in baldness but that dandruff was the form most likely to do so. When Dr. George Elliot read a paper before colleagues in 1892, he claimed the overwhelming number of cases of baldness were due to seborrhea. He got a certain amount of flak from those peers who believed other causes were at work. To refute those critics, Elliot studied 344 bald patients during the next 2½ years. He concluded that 4 cases were due to heredity, 24 were due to malaria and other factors or were untraceable, and 316 were caused by seborrhea, more precisely, dandruff. Dr. Ellice Alger concurred by saying that in a larger proportion of baldness cases "an unmistakable cause" is dandruff. Joining this group with his evidence was the resurfacing Dr. George Jackson, a Columbia University Medical School dermatology instructor. After studying 300 of his bald patients, he found that dandruff was present in 218 of them. Of the role of dandruff, he concluded, "It must be regarded as the most active exciting cause of alopecia." Curing the dandruff stopped the hair loss, he claimed. Yet another study done by a medical man stated that of the main causal factors in baldness (more than one per case allowed) he found in his 794 cases, dandruff led the way, being present in 79 percent of the cases, followed by "maltreatment" of the scalp at 50 percent, heredity at 30 percent, systemic depression at 20 percent, and fever at 11 percent.[44]

Many decades later Dr. Irwin Lubowe stated in his 1960 book on hair care: "As to seborrhea, there can be no doubt that this overactivity of the sebaceous glands, which is the most common cause of excessive dandruff, is a prime culprit in baldness." For evidence Lubowe cited Elliot's study from the 1890s, without mentioning when the study was done.[45]

Considering the phenomenon of baldness around the time of World War I, Dr. William Brady noted that American Indians did not go bald, "but then, they never visited a barbershop, so they harbored no microbacilli to destroy their hair. A man should lose no time in getting home from the barber shop to take a thorough shampoo." Brady offered the thought that premature baldness would prevail until the coming of the "aseptic barber."[46]

When physician Isadore Dyer, a professor of skin diseases at Tulane University, read a paper at a medical meeting in San Antonio in 1912, he claimed the barber shop was the most frequent place to pick up the infection that caused baldness. Also important was the community comb found in private dwellings, which to his mind explained so-called hereditary baldness.

Prevention was simple—throw out that comb or brush which was a "nest of infection." To treat existing baldness, Dyer advised frequent washing of the scalp with antiseptic soaps followed by daily use of antiparasitics. Some recommended agents were sulfur, the mercurials, the naphthol group, and carbolic acid. Also recommended for use on bald areas were stimulants such as capsicum, veratrina, castor oil, and cantharides (better known as the reputed aphrodisiac Spanish Fly).[47]

One journalist reported that the only sensible suggestion was that the head should be kept clean, not ordinary cleanliness but "surgical cleanliness." That was necessary because men went to barber shops where the same implements were used on head after head, because men regularly used combs and brushes provided for common use in hotels and railroad cars, and because men were careless in regard to trying on hats that had been used by others and were "fairly reeking with the secretions and vegetable parasites of the hair." To turn the tide against baldness, readers were advised to take hygienic care of combs and brushes. The young in families were not to use implements used by bald family members. "Frequent boiling in a soda solution must be the rule" for the nursery comb. Hair pomades were to be avoided because they "swarm with bacteria." If it required a large effort, it was worth it, thought the reporter, since a decrease in the number of baldies was "a consummation devoutly to be wished and faithfully to be striven for, even with considerable trouble, since the present tendency to baldpatedness is eminently to impair the natural dignity and impressiveness of the manly countenance."[48]

Dr. Guelpa of France blamed barbers because "the shampooing, frictions and manipulations commonly employed by barbers constitute a perpetual attack on the very life of the hair." Following such treatment the sebum from the sebaceous glands thickened, eventually destroying the hair. One of the few to disagree with the theory that microbes caused seborrhea, Guelpa remarked that Sebouraud was mistaking effect for cause: "One does not accuse the vultures on a field of battle of having slain the corpses they tear to pieces." Guelpa believed microbes were attracted to bald heads due to the "physiological poverty of the scalp."[49]

Avoidance of hair pomades was not advised by Dr. M. Joseph Tyson, who blamed baldness on many factors, two of which were constant washing and the failure to use some oil or pomade. Tyson thought many men applied no pomade at all to their head because of a common notion that greasing the hair was vulgar. He urged men to wash their hair—no more than once a week—and then apply some form of "simple grease or oil" to their hair. If the hair was already thinning, then adding material such as ammonia or cantharides to the oil would "increase its good effect." On the other hand, George Jackson urged that no pomades be used. He believed that hair dressings "by becoming rancid are apt to irritate."[50]

Among the 1913 letters received by the *New York Times* was one from

Dr. H. B. Sheffield, who wrote because he believed many of the *Times* readers were greatly perturbed over the "ridiculous explanations" given in regard to the topic. His own theory was that germs caused baldness and that the germs reached the head "principally by the common use of combs and brushes, as practiced by barbers' shops." To Sheffield, this explained why baldness ran in families—everybody used the same comb and brush. It also explained, in his opinion, why females didn't go bald because they almost never went to barber shops and were more particular in using their own brush. Men were advised to take their own comb and brush to the barber.[51]

Other letters also supported the germ and blame-the-barber ideas. One correspondent urged that barber shops be required to sterilize instruments after use on a customer. This correspondent said he had searched diligently but could not find a single barber shop in New York City that observed those precautions. Many letter writers severely criticized Sheffield's ideas, however. One attacked the germ theory since baldness never appeared below the hat line; he voted for the hat theory. Another writer, a barber by trade, scored the idea of common brushes as a factor, noting many rich men had a barber come to their home and provided their own clean instruments. Some of them were bald. The barber also noted that women frequented hairdressing parlors, where the same implements were used over and over on different customers without cleaning. Such criticism caused Sheffield to respond angrily to these attacks from the unwashed rabble, saying that the idea that baldness was caused by a microbe "is no idle dream, but a fully established fact." Addressing the hat-line criticism, Sheffield argued that baldness remained on the upper portion of the scalp because that area was the thinnest and least nourished. Backing away from his earlier statements, he said the germ had many ways of entry and did "not necessarily" enter through the means of a barber's common comb and brush. Nonplussed over the valid criticism that female hairdressing parlors had the same dubious hygienic levels as barber shops, Sheffield could only worry that it "tends to strengthen my view that a great many of them, like the men, will soon become afflicted with baldness if they do not soon awaken to the importance of using their own comb and brush."[52]

As early as 1902, the popular press had suggested it would be worthwhile for its readers to appeal to their legislators to help out by drawing up regulations that would require barbers and "all purveyors of combing implements" to sterilize these implements after each use on a patron.[53]

An anecdotal account, perhaps apocryphal, appeared in the popular press in 1917 when a journalist reported going into a Chicago barber shop where he witnessed the following "horror." A woman brought in her little boy who was recovering from a scalp infection. Worried he might get it again, she asked the barber if he ever washed his implements between customers. He replied no. She asked him to make an exception this one time for her son, but the barber declined. "This is not fiction. It is the daily story of the average barber shop. It is one of the greatest reasons why men are bald," wrote the journalist. To reinforce his theory, he erroneously stated that when a woman went to the hairdresser, even a "mediocre" one, she had a sterilized comb and brush used on her head.[54]

Several years later, in the 1920s, physician S. Dana Hubbard, director of the Public Health Education Division, New York City Board of Health, warned his audience to "employ only careful barbers" because he believed unclean shops were the most fertile source of scalp diseases. By then antibarber sentiment had led New York City to adopt regulations governing barbers. A barber couldn't use any implement for more than one customer without disinfecting it, the chair headrest had to be covered with a fresh cloth for each customer, and the barber himself had to be free of scalp diseases and was required to wash his hands after each patron.[55]

There was even a barber who engaged in barber-bashing. In Los Angeles, where they did not yet have the New York City hygiene regulations, James O. Shannessy, president of the Journeymen Barbers' International Union, warned in 1926 that baldness was inevitable among women as well as men unless sanitary conditions were improved in hair-cutting facilities. "It is not a wild dream that baldness may come to plague women. Baldness afflicts many men, not because they wear their hair short, but because they encounter scalp disease in barber shops. The remedy is State supervision of the trade to enforce hygienic conditions," he said.[56]

The idea that seborrhea caused baldness but did not result from germs appeared occasionally. Dr. William Cunningham, Harlem Hospital assistant dermatologist, wrote in 1915 that seborrhea "is the disease responsible for most of the overt baldness in men." In his theory, sebaceous glands excreted excess amounts of sebum which inflamed and eventually choked the hair follicles. He believed the prognosis for the disease was problematic.[57]

Over a decade later, a writer argued that dry seborrhea—dandruff— caused baldness and that dandruff was full of germs. He did not argue, however, that germs caused dandruff or that dandruff attracted germs; he was apparently confused on the point.[58]

As late as 1948, French dermatologist Dr. Darier asserted that most baldness was caused by seborrhea. Heredity played no role except in that there was a hereditary predisposition to overactive sebaceous glands. Darier was also confused on the role of germs, thinking that if they did not cause seborrhea then perhaps they aggravated it. Further evidence heredity was not a factor, in his view, was that appropriate treatment would in many cases check, if not prevent, the loss of hair. That treatment was simple—and by then out of date— "keep all combs and brushes clean."[59]

Maurice Bodington unburdened himself in print against barbers in 1948 in more general terms when he mentioned how annoyed bald men were when they went to the barber shop and heard the same tired old jokes about baldies time after time, such as "Make a good skating rink for flies." Also irritating him was the fact that baldies were expected to tip the barber, just as was a hair-bearing man. If baldies complained at all, the barber answered that it was a difficult job: "It's hard to find any hair to cut." Bodington issued a plea to the influential newspapers to begin a campaign to urge the local barber/humorists to hire good script writers. "We would honestly welcome any new gags coined on our behalf," he concluded.[60]

Another attack on barbers took place around the same time when R. J. Wilkinson, Jr., a bald Huntington, West Virginia, city councilman, unsuccessfully tried to sneak through a city bylaw forbidding barbers to charge bald customers more than 25 cents for a haircut. Perhaps the councilor had been the victim once too often of a barber who taunted him with this joke: "Then there was the barber who said to the bald man passing his shop, 'Come on in—what've you got to lose.'"[61]

A few years later Dr. Peter Flesch was working away on skin cancer research at the University of Pennsylvania when he learned that a large number of employees of a plant manufacturing synthetic rubber suddenly lost their hair temporarily. That hair loss was traced to six chemicals, three of which were found in sebum. Reinventing the wheel, Flesch painted sebum from baldies on the skin of mice and rabbits; within ten days all of the rabbits and most of the mice lost their hair from the painted spots. Flesch hoped his findings would lead to the checking of baldness in humans, but other researchers analyzed the sebum from baldies and hair-bearing men and found no difference.[62]

3

EVERYTHING UNDER THE SUN

Say, you know Irving, your hair is getting thin? So who likes
fat hair?
Newsweek, February 16, 1959

For a young woman to dream of a bald-headed man is a
warning to her to use her intelligence against listening to
her next marriage offer.
Gustavus Miller,
10,000 Dreams Interpreted

If hats caused baldness, the simplest remedy would be to remove them permanently. That meant exposing the hair to the sun, however, and there were two schools of thought regarding that practice. Around 1900 one school believed that exposure to the sun was a baldness preventer. A German physician named Seeger advised that "In the summer it is well to expose the head morning and evening to the sun." Another medical man speculated that exclusion of light and air had much to do with the predisposition to baldness. At the time of World War I, Dr. William Brady thought that if there was an agent which, without seriously injuring the scalp, possessed real germicidal power in the tissues of the scalp, it was light. He subscribed to the idea that underlying baldness was an infection. Brady advised that "All the sunlight the scalp will stand, short of sunburn or sunstroke, is beneficial to the vitality of the hair." He argued, without explanation or evidence, that dark-haired people more commonly went bald than light-haired people because dark hair excluded light from the scalp. During the mid 1920s, one physician advised those men going bald to get sun on their heads, but only in the mornings.[1]

Believing natural sunlight was able to prevent baldness, some extended this idea illogically to tout artificial sunlight as a cure for baldness. As early as 1912, a Dr. Harris was giving the hairless half-hour exposures of the bald areas to ultraviolet rays, "protecting" the area with blocks of ice. Treatment at a specific area was stopped and moved to another area when the skin reacted painfully. Duration of treatment varied from three weeks to thirteen months. Harris claimed excellent hair regrowing results in nine of eleven cases, with one failure. The eleventh subject reportedly discontinued treatment after his hair started to regrow. Within a few years, other doctors such as William Dieffenbach of New York and Franz Nagelschmidt of Berlin claimed to have successfully treated baldness by means of the ultraviolet rays emitted from a quartz lamp.[2]

Brady also favored exposure of the bald head to artificial light, if sun exposure was not possible. He favored the ultraviolet ray obtained from a powerful electric light which was passed through a lens in which cold water continuously circulated, absorbing the heat but not the light. Then the cool ray was focused on the area of baldness to be treated through a quartz lens, not an ordinary glass lens. Calling the violet ray "comparatively useless" and not to be confused with the colorless ultraviolet ray which was capable of inducing powerful physiological changes, Brady concluded, "Perhaps the ultraviolet ray—which of course no barber or other unskilled operator can manage—and massage offer the greatest hope to the victim of premature loss of hair."[3]

In the 1930s the popular health magazine *Hygeia* reported that sunlight's "beneficial effects upon hair growth have been demonstrated experimentally. Artificial sunlight in the form of ultraviolet radiation is now largely used in the treatment of falling hair." Baldies could take a trip that same decade to the Dermalav Laboratories which promised to grow hair on the shiny dome for only $10. For its fee, the company applied an unnamed caustic solution to the bald parts, which caused the scalp to peel off, exposing the "dormant" follicles to the environment. Sunlight did the rest, causing them to send up new hair.[4]

A second school of thought believed sunlight caused baldness. Boston's Dr. George Harding observed in 1910, after studying 312 cases of baldness in young men, that "exposure to the sun was harmful rather than beneficial to the hair and scalp." All of his subjects had spent one or more years going about in the open without head covering. More than 200 of the men spent their summers at the seashore; in these cases the baldness was most pronounced. Those who had only a year or so of exposure to the direct sunlight responded well to some unspecified treatment, but for those men with several years or more exposure to the sun there was no hope at all.[5]

Dr. Gottheil, who agreed that tight hatbands were harmful, was against discarding headgear since he condemned the sun on several counts: "Overindulgence in sun baths is prejudicial to the human organism, causing irritability and nervousness, cardiac and circulatory disturbances, and dermal lesions, sometimes of a serious nature. Well-known authorities on skin diseases state their belief, found on long experience, that extended exposure to the rays of the sun finally causes marked baldness."[6]

Charles Pabst was the chief dermatologist at the Greenpoint Hospital. In 1921 he advised that exposure to natural sunlight should be undertaken only when the sun's rays were properly regulated, and under the direction of a competent physician. Seven years later he argued it was not a good idea to go hatless and expose the head to sunlight for a long period of time as he knew of cases "in which this resulted in complete loss of hair." The *New York Times* editorialized against going bareheaded in the sun. Agreeing that a small amount of exposure to the sun might stop or cure baldness by killing bacteria, the editorial writer believed too much exposure of the head to the sun was worse than none. In hot and sunny countries, he said, observers "will see that the upper classes, presumably the more intelligent, always wear heavy head covering when they go out of doors, while the peasants and coolies, always more heavily pigmented than their social betters, do all the baring of heads that is done." Strangely, the editorial writer did not state whether the upper or lower classes, hatted or hatless, went bald in those places.[7]

Anyone who argued that sunlight caused or cured baldness faced the impossible task of integrating females into his theory. It was even more difficult logically than to squeeze them into the hat theories. Consequently, none of the sunlight theorists ever mentioned females at all. As late as 1952, in a roundup article on the causes of baldness, *Science Digest* asserted that the practice of going bareheaded "often does harm" to the hair by drying it out. The magazine did note, however, that there was no basis for the theory that hats caused hair loss.[8]

Oddly enough, water was even considered a cause of baldness, or at least something which should not often make contact with the head. One late 1880s physician solemnly stated: "It is a very common practice for men to souse the head daily in water." He noted that habit in 85 percent of his bald patients. Another physician warned that too constant washing of the hair was not only unnecessary but harmful; once a week was enough, he believed. Less liberal was a German physician who counseled that soap and water were rarely required for the head. Dr. Condict Cutler warned against the constant application of water to the scalp as "It undoubtedly tends to produce dandruff." In his opinion, dandruff led to baldness. Physician Ellice Alger declared one cause of baldness to be "frequent soaking of the head."[9]

The idea that water contributed to baldness continued to be popular well into the 1900s. Writing in the popular press, Lester Reynolds argued against too frequent washing of the head because it was "one of the commonest causes of baldness especially with men who are given to washing their hair daily." He believed that washing the hair with soap and water once a month was sufficient for the average head. "Instead of washing the hair daily, wash the brush daily. Surprising results are obtained with this method," he urged.[10]

William Cunningham, Harlem Hospital dermatologist and New York Skin and Cancer Hospital clinical assistant, counseled: "Water should be employed as sparingly as possible. Even for the removal of accumulated debris it is of doubtful utility" since it aggravated the seborrhea, leading to hair loss. Professor Ellinger considered wetting of the hair to be an important cause of premature baldness because it formed an emulsion with the natural oil secretions of the sebaceous glands that dried and plugged the hair follicles, damming up the sebum in the follicles and killing them. Medical man Charles Pabst warned against wetting the head with soap and water more than once every three weeks, while S. Dana Hubbard, director of the New York City Board of Health's Public Education Division advised washing the hair only once every two to four weeks. Excessive washing, he thought, robbed the hair of its natural oils, drying it out and eventually destroying it.[11]

As late as 1930, an article in *Hygeia* advised that shampooing the head once every two weeks was enough, although the writer did admit that "Contrary to a widespread belief, water does not injure the hair nor does it cause loss of hair." Six years later when the American Medical Association offered advice on how to treat thinning hair, one stricture was that the patient should not wet his scalp daily in order to comb his hair easily.[12]

Back in 1906 a physician named Lassar took a contrary position with respect to water. Acknowledging that baldness could not be cured, Lassar advised that one of the more important prophylactic measures consisted in "frequent ablution of the head, a measure that is still considered injurious by many people." Frequent shampooing of the head was, he believed, "the best preventative of baldness." Lassar stood almost alone among medical people in not condemning frequent head washing.[13]

One way of turning baldness into a positive characteristic was to link it with a valued trait such as intelligence. Writing in the mid–1800s, a British investigator demonstrated that "butcher-boys, valets and the lower classes of the Irish" rarely went bald, whereas legislators and lawyers did. Around the same time, American medical students were taught that "slaves, Indians, women and donkeys" were immune to baldness because of their "pea brains." Dr. Anderson argued men grew bald while females didn't because of greater "excitement of the brain which their pursuits occasion." Warning women seeking an education, Anderson asserted that "ladies who follow the pursuit of literature" would find the price they might pay for their book learning was a wig.[14]

Medical journals gave coverage to the idea with an 1886 issue of the *Medical Record* that answered its own question as to why there were so many bald men by writing: "The American nation is threatened with the catastrophe of a universal alopecia.... The answer has almost always been that it is due to the excessive strain and ceaseless mental and physical activity to which American methods of business and modes of living conduce." It was an affliction of the overclass. The next year Dr. George Jackson expanded on this idea. Speaking before a New York County Medical Society meeting, he confirmed that thinkers and brainworkers were often bald. Thinking was to blame because "In active intellectual effort the circulation of the head is increased and the scalp sympathizes and becomes warmer than usual." In some unexplained fashion, the resultant sweating of the scalp led to baldness. Over a decade later, Jackson discussed the idea that heredity was a factor of marked influence in baldness. Nonetheless, he said that nearly all of his bald patients belonged to the intellectual class, which led him to conclude, "It may, then, be fairly inferred that an intellectual, indoor life, specially when coupled with worry and nerve strain, is a predisposing, if not a determining, cause of baldness."[15]

Medical thinkers from around the globe nodded in agreement with this theory in the early 1890s. A German physician believed intellectual application was to blame, but only indirectly. It was the thinkers' neglect of physical exercise and "regularity" in their general conduct of life that was responsible. Writing in the *Lancet*, Dr. M. Joseph Tyson added his voice to those blaming excessive mental work and worry. Putting this idea into a more evolutionary perspective, T. J. Hutton of St. Paul, Minnesota, stated: "Nature having fixed man's form to her satisfaction is now putting a head on him, enlarging and fertilizing his cerebrum." According to Hutton, this increasing intelligence of evolving man meant an increased supply of blood went to the brain, with a correspondingly lesser amount of blood going to the scalp. This decreased nourishment to the hair led to the increased baldness of the population. Hutton believed the average twelve-year-old boy thought more in one day than his great-grandfather of a century earlier had done in a full week. Still, Hutton was content with the situation since "We get brains for hair—a profitable exchange."[16]

When Lucien Jacquet surveyed the area in 1906 for a medical journal, he concluded baldness was more common among intellectual persons than among others. As civilization advanced, so did baldness. Also noted was the "curious fact" that since females had devoted themselves to "intellectual pursuits, and have grown accustomed to employ their cerebral centres in a more intense manner," baldness was becoming progressively more frequent among them. No evidence was presented for the latter idea. None existed.[17]

Around the time of World War I, the idea that intelligence caused baldness could be found in popular magazines. Writing in *Cosmopolitan*, Dr. Woods Hutchinson observed that baldness occurred among all classes. Nevertheless, he went on to state that "perhaps it is a trifle more common among those of sedentary occupations and among brainworkers." A little later a Professor Jamieson vigorously upheld the theory that baldness was indeed more frequent among brainworkers, arguing that since the same nerves supplied brain and scalp, any congestion of the brain automatically disrupted scalp nutrition. The *Literary Digest* commented that many authorities and experts agreed "that premature baldness is common in those who perform intellectual work."[18]

A more evolutionary outlook was offered by Harry Storm, author of books such as *Man, Mind and Hair*, whose thoughts were presented in a 1933 issue of *Fortune* magazine. "What caused our forefathers to lose their hair from the face and ears was caused from the heat created by thinking, but the more continuous thinking of man today loses the hair upon the head," concluded Storm. Over a decade later, another business magazine brought up the theory, perhaps offering comfort to its many bald readers. Journalist Norman Kuhne observed that "baldness is a true triumph of mind over matter—that there is a constant struggle between the gray cells and the hair cells—and that the more a man has inside his head, the less he will have on top of it." As an example he noted that in sports, "The lads who provide the brawn are hairy and the coaches who provide the brain frequently are bald."[19]

In 1956 Dr. M. Wharton Young of Howard University presented his 20 years of research to buttress his contention that people lost their hair due to growing brains. The expanding brain pinched the scalp's blood vessels, cutting down the flow of nourishment to the hair. To explain why the brain expanded in the first place, Young compared it to a muscle, saying that the brain grew with exercising—thinking in this case. According to this theory, baldness was a case of your brain work showing through. Said Young, "In brain workers the brain continues to grow through the fifth decade or longer, and many intellectuals are bald, but idiots and morons are seldom so." Added Young, "Primitive man was not afflicted thus (with baldness) nor do women, with their smaller brains, suffer such a fate." Irwin Lubowe included Young's theory in his own book *New Hope for Your Hair*, published in 1960. While Lubowe tried half-heartedly to distance himself jokingly from Young's blatantly misogynistic remarks, he did refer to Young as a "brilliant anatomist." Later still, in 1978, a journalist writing in the *San Francisco Chronicle* summarized Young's theory in a serious manner, concluding the reduced blood supply caused by the growing male brain was an "important" factor in baldness. A slight revision was added in that according to this summary, women didn't go bald because they had a thicker layer of fat, which aided circulation.[20]

Personal habits from eating to drinking to obesity could also endanger your hair. French physician Dr. Guelpa claimed in 1912 that vegetarianism was an effective remedy for hair loss. He believed a meat diet produced toxins which injured the functioning of the body's organs. One negative effect from a meat diet was excess acidity, which altered nutritive properties of the blood, thus diminishing hair vitality. Charles Pabst observed that "baldness is not as common in vegetarians as in meat eaters." His general recommendation for treatment involved tonics and exercise along with moderation in drinking, eating, and mental effort. Another writer thought both hair loss and tooth decay were caused by poor food habits such as using refined white flour instead of whole grains as well as the use of adulterants, chemicals, and colorings in foods.[21]

Dr. S. Dana Hubbard explained; "Every hair on your head is like a little plant, growing on the scalp as in a garden. The blood is the stream that nourishes this garden…. I know a man who is bald because, for years, he indulged too frequently in Welsh rabbits. This food kept his digestion continually disturbed. He suffered many bad results and among them the loss of hair." Hubbard added that "one of the greatest factors in baldness is constipation. It shows itself in sallow complexions, lack of energy, headaches, nervous and mental depression—and ultimately in the loss of hair." Proper diet and physical exercise were the remedies in that case. Professor Earl Butcher of Hamilton College, New York, agreed that poor nutrition led to baldness. He found that white rats normally got a new growth of hair every 30 days but only every 50 to 60 days when they were underfed, if at all. According to Butcher, "less worry and better appetites, more rest and less energy-consuming activity should be the salvation of America's hair problem." Dr. C. N. Myers of the New York Skin and Cancer Hospital claimed in 1930 that his investigations showed that "a large number of cases of either partial or total baldness are due to the absorption of systems susceptible to toxins of amounts of arsenic and lead that have become more abundant in our present-day environments." He worried about the increased use of arsenic in the spraying of fruits and vegetables as well as its increased presence in food, drugs, and some beverages. Myers stated that in cases of baldness traced to this cause "in a very large percentage of them a cure was effected."[22]

In 1895 one Southern physician claimed that one of the most common causes of hair loss was dyspepsia (indigestion). According to his theory, all parts of the body normally got an appropriate amount of blood supply to keep them well nourished, but in an emergency or when a full supply was not available, the body would direct available blood to important areas such as the heart and lungs, cutting it down to relatively unimportant areas like hair and nails. That was what happened with indigestion. In this theory a common cause of dyspepsia was the irregularity of meal hours. The stomach worked best when fed at regular times. Taking meals at irregular hours caught the stomach by surprise when it was not in a state of perfect readiness. "Be more careful about what you eat, when you eat it, and you will have less dyspepsia and fewer bald heads," he advised.[23]

Teeth also played a role in baldness. In 1900 physician M. Jacquet checked 40 baldies and found 6 with mediocre teeth, 31 with defective teeth, and just 3 with perfect teeth. He believed a close relationship existed between baldness and bad teeth, with both indicating an absence of some of the essential mineral salts in the body, especially sodium sulfate, potassium sulfate, sodium chloride, and calcium phosphate. J. Deroide of France argued that "alopecia is excited by peripheral, visceral or central foci of irritation, situated most frequently in the teeth." No elaboration of that idea was presented. Frenchman R. Sebouraud called attention to the similarity in composition of hair, teeth, and nails, explaining that in men with male pattern baldness, "dental abnormalities are almost regularly to be found." A tendency to baldness often dated back as far as the period of formation of the teeth. Even though the baldness was then not apparent, Sebouraud believed it was there, "existing in a latent, potential form." Dental abnormalities included odd shaped teeth and abnormal spacing. In addition, he also found evidence of syphilis: "Among cases of extensive alopecia many exhibit both the dental abnormalities referred to and a positive serum test (Wassermann). Evidence of syphilis should therefore henceforth be carefully sought in all instances of extensive alopecia."[24]

The idea that food had a major role in causing hair loss died by the 1930s, to be resurrected in the 1970s by Dale Alexander, something of a new age guru, in his book *Healthy Hair and Common Sense*. He wrote other popular books such as *Arthritis and Common Sense*, but he considered his book on hair to be "my chief endeavor, perhaps the culmination of my life's work." Alexander wrote that he had learned how to stop his own hair loss and regrow the lost locks. "I found the right combination of germinating foods, foods that nourish the 'hair seed' that is responsible for the growth of new hair," he explained. His experience was that it took about 40 to 60 days for a constant diet of harmful foods to manifest itself as dull hair or dandruff and even longer for the hair to start thinning. Alexander considered ice cream to be bad for the hair, yet he believed it would take 90 to 180 consecutive days of ice cream eating before its damage to the hair became noticeable. An excellent hair food, thought Alexander, was a raw, fertile egg, drunk in a specially formulated milk shake. "The answer to the startling growth of baldness in the last several decades, I maintain, is the supplanting of a mineral-rich diet of natural, organically grown foods by a menu of diluted, refined, preserved, overcooked foods whose value to the human body has been sharply reduced," said Alexander. "In the century since the Civil War, baldness and hair problems have increased enormously." He presented no evidence for increased baldness in recent years, but he grimly warned: "Our society has become the great hair equalizer! If all races continue to eat the American diet of synthetically fertilized, artificially prepared foods, those who predict a totally bald human race for the future may well be right.... In my opinion it is diet that is chiefly responsible for most cases of baldness."[25]

Alexander thought that constipation could also lead to hair loss because chronic constipation led to frequent headaches which in turn led to changes in the blood circulation of the scalp. He believed that "in this indirect way, constipation could also contribute to baldness." The remedy for that was the Ps and Qs—prunes and a quota of raw vegetables. Alexander cured his own constipation by that method.[26]

Enumerating the causes of baldness in 1893, a German physician cited "excessive indulgences in alcohol and tobacco." Thirty years later Dr. S. Dana Hubbard told of a young man with thinning hair who would soon be bald "largely because of his habit of excessive smoking." Actually the causation was indirect, with smoking causing indigestion, which in turn caused baldness. These men may have been off-the-wall with the idea that smoking caused baldness, but they were ahead of their time in something that only became fashionable after the 1960s—tobacco bashing.[27]

When French physician Dr. Guelpa dissected two corpses, one bald, one hair-bearing, he found a bigger fatty layer in the hairless scalp, which led him to assert, "This simple fact explains the predisposition of the obese to baldness."[28]

Then there was the theory from J. Deroide, another French medical man. Two male patients came to see him independently, each with classic male pattern baldness. An examination of the mouth, teeth, nose, and chest found all to be normal in each man. The doctor removed earwax from each patient's blocked ears, however, and concluded: "A wax earplug was clearly the exciting factor of alopecia…. In the second week after removal of the wax, hair began to grow in the alopecia patches, and later it became firm and abundant."[29]

Even something as seemingly innocuous as brushing the hair came in for attack. One writer explained that there was no remedy for baldness but there was a preventive. The cause of baldness was the stiff bristles of a hair brush. Decades earlier a barber had told this man that the sharp point of a bristle punctured the blood vessel at the hair's root, causing the follicle to die. Immediately this man stopped using a hard brush and switched to a comb. His hair, which had been falling out, stopped doing so. He believed baldness struck certain areas of the head and not others because of the angle of brushing, which was most injurious to the top of the head. People with thin hair were at greater risk, while men with thick, coarse, curly, or kinky hair had less baldness since their thicker hair gave more protection to the scalp. Women didn't go bald because they had thicker hair and brushed differently than men did.[30]

In 1934, Dr. George Carlson of Lincoln, Nebraska, told Nebraska optometrists that nine out of ten baldies had some kind of eye fatigue. "Nerves and muscles of the head are deprived by eye strain of energy that should go to the roots of the hair," he explained.[31]

In a more spiritual vein, the writer of a 1913 letter to the *New York Times* commented that 99 percent of "sincere" religious leaders had full heads of hair and that he had never seen an elderly religious leader who was bald. That prompted a second man to write in agreeing with the first letter. Among a score or more of elderly clergy that the second writer could recall, not one of them was bald.[32]

Bald men worried about their hair loss, and this worry could be bad for them because there was a long-lived school of thought that worry itself, or tensions and nervous strains, was a cause of baldness. One more thing to worry about. Worrying made you bald, which caused you to worry more, which led to a greater degree of denudation.

One of the earlier references to that idea was by Dr. George Jackson in 1887; he advised as a treatment or preventive that "worry and anxiety of mind should be combated by the cultivation of a more cheerful habit of thought." A few years later Dr. M. Joseph Tyson indicted several items for causing baldness. One of them was excessive worry, but he offered no prescription. Slightly more wide-ranging was a German physician who implicated emotion, anxiety, grief, fright, and certain "reflex influences" as causes of baldness. When Dr. Ellice Alger considered the affliction, he declared that "nerve-strain ... is beyond question a factor in many cases."[33]

More long-winded was physician A. Ohmann-Dumesnil, professor of dermatology and syphilology at the St. Louis College of Physicians and Surgeons. He thought baldness was due either to a parasite or nervous influences, or both. From his experience, he thought neurotic baldness occurred more frequently than the parasitic type. Most of the cases he treated were "light blondes." While all of them were in good physical health, he noted: "The nervous system lacked that stability and repose which should exist in the normal individual and which is so essential to proper assimilation.... Those that did not exhibit the grosser phenomena of nervous disturbances exhibited psychic phenomena plainly indicative of nervous instability. Irritability upon slight provocation, anxiety concerning trivial affairs, depressions of spirits out of proportion to the exciting cause and similar perturbations showed themselves as evidence of the neurotic condition present in the individual." A prominent feature Ohmann-Dumesnil found in these patients was their "hopelessness" as to the ultimate result in the treatment of their cases. Ohmann-Dumesnil thought there was very little promise of hair recovery for those people, but stated: "A little moral suasion has quite an effect in improving the condition, and success is not the impossibility it might at first appear to be." To treat nervous baldness, this physician gave pills to ameliorate the nervous condition. In several cases he claimed to have obtained marked growth of hair.[34]

In 1900, Jackson was still arguing that, among other things, worry and nervous strain were predisposing or determining causes of baldness. Dr. Pincus believed that "anxiety of the mind, depression of the spirits" led to something called a "tight scalp," which led to an unexplained fashion to baldness. Another observer declared that worry and depression caused the formation of uric acid around the brain tissue. This acid then acted to kill the hair roots. "Complacent individuals and those with unruffled spirits," he said, "always have plenty of hair."[35]

In the 1920s, Dr. S. Dana Hubbard reported on a famous millionaire who was bald due to prolonged nervous strain. All of his worrying affected his digestion, circulation, and nervous system, causing poisons to accumulate in the blood. That starved the hair, causing it to fall out and never return. A decade later physician Herman Goodman held forth with a theory of "nerve baldness." Hair growth was governed by the sympathetic nervous system.

When that system was disrupted, as it could be by nervous strain or shock, said Goodman, then hair loss followed.[36]

In London, during World War II, the nervous strain from the war and working long hours was causing workers to lose their hair. According to Herbert Agar, special assistant to the United States ambassador to England: "Once it starts there doesn't seem to be anything to do about it, but go on losing your hair until it is gone. The London doctors tell people that the only thing to do about it is to go away for two or three weeks of rest and peace." The government refused permission to its clerical workers to take a vacation as a hair restorer, however, believing that to do so would open the way for many other such requests.[37]

One of the more fully developed of the nervous strain theories came in 1950 from two Chicago psychiatrists. One was Alan Robertson; the other was Thomas Szasz, who went on to bigger and better things as an iconoclastic critic of the establishment. It was their theory that long continued nervous tension affected the scalp and caused baldness. They believed that nervous tension caused the scalp muscles to become taut, pinching the blood vessels and resulting in hair that could not grow normally. Their idea came to them from working with psychiatric patients. They thought their patients' physical ills and baldness might be related to emotion tension. Studying the patients, Szasz was struck by the fact that "many bald men, particularly those who start to lose their hair at an early age, have expressions suggestive of a pronounced and chronic tension of the facial muscles. In many, we encountered various types of 'fixed smiles,' and in a few, a rather striking, characteristic expression best described as a 'toothy smile.' Such rigid facial patterns are thought to reflect psychologically speaking, defensive attitudes." This tension was a stretching of the facial muscles which could be very subtle in a condition of mental anxiety or fear or anger. That tension of the facial muscles was passed by the nerve system to the ears and scalp, weakening the elements in which the hair grew. Unless that tension was diminished, loss of hair continued.[38]

As evidence, the doctors cited investigators who agreed with them that scalp tension was important in baldness and others who claimed there was less of a fatty layer in bald scalps than in hair-bearing men and women. Also cited by Szasz was M. Wharton Young, who claimed to have produced baldness in a monkey by taking out a section of scalp, producing increased scalp tension. Szasz and Anderson did, however, disavow themselves from the blatantly sexist elements of Young's theory.[39]

The two doctors believed all that scalp tension produced shearing forces which decreased circulation to the scalp. In conclusion they stated that "ordinary human baldness is the result of chronic hyperactivity of the scalp muscles." To treat this excess scalp tension would require blocking the nerve signals passing from the face to the head, especially the region most prone to baldness. If accomplished, the blocking would at least arrest the balding areas and possibly lead to regrowth of hair in areas with relatively minor structural damage. Blocking could be accomplished, they thought, with injections of procaine or pure alcohol into the branches of the facial nerves innervating the occipitalis muscles on both sides of the head. More drastically, they believed bilateral section would provide a more permanent and complete type of severance. Only those branches of the facial nerves which innervated the occipitalis muscles needed to be sectioned. Either way the doctors reassured their readers: "This should be a relatively simple and harmless procedure." Szasz hoped dermatologists would use these methods on their bald patients.[40]

Heredity played no part in Szasz and Robertson's theory, although they believed testosterone played a part in that it interfered with and decreased the fatty layers that protected the scalp muscles. "It is this fat padding of the scalp which, we believe, affords protection against baldness to women and prepubertal boys." While they seemed to argue that virtually all baldness stemmed from the effects of nervous strain on the scalp muscles, the pair spread their bets around a little by advising it might be helpful in treating or preventing the affliction to keep the hair dry, to avoid the use of tight hats, to avoid headgear worn by others, to massage the skull, and to treat the scalp with ultraviolet rays.[41]

Two years later *Science Digest* writer John Gibson dispelled some of the untrue information about hair, such as the theory that hats caused baldness. He noted, however, that science had discovered that emotional factors played a role. Thus he advised: "Practice mental hygiene. Do everything possible to avoid worry, anxiety, and other destructive emotions. For scientific studies indicate that what goes on inside your head has a very definite effect on what grows on top!"[42]

Time magazine once reported that if anxiety changed into anger, a man could be in trouble because "Repeated scares or fits of anger may cause baldness by causing the capillaries of the scalp to constrict." Even if one overcame the worry and anger, trouble still lay ahead. Two psychiatrists suggested in the 1980s that laughter could be a cause of baldness. The facial nerve had branches that activated the scalp muscles. If you laughed a certain way, you pulled the muscles tight, cutting off the blood supply, they theorized.[43]

Turning to sexual activity to take one's mind off worry and worry about worrying was not the answer, at least for your hair. Early researchers who tried to tie sexual activity to baldness believed that excessive sexual activity was a cause of baldness. Medical practitioner M. Jacquet announced in 1900 that in the treatment of the condition, "All excesses, especially sexual, must be avoided." Researcher Dr. Sebouraud observed the "high frequency of baldness among the sexually precocious." U.S. Public Health surgeon J. O. Cobb remarked that when a man started to go bald, his friends "begin to slap him on the back, and nudge and wink and point the accusing finger at this early sign of their overtasted forbidden fruits. A young man thus afflicted springs into prominence at once as a person who is more or less of a rake." During World War I, Dr. Louis Mount, speaking of younger bald men, declared, "It is often excesses at the shrines of Venus and Bacchus that are at the bottom of their trouble."[44]

The idea that too much sex caused baldness was not one likely to sit well with baldies. While the cure was obvious, it was also drastic. Better to recast the theory to see the two aspects stemming from another source. Thus in 1948 a journalist reported the same chemical processes "that make a man sexually prolific, cause him to lose his hair." An example given was that if your great-grandfather was of an "amatory bent and bald, you may well have inherited both characteristics, one the natural consequences of the other." A few years later the British Medical Association's magazine *Family Doctor* argued that bald men were likely to be more virile than those with a full head of hair. That was a distortion of the genetic theory that baldness came to people who had the genetic material and normal levels of male hormone—virtually every male. Nevertheless, the journal inaccurately contended that the more hormones, the greater the likelihood of baldness.[45]

Even more comforting to baldies was the further recasting of this theory in the 1980s to hold that bald men were indeed more sexually active and it was precisely because they were bald. Dr. William Rosenberg, professor of dermatology at the University of Tennessee College of Medicine in Memphis, claimed that baldness caused men to be more virile. He had no plans to apply minoxidil to his own bald head, and he advised all his bald patients to avoid wigs, operations, and creative barbers and to get as much sunlight on their domes as possible. Sunlight had the ability to penetrate through the skull and scalp to affect the pineal gland. In turn, the pineal influenced the endocrine system, which regulated the amount of male hormone testosterone produced. Since more sunlight got through the bald head than the hairy one, more testosterone was produced, resulting in more manly, virile men. The question of how sunlight could penetrate the skull but not the hair was left dangling.[46]

As might be expected, this image of the macho bald guy was happily accepted, at least by baldies. Senator Alan Simpson of Wyoming began to lose his hair in his 30s. He declared he wasn't going to waste any of his hormones growing hair. At the tenth anniversary meeting of the Bald-Headed Men of America club, President John Capps remarked, "Most any intelligent woman will tell you bald men don't waste their hormones growing hair."[47]

Researcher Albert Damon reported on the topic of baldness and paternity in 1965. The only study he uncovered prior to his own was a 1951 Italian report which found that bald men had 40 percent more male offspring than men with full hair or with receding hairlines that had not developed into full baldness. Damon did not accept that conclusion putting the result down to chance instead. Using the 1,297 men who had entered Harvard College between 1880 and 1912, Damon classified them into categories, 93 having no baldness, 593 with slight baldness, 413 having moderate hair loss, and 197 with marked to total baldness. To classify those men, he used their 25th class reunion pictures. With regard to the 1,008 fathers from the group, Damon found no association between baldness and either the number or the gender ratio of their 2,775 children. Damon added that to his knowledge no association had been established in the general male population between sex hormone levels and fertility or the sex ratio of offspring.[48]

One of the oddest theories to come along was the idea that a certain form of breathing caused baldness. Physician Delos Parker was a lecturer at Detroit College of Medicine, where he had researched baldness for over a decade. In 1901 Parker released his accumulated wisdom. He thought that baldness was caused by a poisonous material circulating in the bloodstream, a pathological condition resulting from an "auto-infection" whereby the toxin was absorbed by the blood from the lung tissue. This toxin formed in the lungs from the decomposition of organic material normally present in respired air. Due to inappropriate breathing, it remained in the lungs instead of being expelled. It was residual air which hung around in the lungs to incubate into a toxin over time, instead of being expelled as in the case of a good breather. Parker called the process when the upper ribs took part in breathing "superior costal type." When only the lower ribs and diaphragm took part—the upper ribs remaining immobile—he called it "inferior costal type." Both were appropriate, he believed. If only the diaphragm was involved, Parker used the term "diaphragmatic or abdominal" breathing. If there was no movement of a portion of the chest wall in breathing, no air was received or expelled by lung tissue lying beneath the position of the chest wall under consideration. Any air in that location just sat and incubated, said Parker.[49]

Citing a couple of medical texts, Parker announced that costal breathing was common in women, while abdominal was common in men. One reason for that difference was the dress style of the day, which in the case of females greatly restricted the descent of the diaphragm, making costal breathing a necessity. A second factor making costal breathing easier for women was the fact, claimed Parker, that female ribs were more mobile than male ribs. It should come as no surprise that the physician could cite no authority for that statement. People who led sedentary work lives were at special risk for baldness because the head-bent-forward posture of a desk worker tended to mitigate against costal breathing. These factors all meant that abdominal breathing men went bald while costal breathing women did not. In over ten years of research involving observation of thousands of individuals, Parker said he had never seen baldness not associated with abdominal breathing, nor did he ever see a baldie who was a costal breather.[50]

To prove his theory, Parker conducted an experiment. Taking respired air from a baldie, he put it in a flask with distilled water and then let it sit for a while to allow time for organic material to decompose in warmth and moisture as in the lungs. Next he injected a dog and a chicken with this material. Both went bald. Colleagues complained, however, that the doctor had used no controls. Parker countered by doing a more controlled experiment in which chickens one and two got respired, incubated air from a baldie and nonbaldie, respectively. Other chickens got atmospheric air, freshly respired air, or water only. Only chickens one and two went bald. Although the experiment was marred and abruptly ended when chickens one and two got into a fight. Chicken number one slam-dunked number two into a pan of cold water. When found later number two was cold and exhausted and soon expired. Seeking a name for the toxic substance produced from improperly respired air after incubation, Parker chose trichotoxin.[51]

Six years later Parker presented another paper on his theory in which he reiterated that the fundamental cause of common baldness was "a form of respiration that leaves residual air undisturbed…. [The] fundamental cause of common baldness is absence of upper chest breathing." Parker's readers now had the advantage of 20 years of his accumulated wisdom. Having been queried as to why the toxin only killed the hair on top of the head, he replied that those hair roots had low vitality compared to roots in other parts of the head because of the hard, more bloodless top of the head. He maintained there was "not a single exception to the rule that persons affected with common baldness do not employ upper chest breathing." Nonbaldies always employed upper chest breathing. Parker said he had treated many men for the condition over the past decade by giving them directions to constantly practice upper chest breathing. Some had followed his instructions exactly, some not at all, and some were in between. Success in hair restoration was a function of how closely one had followed the doctor's directions. Those that followed his instructions exactly grew hair. Those that didn't, didn't grow hair. Hair grew on men on spots that had been bald for 20 years, Parker claimed.[52]

Still experimenting, Parker injected dogs, pigeons, chickens, rabbits, and guinea pigs with his strange mixture of air and water; he even had some creatures drink it. Although he claimed most creatures who got incubated, respired air went bald, he did admit that it did not happen to the guinea pigs and rabbits. He explained that there was an "anatomical reason for this that need not be explained at this time." According to Parker, all the bald creatures regrew their covering when he stopped the injections. Six years after first identifying trichotoxin, Parker admitted he was no closer to determining its composition, although he claimed to have taken photos of it through a microscope. By this time he was convinced that trichotoxin began to form after six hours and the process was complete in four to five days. He was more convinced than ever of his theory, vowing to solve the mystery of trichotoxin.[53]

This theory was reported in both medical journals of the era and in the popular press and was not derided. One journalist suggested that since chest-breathing women kept their hair, men should limit abdominal breathing by wearing constrictive garments, as women did, in order to secure "the thoracic respiration so conducive to hair health."[54]

The idea that heredity played some part in producing baldness was discussed for well over a century. Many issued a flat denial for a heredity role in denuding the scalp. In 1895 physician George Elliot declared that no "warranty exists for accusing heredity as a direct causal factor" in baldness. Dr. Isadore Dyer, professor of diseases of the skin at Tulane University, stated in 1912 that "hereditary baldness cannot be proved—as in most instances some presenting factor may be found in all such cases, able to explain the cause of the loss of hair." Speaking around the same time as Dyer, physician Arthur Reynolds, a former Chicago health commissioner, asserted that baldness could not be due to heredity since men went bald but women did not.[55]

Some experts did blame heredity, but for unusual reasons. Faced with some cases of baldness he couldn't explain away with other theories, Dr. George Jackson believed heredity was the cause, but only in the sense that the victim inherited a scalp type predisposed to press downward, ultimately killing the follicles. During World War I, a physician named Pincus touted a similar idea when he argued that premature baldness was due to heredity in that some individuals received a tight or stretched scalp muscle that was peculiar to certain families.[56]

From time to time, someone would state heredity played a role, but would then ignore the statement. A confused Jackson resurfaced a dozen years later in 1900 to declare that "heredity is a factor of marked influence, a strong predisposing cause of loss of hair at least, if not in many instances the actual cause of baldness." Nonetheless, he went on to cite dandruff as the "most active exciting cause of alopecia," as well as to cite the indoor intellectual life and nerve strain as predisposing if not actual causes of baldness. Another physician of that era named heredity a powerful predisposing factor in the affliction but went on to claim it was mostly the fault of hats. More number oriented was medical man C. J. White, who studied 794 cases of baldness in 1910 and claimed to find heredity involved in just 30 percent of them.[57] One of the earliest reports to blame heredity in an unequivocal fashion was an 1868 editorial in the *New York Times* which said of baldness, "The defect is often hereditary, and runs through generations; and nothing will do any good, except the strictest hygienic treatment, adopted at a very early age and continued while growth lasts." It was an idea rarely espoused or accepted by the scientific community.[58]

More than six decades later, biologist Laurence Snyder said that pattern baldness seemed beyond doubt to be due to heredity. After extensive study of 4,000 men and women over the age of 35 at asylums for the insane, Snyder concluded that "baldness is more common in men than in women, that it is generally transmitted directly from a father to half or more of his sons but only to an occasional daughter, that a woman never shows it unless her father showed it, and that the sons of a bald woman will all be bald." He found 43 percent of the men were bald, while 8 percent of the females were bald. Snyder selected insane asylums for his study because women there didn't try to hide their baldness.[59]

Snyder was working with a hereditary concept which dated back to 1918, when D. Osborne advanced the idea that baldness was hereditary as a single Mendelian dominant in the male and as a recessive in the female. The major problem in explaining baldness by heredity was the sexual dimorphism manifested by this condition. In the 1930s one researcher believed the inheritance was dominant and that its different manifestation in males and females was due to the difference to be found in the activity of the sebaceous glands and their general metabolism.[60]

The person whose work proved that baldness was due to heredity and hormones was Dr. James B. Hamilton, whose 1942 work is still accepted as establishing the causes of baldness. He investigated 104 eunuchs and eunuchoids (testes present but not functionally normal). Men who failed to mature sexually, he found, did not become bald. Even the recession of the line of hair on the temples and foreheads that was observed in the majority of normal men failed to appear. Of those castrated in adulthood, some already exhibited states of baldness at the time of castration. Castration prevented all further extension of baldness, although, of course, the bald areas did not experience any regrowth. Twelve prepubertial castrates were treated by androgenic therapy (testosterone injections). Four started to go bald; all came from families in which baldness among the normal males was a frequent event. The other eight came from families showing no tendency to baldness. When the treatment was stopped, the baldness halted. When it was later started again, the baldness again proceeded. Hamilton concluded that the hereditary tendency to baldness would only manifest itself in the presence of an adequate level of androgenic hormone secretion in the body. That level was only rarely reached by females but was present in all normal adult men. Baldness never developed before puberty, adult eunuchs castrated before puberty never went bald, and adult eunuchs castrated in adulthood had any already developing baldness halted at that point. Adult eunuchs treated with testosterone as therapy continued to go bald (if genetically predisposed) as long as therapy continued. A cessation of therapy once again halted the progression of baldness. Hamilton found that in the eunuchs he studied, the one with the highest daily average level of androgenic secretion was at 20.5 IU, while in normal adult men the average daily level of androgenic secretion was 65 IU. Thus, said Hamilton, the minimal androgenic stimulation required to induce baldness was a value between that present in normal men and that in castrates and eunuchoid men. "Induction of common baldness is an example in the human of a mechanism by means of which a genetic predisposition becomes expressed. Inherited susceptibility results in the development of common baldness if the gonads differentiate as testes, since in the usual course of events these glands provide androgenic secretions, incitants of baldness," he wrote.[61]

Hamilton's work should have put an end to the heredity issue and to the many theories about other causes of baldness, such as wearing hats, but it did not. Four years after Hamilton's work, eugenicist Harry Harris supported the idea that baldness was inherited as a simple Mendelian dominant but also said, "The hypothesis that both late and premature baldness are determined by the same gene do [sic] not fit." *Science Digest* summarized Hamilton's findings, noting that no amount of androgenic stimulation given to a man would produce baldness in him if he lacked a family genetic predisposition to baldness. Although Hamilton made it clear that only a minimal amount of hormone secretion, found in virtually all adult men, was enough, this magazine headlined its piece "Baldness—He-Man Complaint." Hamilton had never suggested, nor was it true, that a man with twice the normal androgenic level would go bald twice as fast or start losing hair earlier. Reaching the trigger level started the process; any amount over that was irrelevant.[62]

Chicago dermatologist Herbert Rattner argued in 1948 that baldness was due to heredity but said it was a recessive trait in females. Somehow the erroneous idea that baldness was a recessive trait in females was illogically extended to a fairly prevalent piece of folklore: women were responsible for baldness. Typical of such pronouncements was a 1955 article in *Americas* magazine which stated: "As for us at 'Americas,' what seems most unfair about the whole business is that women, who rarely suffer from baldness, are the ones who blithely pass it on from generation to generation. Your grandfather really had nothing to do with it, except that he married your grandmother." Genetically, baldness is passed on equally from either parent and is inherited with equal probability by sons and daughters. Whether hair loss then ensues is a matter of hormones.[63]

As late as 1960, Hamilton's work was still not accepted, at least not everywhere. In his book, Dr. Irwin Lubowe, a dermatologist at the Metropolitan Hospital Center in New York, declared heredity was not the only cause. Lubowe claimed that Hamilton suggested "that excessive production of the androgens, the male hormones, is an important contributory factor in pattern baldness." Lubowe actually changed Hamilton's phrase "normal production" to "excessive production" and changed "necessary contributory factor" to "important contributory factor" to support his own theory. He believed many other factors such as dandruff, hats, and circulation were important. The shape of the skull and "a continuous overstimulation of machinery for the production of androgen" were factors Lubowe considered to be inherited. When *Newsweek* summarized Lubowe's work, it stated that while the baldness gene could be inherited with equal likelihood by either sex, its behavior differed between the genders because "The male need inherit only one baldness gene to develop the pattern of baldness. A woman must receive two baldness genes in order to be afflicted by a thinning or loss of hair."[64]

Curiously, the same Dr. Lubowe is the expert who contributed the signed article on baldness in the 1994 edition of the *Encyclopedia Americana*. One line from that entry stated that a certain type of diet "may eliminate excess oil and dandruff that contribute to baldness." Another sentence read: "The use of hormonal (testosterone) lotions on the scalp may also be helpful" in treating baldness. Both statements are incorrect.[65]

Early in 1994 the media gave a certain amount of attention to London scientists who announced they were close to finding the gene responsible for MPB. It was a discovery, they thought, which could pave the way for development of drugs to counteract the gene, preventing baldness. Dr. Adam Carey of St. Mary's Hospital Medical School in London said his team was close to finding the bald gene. Trained as a gynecologist, Carey was researching polycystic ovary disease—a condition in which women can become infertile because of hormonal disturbances and the failure of the ovaries to ovulate—when he stumbled onto his supposed discovery. In an attempt to establish that women were genetically predisposed to the condition, he interviewed their parents and siblings. Carey was struck by the large number of fathers and brothers who showed signs of baldness. His analysis showed 50 percent of these men were bald. "That is very striking when you realize that only seven percent of men in general are bald," Carey concluded. He decided a mutated gene caused both complaints, one in each gender. The problem here was Carey's odd idea that seven percent of males were bald. Actually the 50 percent figure was about what one would expect in the general male population.[66]

4
RUBBING, BLISTERING, AND ELECTRIFYING

Of ten bald men, nine are deceitful; the tenth is dumb.
Chinese proverb

The only thing that stops hair falling is—the ground.
Journal of the American Medical Association,
February 15, 1965

Massage of the scalp was an often recommended treatment/preventive of baldness. One 1890s doctor declared that the occipito-frontalis muscle should be exercised several times in the course of a day if baldness had already set in. Another medical practitioner argued that for stimulating growth of hair the only remedy was massage, with the "patient pinching up the scalp between the ends of the extended fingers of both hands for five minutes night and morning. Massage must not be used until the dandruff is checked." One of the stranger massage techniques recommended in the medical literature was stroking "the nape of the neck with a coarse bathing-glove, that may be warmed if necessary."[1]

The problem, explained Dr. George Elliott, was that the skin of the scalp had no underlying muscles to exercise it. Only the infrequent action of the occipito-frontalis muscle caused the skin of the scalp to move. It was not enough for a healthy scalp. Women had well-exercised scalps from the combing, plaiting, and throwing of the hair from side to side, while men barely gave more than a moment to the brushing and combing of their hair. Indications for treatment pointed to regular scalp massage before the absorption of the underlying fat and atrophy of the occipito-frontalis muscle. Massage had to be applied early in life to be an effective preventive.[2]

U.S. Public Health and Marine Hospital Service surgeon J. Cobb urged that every man should devote a short time before going to bed and after he got up in the morning to scalp massage. "During the brisk friction he should grasp his hair in handfuls and draw the scalp back and forth many times, to make it slide over the skull. That will prevent binding and thinning of the scalp and preserve the cushion of fat on the top of the head," he said.[3]

Around the time of World War I, a letter writer to the *New York Times* declared that a man could easily develop in his scalp "most remarkable muscles." Since almost any man could raise his eyebrows, a man who put his mind to it could learn to raise his forehead for several inches above his eyebrows "and it will then be only a short time before he can move his scalp in any direction he pleases. As soon as this has been learned all fear of baldness is gone.... This method tried for six months will give a good head of hair." The letter writer claimed to have cured his own baldness precisely that way. Ten days later a second letter writer, in reply to the above, stated that this scalp wriggling would, if it did anything, cause rather than cure baldness because developing the scalp muscles would reduce the blood supply to the follicles.[4]

In 1917, Dr. William Brady recommended that massage was a good remedy, but only when done by the individual himself, not by the barber. Massage should loosen the scalp, with the man lifting it up in folds and rolling those folds between the fingers. "Grasp the scalp with the wide open hand, forcibly draw the fingers toward the palm, heaping up a little fold of scalp under them. Go over the entire scalp in this way, changing hands occasionally, for the hand soon tires, until the whole head glows," explained the doctor. Advice from the American Medical Association in 1930 on how to treat thinning hair included a recommendation of five minutes of scalp massage with the fingers, morning and night. So popular and widespread had scalp massage become by then that some establishments had replaced human fingers with rubber, fabric, or leather fingers in machines.[5]

Dr. William Fitzgerald of Hartford, Connecticut, reported the results of zone, or pressure, therapy in the medical literature. He claimed that rubbing the finger nails of one hand against those of the other hand, including the thumb nails, very briskly for two or three minutes a few times daily would cause the scalp to tighten, thus decreasing or altogether stopping the loss of hair.[6]

During the 1880s and 1890s, one of the popular baldness treatments used by the medical profession was blistering (vesication) of the scalp. Irritating the area in this manner was believed to produce pooling of blood in the scalp (hyperemia), which provided more nourishment for the follicles there, causing hair regrowth. Physician M. Vidal had used cantharides (crushed insects better known as the reputed aphrodisiac Spanish Fly) applied to the scalp to produce blistering. He often found these blisters painful for his patients, however, and liable to cause cantharidism—a poisoning effect from the insects. Searching for something better, he turned to a blister recipe devised by a former pupil, M. Bidel. After the bald head was cleaned, Vidal applied two or three coats of his mixture with a brush, happily finding "complete vesication took place, without any considerable pain, in about two hours and a half." His formula combined crushed bugs with acetic acid in a solution of 90 percent alcohol. While the mixture contained 1.2 percent insects, there was said to be no poisonous effect to the patient.[7]

A formula recommended by a different medical man required the hair to be cut short and the scalp to be reddened with a mild sinapism (mustard plaster). For the following five days, the scalp was treated daily with a mixture of equal parts chloroform and acetic acid. In addition, an ointment consisting of one part salicylic acid, four parts precipitated sulfur, and twenty parts Vaseline was applied.[8]

Considering baldness a disease of the skin and not the hair, Dr. Sebouraud accordingly recommended "the heavy layer of skin be destroyed by vesication" so drugs applied could have a more direct effect. His method was to apply an unnamed liquid which caused a blister and then on the next day to apply nitrate of silver to the denuded surface. It was a treatment said to be rapid and effective.[9]

France's Dr. Jacquet claimed all dermatologists agreed that "cutaneous irritation is the first principle in the treatment of baldness," although he did admit there was no agreement on just how much irritation to apply. Jacquet thought temporary irritation was more effective than permanent irritation. To his credit, he eschewed the use of chemicals, recommending, "Transitory hyperemia can best be caused by repeated slapping of the scalp with a sharp brush, made of good pig's bristles. The brush should be applied all over the bald area, and along the margins of the hair. In a few seconds the scalp will become red and pulsating, a condition which will last for half an hour or more. The treatment should be repeated morning and night." Jacquet had obtained more rapid results in a few cases with more frequent applications of his scalp spanking, five or six a day. He preferred a rubber-backed brush with wire bristles because he thought it was easier to clean.[10]

Discussing the use of cantharides, Dr. Ohmann-Dumesnil noted they varied in composition and were irritants. Admitting their effects were "the best," he acknowledged the inconveniences resulting from their use made the method "anything but a pleasant one to the patient." They caused the hair to mat, were difficult to remove, and didn't look good. Instead of cantharides, Ohmann-Dumesnil used carbolic acid to create blistering on his patients. Once or twice a week he freely rubbed the entire bald scalp with the acid. Any parts which showed an inflammation reaction were skipped at the next treatment. Not satisfied with the ordinary 95 percent carbolic acid, he secured some "pure English carbolic acid," which reportedly gave faster and more marked results. Referring to his method, this physician declared: "The impulse given to the growth of hair by this procedure was quite noticeable…. Such treatment, while rather painful, is efficacious."[11]

A Dr. Balzer from New York State practiced "friction of the bald part" on his patients daily with a 30 percent solution of lactic acid until the skin became inflamed. Treatment was then suspended for a few days until the inflammation subsided. Balzer claimed he regularly observed a new growth of hair on his patients in the course of three weeks.[12]

One naysayer regarding the use of blistering agents was Dr. Condict Cutler, who argued that by setting up inflammatory conditions, those agents dissolved the natural oil of the skin, produced scalp dryness, and "in fact, may be the direct cause of the disease."[13]

Another treatment method was the vacuum cap. One of the earliest mentioned was in 1899, when the *Canadian Lancet* reported on an advertised cure for baldness based on the theory that hair loss was caused by a diminished blood supply to the scalp with a resulting atrophy of the hair follicles. A hollow rubber cup called a "capillary chalice" by the maker was placed over the head. Some air was then sucked out to create a partial vacuum. Supposedly this procedure increased blood circulation to the scalp and stimulated normal growth of hair. Surveying that method of hair restoration, the *Medical Record* declared it was left "in no doubt as to the efficacy of the treatment" because the company ads for the product contained a number of before and after photos in which "A number of men are shown with remarkably smooth pates, and later we see the same heads covered with hair that would be the envy of any barber in the land."[14]

In 1920 it was reported that the vacuum method had been recently tried in the United States. It was much the same process except that this one featured a tight fitting metal hood that attached to the head. When the air was sucked out, a full vacuum was said to be achieved. In the 1930s, ads for these vacuum suction caps were still appearing in the daily press and in magazines. A hot mail order item early in this century was the Evans Vacuum Cap. If the patient had a red scalp after 10 minutes of use, it was a sure sign the machine was working. Marketing the cap with a money-back guarantee, the Evans company claimed only 5 percent of the users took it up on that offer. Then there was the Inter-Vac Hair Rejuvenator aluminum vacuum cap, which promised to draw "life-giving blood into the starved hair roots."[15]

The state of the art in that technology was reached in 1936, when the new and improved vacuum model was featured in news articles in the major weekly newsmagazines. Dr. Andre Alexis Cueto of Cincinnati was offering the medical profession a machine to grow hair on heads whose hair follicles were not dead. It consisted of a hood that fit over the head. By means of an air pump, Cueto created an alternating vacuum and pressure upon the scalp which exercised the capillaries, bringing reviving blood to them. The action of the machine was described by one journalist as "sucking and blowing, thus kneading the surface and underlying tissues." Cueto claimed he had treated 150 patients with his machine, achieving "one hundred percent results." Asked to comment on this vacuum treatment, Dr. Morris Fishbein, the bald editor of the *Journal of the American Medical Association*, replied only that he was skeptical.[16]

Then there was the Frankenstein method of treating baldness with electricity. In the 1890s a German doctor named Seeger recommended the application of frictional electricity to the scalp by means of a gutta-percha plate (with an insulated handle) that was rubbed over a dry cloth or piece of soft leather and then rubbed over the bald areas a couple of times a day.[17]

Dr. Samter was another German who tried electricity around the same time as Seeger. Samter used faradic current on baldies for weeks on end but got no results. The faradic-induced electric current circulated around the subject's head but made no direct contact.[18]

More successful was the static electricity treatment reported by Drs. R. Pivani and J. Blasi, who claimed to have effected a complete cure in four out of five patients subjected to their treatment. About 20 to 30 sessions, or "seances," were required in which "The electric bath with sparks discharged on to the bald patches was the method employed."[19]

Deeply into this type of torture was Dr. George M. MacKee of New York State, who in 1900 reported a success rate of close to 100 percent over three years. MacKee, who taught dermatology at New York University, thought the major problem in baldness was poor blood circulation in the scalp, which starved the hair, and bacterial invasion. After unsuccessfully trying various irritants and corrosives on the scalp, MacKee hit upon his successful method: using high frequency electric current applied to the skin in the form of a spark. This produced a hyperemia which lasted for some time after the treatment was given. During the 6 to 12 hours the hyperemia persisted, the hair follicles received an increased blood supply and resistance to germ invasion. It was important the hyperemia cease after some hours lest it become a chronic congestion with "untoward results." MacKee called the treatment "practically painless" and thought the spark was both a stimulant and a bacteriacidal. The latter effect was supposedly penetrating and powerful because of the properties of the spark, heat effects, and the production of large amounts of ozone. MacKee knew ozone was produced because its odor could be detected for hours after the treatment. An electrode was used to apply the spark to the head. The spark gap had to be a certain distance or else "it condensed into a heavy spark which is unpleasant to the patient and is not productive to the desired results." Five to ten minutes of treatment was sufficient to produce an active hyperemia. Successful treatment could take many, many months of two to three treatments per week. As a last caution, MacKee noted, "While applying the spark the electrode should be kept in contact with the hair and in motion, so as to avoid the heat effects which are strong enough to burn the hair if allowed to remain stationary for several seconds."[20]

Despite MacKee's success, this was a treatment that lay dormant for well over half a century until the late 1970s when Marcella Ferens administered her version of the electric cure while working out of a secluded farmhouse near Darragh, Pennsylvania. The first step in her treatment consisted of running a rake-shaped glass instrument filled with a purple gas across the head to sterilize the scalp. Then the subject held a wire hooked to an electrolysis machine while the operator massaged the bald area with a secret formula consisting of herbs, vitamins, and minerals, holding a second wire to complete a low current. Said Ferens, "We sterilize the scalp and then force the formula in by electrolysis." She claimed she could grow hair on anybody with her technique. At least some customers agreed. Car dealer Richard Lipecky remarked, "It's true. You wouldn't believe it. I look in the mirror and see it happen every day. My head was bald from the front to the back and now I've got hair all over." A Roman Catholic priest who wouldn't give his name said he had tried many treatments, but only Ferens's method worked: "I'm a believer. I'm seeing something happen up there." Reportedly about 20 bald men made the trip each day to the farmhouse to receive the $20 treatments.[21]

Undoubtedly, the ultimate electrical treatment was that delivered from on high. On June 4, 1980, Edwin E. Robinson, 62, was out in his backyard in a Portland, Maine, suburb looking for his pet chicken. Over the years he had gone bald in the usual manner. Robinson also went blind and deaf after a head injury sustained in a 1971 traffic accident, although there was no physiological reason for it. During a thunderstorm that June day, Robinson was struck by lightning. His vision and hearing slowly returned. Then his hair grew back. Family doctor William F. Taylor agreed the hair was returning, and some days later, Robinson's wife Doris said, "It's coming in thick." People deluged Robinson with letters and phone calls. Among them was Hollywood producer Drew Cummings, who announced he would make a movie about the event. Nothing more was heard about Robinson, however.[22]

Hair-raising by electricity got another 15 minutes in the media spotlight after University of British Columbia dermatologist Dr. Stuart Maddin published a study in 1990 which claimed that 25 of 30 treatment subjects grew hair and all but one of the subjects experienced no further hair loss. Subjects sat under a hairdryer-like device that created an extremely low-level electrostatic field around the scalp. In Maddin's study, subjects received 15 minutes of electrical pulses once a week for 36 weeks. That study was done for a Vancouver company, Current Technology Corp., whose stock was then trading at $6 per share. Current Technology had its treatment approved by the Canadian federal government and began offering it to the public within months. Cost of the treatment was $50 per weekly treatment for 36 to 52 weeks, by which time the maximum effect would be reached. After that one maintenance treatment a month was necessary, forever.

The device itself did not actually touch the scalp, and the treatment had no known side effects. Researchers could not explain how this process, called electrotrichogenesis, worked. Current Technology was quick to explain that the type of electrical field used in the process bore no relationship to the type of electromagnetic field then in the news with regard to its possible role in causing cancer. The company planned to market its device exclusively through medical practitioners. Maddin believed the prime candidates for treatment were men just starting to go bald. "People with well-established wide areas of baldness are not candidates for this. You can't grow where there's no seed," he added. Some initial financing for Current Technology was provided by Don Farrell, described as a "Vancouver financier and stock promoter." Although the stock price had moved up to $6 per share, the company had no revenue. A major problem, of course, was to convince the public it worked. Company president Anne Kramer remarked, "There will always be those people who are skeptics." Geoff Warne, president of the Toronto outlet of the U.S. hair weaving chain Hair Club for Men, commented, "My opinion is that we're not looking at any significant cosmetic effect with Current Technology." He thought, however, that it might increase his own business as minoxidil did because "Rogaine wasn't a cosmetically significant benefit to the client but it increased expectations."[23]

A few years later it was reported that Current Technology was conducting tests at 16 sites in Canada and the U.S. and that the company was hopeful it would be ready to submit results to the FDA for evaluation sometime soon. An unidentified businessman reportedly flew coast to coast once a week just to receive the treatment. Speaking of the effects of the remedy, he observed, "There's much less hair in my brush in the morning and there's much less hair in the bottom of the shower." Nothing more was heard from Current Technology, whose prospects apparently dimmed. In 1994 their stock was still trading on the Vancouver Stock Exchange, but at under $3 per share. Finally, it appeared, the electric hair-raising idea had gone out.[24]

Hormone therapy was once touted as a baldness treatment. In the 1930s dermatologists using hormones believed they could make a man as hairy as a gorilla, but they couldn't put the hair where it was most desired—on the top of his head. By the 1940s the power of female hormones was reported. Using bald penitentiary inmates, a dermatologist regularly injected them with female hormones. The lost hair returned to their heads with "amazing rapidity," but the men took on the characteristics of the opposite sex. When the injections stopped, this difficulty disappeared, but so did all the new hair.[25]

Speaking in the 1980s, dermatologist Sorrel Renick remarked: "We haven't got anything that will regrow hair other than hormones. But we can't use female hormones in men." When the female hormone estrogen was rubbed on a man's scalp it could restore hair, but it could also turn a man's voice from bass to soprano, reduce his libido, enlarge his breasts, and produce other female secondary characteristics. Dr. Norman Orentreich added, "This is obviously too high a price to pay to grow hair." Some did pay, though. In Europe, antiandrogens were available in topical form for the treatment of baldness. One of the products, Androcur, was originally developed for the treatment of sex offenders in Sweden. Germany and France both developed similar products but no such product was available in the U.S. Adding personal experience was Dr. Renee Richards, the well-known ophthalmologist and tennis coach. Before surgery that changed her from male to female, Richards underwent hormonal castration. She said: "Female hormones do some marvelous and radical things. They make you grow breasts, they shrink your testicles, they change the outline of your body, and they'll even stop you from going bald." Other feminizing effects included reduced musculature, increased fat deposition, and hot flashes, as well as loss of the ability to have and maintain an erection.[26]

Although the male androgen testosterone caused baldness in adult males with genetic predisposition, some researchers considered using that very hormone to treat baldness. A journalist in 1948 reported that if an ointment preparation of testosterone was applied locally, it would cause the growth of hair on the abdomen in both men and women, but it had no effect on head hair.[27]

During the 1960s, Drs. Christopher Papa and Albert Kligman at the University of Pennsylvania School of Medicine showed the capacity of topical, but not systemic, testosterone application to stimulate hair growth in the axilla and on the forearm of aged skin. Said Papa, "Once we saw that testosterone stimulated hair growth in the armpit we felt it might work on the head." They applied a one percent testosterone propionate cream to the scalps of 21 men with severe baldness. Within five to twelve months, 16 of the subjects displayed some degree of terminal hair regrowth in sites previously supporting an almost invisible downy fuzz. Testosterone could be synthesized and taken internally to treat various conditions of old age. When taken internally, however, the hormone could produce serious side effects, such as stimulating prostate cancer and causing the accumulation of body salt to a degree dangerous for someone with heart disease. None of the subjects used in the control group showed any evidence of hair regrowth. Papa and Kligman regarded their study as a breakthrough because "Despite manifold claims from legitimate and not so legitimate sources, no verified instance of hair growth of any type has ever been authenticated in common baldness. In view of the futility of past experience we submit, with trepidation, an indisputable demonstration of at least partial regrowth of hair."[28]

When they were asked to explain why there was not a complete regrowth of scalp hairs approaching the original density, the researchers stated that many follicles were dead and could not be brought back to life. That meant the possibility of hair stimulation was absolutely dependent on the survival of competent follicles. "We are not growing hair on a marble top. There is hair present but it is downy hair that is not visible. There is something to work on." The researchers believed their study demanded that physicians reexamine their skeptical outlook that baldness was a totally irreversible process. That outlook stemmed from a long line of unfulfilled therapeutic claims and the rampant commercialization of various worthless trichological enterprises. Presenting their data, Papa and Kligman remarked: "We are fearful of the misinterpretation and misapplication of this work in the face of such intense feeling. We would strongly counsel against the indiscriminate use of testosterone. This is a potent hormone and its long-term use in an unsupervised population is to be condemned."[29]

When queried about the contradiction involved because scientists accepted the fact that testosterone caused baldness, Papa stated: "Perhaps this fact has caused other researchers to shy away from testosterone up to now." When asked why testosterone could cause baldness in genetically prone males, stimulate the growth of beard hair in men, and at the same time regrow hair on baldies when rubbed on the scalp, Papa admitted it was a mystery. Nevertheless, he believed his results to that point indicated the possibility of an effective prophylaxis against common baldness. Papa said he planned to do a new study of his discovery on younger bald men. Again the researchers urged caution: "We know only too well that bald people grasp at hairs and cherish every fiber. They are ready to be gulled, deceived and deluded.... We do not regard that we have achieved a useful treatment for common baldness." When their research was published in the *Journal of the American Medical Association*, the same issue featured an editorial on the topic. Noting there was "much to be desired in the quantity of hair restored," the editor optimistically agreed the research nonetheless supported the idea that baldness was not an irreversible process. In conclusion the hopeful editor wrote: "In this era of biochemical legerdemain, there can be little doubt that a safe androgen will be developed whose hair-growing capabilities are divorced from these side effects. For physician and patient alike, however, the present study brings only hope, and a caution for patience and forbearance." In spite of the caution urged by Papa and Kligman, soon after their research was published they were inundated with demands for help. They received thousands of letters from all over the world asking for the salve, for its formula, or for treatment.[30]

A few years later a researcher tried to duplicate Papa's results. Of the 51 patients he used, not one showed growth of new hair or the appearance of longer, stouter terminal hair, not in the testosterone treatment group or in the placebo group. Patients rated themselves, as did the researchers. All reached the same conclusion. While some subjects in the active group reported a perceived decrease in the rate of hair loss, so did an equal percentage of men in the placebo group. Researchers noted that those self evaluations were "certainly not substantiated" by any evidence. Each patient was his own control by using active and inactive lotion on the two sides of his head in that double-blind study.[31]

Nothing more was heard from Papa and Kligman and their testosterone treatment. Two decades later Albert Lefkovits, an assistant clinical professor of dermatology at the Mount Sinai School of Medicine in New York, was asked about hormone therapy for baldness. His comment could be applied generally: "If something were really good, there wouldn't be any baldheaded dermatologists."[32]

One of the earliest reported uses of a drug to cure baldness was in the 1870s. Dr. G. Schmitz of Germany accidentally discovered the hair-growing properties of the drug pilocarpine, which was used to treat eye diseases. A man of 60 received three injections over 14 days after an eye operation. His eye problem cleared up, and in addition, his completely bald head became covered with a thick down. After four months of continued growth, the hair was so thick that, reportedly, no trace of baldness remained. Another of Schmitz's patients was a 34 year old with a bald spot the size of a playing card on his scalp. After that man received two shots of pilocarpine, his eye problem was fixed and his hair was restored. Over a decade later, at least one other doctor was still touting the miracles of the drug. Dr. Condict Cutler believed that if pilocarpine was taken internally in large enough doses, it could help any hairs that were weak and in need of stimulation. Better results with the drug could often be obtained, he thought, by giving it through hypodermic injections.[33]

Dr. John Kelvin of Glasgow, Scotland, in 1954 prescribed a drug called Roniacol for two of his patients who were troubled with poor circulation in their legs and feet. The intended effect of the drug was to open the arteries that were far from the heart. After the men, who happened to be bald, had taken four tablets a day for two months, both reported to Kelvin they had grown "fine heads of hair." Reporting on this phenomena, the doctor speculated the hair growth was due to improved scalp circulation resulting from the drug's vasodilating (artery widening) action. Kelvin confessed he had not then tried the tablets to cure his own baldness.[34]

Much publicity was generated by Roniacol's supposed powers. Manhattan businessman Lynn Robert Akers, president of the twenty-one unit Akers Hair and Scalp Clinic chain in the U.S. flew to Glasgow, where he offered Kelvin $10,000 a year to become director of a proposed Akers research lab in Glasgow. Twice the doctor visited the U.S. to consult with Akers. As a result, Kelvin ran afoul of the British General Medical Council's disciplinary committee, which accused him of "infamous conduct in a professional respect." While defending himself, Kelvin argued he had been victimized by American advertising and publicity. His discovery, he said, had been overhyped in phony ads; he had been goaded by reporters and the proposed clinic was nothing more than a "mirage." As disciplinary action, the committee placed Kelvin on probation for two years. In Manhattan, Akers brushed aside the doctor's allegations, commenting that Kelvin was only "a little Scottish country doctor who was scared to death in this country." It was then some 15 months after

Kelvin first announced the powers of Roniacol. He still had not tried it on his own head.[35]

In 1973, hair transplant pioneer Dr. Norman Orentreich was busily studying more than 20 different drugs which he thought had some effect in blocking the action of androgens when applied to the scalp. He thought that was the way to cure baldness and had tested the drugs on hundreds of volunteers. Orentreich predicted drugs to prevent baldness might be developed in two years: "It is something I am certain we can do, probably in the next year or two and no longer than five years."[36]

Three and a half years later Orentreich was still at work testing drugs, saying: "I've knocked myself out to grow hair without transplants. I think I see an end. I don't see a goal that's not feasible within a year or two, although this might drag on for five years. We still haven't got a safe, effective product to grow hair, but we will." In 1992, Orentreich predicted there would soon be a pill on the market to block testosterone to prevent it from converting into DHT, which led to baldness. How long would it be? He predicted five years....[37]

Researchers at the University of Miami reported in 1988 that they had found a molecular "missing-link" confirming that baldness was tied to male hormones. According to researcher Dr. Marty Sawaya of the school's dermatology department, oil glands in scalps with male pattern baldness had molecules called receptors with 50 to 100 percent greater capacity for binding the ingredients of the male hormone testosterone. That receptor process short-circuited hair growth, but the researchers didn't know how. "It is uncertain whether the finding will lead to a drug to combat baldness. We're still trying. We have some hormone inhibitors and some compounds in mind, but it's going to take a while longer." Those sebaceous glands were adjacent to hair follicles and produced a protective coating for the skin and scalp. Sawaya argued those glands were different in bald men. Thus baldness resulted from an increased ability to use testosterone, not an increase in testosterone per se. "You're really not more virile," she explained. Researchers came to those conclusions after analyzing small scalp samples from 12 baldies and 12 hair-bearing men. They found the sebaceous glands from the bald men had twice the number of testosterone receptors and twice the enzyme level involved in testosterone metabolism as did the glands from the hairy scalps. Sawaya noted that the discovery alone did not suggest a treatment: "That would require an understanding of what is happening at the genetic level."[38]

A couple of years later Sawaya announced she had isolated three proteins that regulated the balding process in men. Two of them served as receptors for testosterone in hair follicles, while the third acted to suppress the amount of testosterone binding. Hair-bearing scalps contained more of the latter, while bald scalps contained more of the former. As to this announcement leading to a baldness cure, Sawaya cautioned that was still "far off in the future." Nonetheless, soon after the discovery was publicized, Sawaya was besieged by phone calls from desperate men. They heard about her on their car radios, calling her from roadside booths. They tracked her down in her hotel room, where they flattered her and begged her for a cure. They offered to be her slaves, they offered to fly to Miami, they offered to do anything. A television weatherman from a large midwestern city said he would lose his job if people knew he wore a toupee. To all these men, Sawaya said she could do nothing. She discovered her baldness "cause" by accident when, by chance, she took small slices of scalp left over from transplants in research she had been doing for years and started using them to investigate the interaction between hormones and skin cells. Soon she stumbled onto what she claimed was the underlying mechanism of baldness. Hair was not Sawaya's primary concern, however; she said she was interested in "more clinically relevant areas."[39]

Another drug under development as a baldness treatment in the mid–1980s was diazoxide, originally used to treat low blood sugar. Dr. Ken Hashimoto, chairman of the Wayne State University dermatology department researched that drug. A small group of subjects had the drug, mixed with a lotion, rubbed on their bald spots. "The results are quite encouraging," exclaimed Hashimoto. One subject was Warren O. Comer, who commented, "I'm waiting for the day when someone says, 'Didn't you use to be bald?'"[40]

A team of research scientists at Dundee University in Scotland also worked on skin cells in the mid–1980s. They believed the key to baldness and its cure lay in a family of cells called dermal papillae, which grew on the underlying stratum of the body's two layers of skin. Papillae had been grown in the laboratory from cells taken from the hair follicles of animals. Then those lab-grown cells were injected into the bald patches of animals, where they stimulated hair growth. Researchers based their approach on the finding that the papillae cells in adult rats played a crucial role in stimulating the follicle cells. When those cells were implanted into the base of a nonproducing follicle, it became productive. According to researcher Dr. Colin Jahoda, the idea would be to insert lab-grown papillae in the follicles on a bald head. One problem, however, was to mass produce the papillae in laboratory culture because after four cell divisions they apparently lost the ability to stimulate hair growth. Nevertheless, the researchers believed their finding raised the possibility of using cell culture "as part of a human hair transplant process." Jahoda remarked, "The eventual application of this work to human hair replacement techniques can ... be envisioned," while cautioning, "However, I think in terms of immediate hair transplant procedures, that's still a long way off."[41]

Back around 1930 glands were briefly featured as a possible baldness treatment. Dr. F.A.E. Carew of the animal breeding institute at Scotland's Edinburgh University was experimenting with specially bred bald mice when he discovered that hair loss was due to the absence of a certain gland substance. By extracting this unidentified substance from normal mice and injecting it into bald ones, Carew was able to promote the growth of hair again. Carew announced he would continue his experiments to find out if human baldness was due to the same glandular deficiency.[42]

Chicago physician Dr. Bengt Bengtson treated baldness with injections of an extract prepared from the anterior lobes of sheep pituitary glands. He accidentally stumbled onto this method a few years earlier when treating a patient with that preparation for other reasons. Reporting his findings in the *Journal of the American Medical Association*, Bengtson cautioned that enthusiasm was not yet warranted, as more tests and observations were necessary before the treatment could be called a success. Also sounding a caution in the same edition of the journal was publication editor Dr. Morris Fishbein, who wrote: "Probably charlatans may endeavor to reap the usual income from these new investigations. The time is not yet ripe for every baldheaded man to try the new treatment. It is still in the investigative stage."[43]

Just a few weeks later, Bengtson had a letter to the editor published in the *Journal of the American Medical Association*. Because of the publicity his research had generated, the doctor had received several thousand letters from eager baldies. Saying the press statements were overenthusiastic, he added that his experiments didn't "indicate that a complete solution to this age old problem has been realized.... The results have not yet been such as to warrant extreme optimism." In particular, Bengtson was writing to set the record straight because "several nonmedical organizations presumably interested only from a commercial point of view have already attempted to obtain material for promulgation to the public, and several charlatans have stated that they were personally associated with me and therefore competent to administer the method." He emphasized no one was authorized to speak for him and that he had no associates in his research. *Scientific American* noted wryly that Bengtson's research would lead to a "new crop of baldness 'cures' though not necessarily any new crops of hair."[44]

Several researchers worked with mice or rats to try to figure out which part of the creatures would produce hair growth. One unnamed Chinese sage from the turn of the century believed the best thing to do was to take no chances. He claimed eating stewed rats was a remedy for the affliction, saying, "A rat is to the human hair what a carrot is to a horse's coat." One reporter thought it might be worth a try since "Rats are eminently hairy animals and can live to a great age without becoming bald."[45]

More palatable were vitamin-based concoctions. In 1940, Dr. D. W. Wooley of the Rockefeller Institute of Medical Research fed mice a diet which caused them to lose their hair. Trying various methods to restore their hair, Wooley determined that phytin, the salt of inositol acid, was the antibaldness factor. Inositol, a vitamin of the B-complex family, was itself shown to be equally effective, claimed Wooley. A few years later a group of doctors administered large doses of inositol to baldies. Nothing happened, no hair grew.[46]

Nathan Zuntz of Berlin, a well-known physiologist, discovered an effective and comparatively simple means of preventing baldness and restoring lost hair. In the course of his nutritional research during World War I, Zuntz discovered that albuminous substances containing tryosin and cystin "if fed to man or beast, caused a remarkable growth of hair." Mixing the substances with food for men and sheep produced dual benefits—wool for sheep, hair for men.[47]

Some of the better known of the vitamin-based products were those containing biotin. In the mid–1970s, New York family practitioner Dr. Edward Settel announced he had developed a hair cream and shampoo treatment that diminished hair loss and increased hair growth. His treatment was based on reducing the amount of testosterone in the scalp because he believed that "an excess of this substance is responsible for pattern baldness." In the past, Settel's treatment was effective against hair loss but 2.3 percent of his patients suffered an unwanted side effect—breast enlargement. Settel claimed he beat that problem by adding a new ingredient—biotin, a form of vitamin B—which he said metabolized testosterone while restricting the actions of the ingredients to the hair and skin follicles on the subject's head only. His treatment consisted of a daily application of the cream and use of the hormonal shampoo three times a week. According to Settel, 90 percent of his 694 volunteers reported reduced hair fallout, while none of his control group did. Hair regrowth ranged from 50 percent of his subjects up to 74 percent, depending on age. No side effects were reported. Settel supplied some of the many doctors who wrote to him with his products, but they first had to go to New York to take a one-week course with him to learn the proper methods of treatment. One skeptic was Dr. Joseph Jerome, secretary of the American Medical Association's Committee on Cutaneous Health and Cosmetics, who said, "Up to this point, I have never seen an externally applied product that would produce hair growth on the scalp in normal patterns. We're dubious of any of these claims." Jerome wanted to see a neutral lab conduct a double-blind study of Settel's treatment.[48]

Biotin received more publicity when a Finnish doctor discovered that the absence of biotin produced several results, including hair loss. The administration of biotin to patients with that rare deficiency caused a hair loss reversal. From there, it was a short step to the conclusion that biotin was a hair grower in spite of the fact that the Finn stated clearly it was not—it only helped the very tiny portion of the population deficient in the biotin enzyme. Meanwhile, Settel patented his "deep-penetrating mini-emulsion," which he claimed nourished the hair root with enough biotin to regrow some balding men's hair. Then he established Pilo-Genic Research Associates in New York. By the mid–1980s, the company had 67 offices coast to coast and in foreign countries. It was expected to gross $8 million in 1986. The Washington, D.C., outlet claimed that among its clients were a movie star, an undersecretary, and members of Congress. Customers paid $75 for the first consultation, which included one month's supply of shampoo and conditioner, and $55 for each successive visit, every two months. Chicago's Pilo-Genic branch had between 800 and 1,000 clients. The company claimed a 90 percent success rate in stopping excess fallout and a 40 to 70 percent success rate in regrowth.[49]

When a reporter visited Pilo-Genic executive Don Hoyt, the latter explained why their biotin product worked and others did not. The secret lay in "mini-emulsion," explained Hoyt. That allowed the biotin to be carried to the follicle area, where it metabolized the testosterone into a harmless form, while in other biotin products the enzyme just sat on the scalp. Another biotin seller was multimillionaire Glenn Braswell, who advertised heavily in the newspaper, retailing by mail. He marketed products like Bioscala, Biogenesis, Jojoba Extract, and—at $25 an ounce—Bio Prima II. All of those products were attacked by the U.S. Postal Service and the Federal Trade Commission for falsely claiming to retard baldness and regrow hair. Braswell simply formed a new company and put out a new product. Pilo-Genic's Hoyt said Braswell's products were based on a detergent and paint remover that sold wholesale for $6 a gallon but retailed for $25 an ounce. During cases against Braswell, biotin was discredited even by the Finnish doctor. All agreed it would grow hair on no one except the minute number of people with bodies lacking biotin. After Settel died in 1985, his wife, Anita Young, took over running the company.[50]

Admitting her treatment didn't work for everybody, Young did state "those who still have functioning follicles get significant results without side effects." A more recent study done by the company in 1985 purported to be double-blind. Referring to that study, Young remarked, "Of the men treated with our product, seventy-seven percent experienced significant hair growth." When critics suggested the product should be studied at a major neutral medical center, Young said her company was too small to underwrite such testing. Many dermatologists scoffed at claims for biotin. Dr. Ronald Savin called biotin-based hair restorers "snake oil." New York University Medical Center dermatology instructor Dr. Joel Kassimir commented: "There are no hard data to show that it works. Many of my patients have used it unsuccessfully." Critics did agree, though, that it was harmless. An earlier study conducted by Settel from 1974 to 1981 at fourteen of Pilo-Genic's clinics claimed to show that 85 percent of the 18,000 subjects using the product "reported markedly less fallout," with 64 percent of the users showing "visible hair growth." Finally, in the mid–1980s, a small double-blind study of 36 men was conducted under FDA guidelines on the product. Results showed there was no real difference in the amount of hair loss between those receiving the biotin and those in the control group, nor did anybody regrow any hair.[51]

5

DESPERATELY
SEEKING HAIR

I've never seen a part with ears before.
Reader's Digest, June 1983

If you see a baldheaded man in a dream, you will have
troubles with crooked people in your business.
Migene Gonzalez-Wippler,
Dreams and What They Mean to You

In the 1800s, baldness cures, hair restorers, and hair strengtheners were
a staple product of the traveling medicine show. If a bald man somehow
missed the traveling hucksters, he could purchase a nostrum at his pharmacy,
from a mail-order catalog or from a general traveling salesman. The hairless
purchased elixirs with ingredients such as the blistering cantharides, olive oil,
borax, sulphur, bone marrow, and lead acetate. Writing in 1893, Dr. Condict
Cutler remarked on the number of available products, saying, "The remedies
which are recommended and advertised for the cure of this affliction are only
exceeded in number by those given for the relief of vomiting in pregnancy."
One of the most widely advertised products in that era was Barry's Tricoph-
erous, "a balsamic hair renewer" whose makers proclaimed that "the hair cannot wither or become thin, but must grow and flourish." Springfield, Massachusetts, paper chemist John Breck set out in 1908 to cure his baldness by
concocting various hair potions. When he died a millionaire in 1965, Breck
was America's leading shampoo manufacturer but was still bald. Film director, D. W. Griffith sold a baldness treatment in 1908 called "yuccatone" before
he went on to success in the film industry. That product was made from the
yucca plant, a regular part of the diet of the American Indian. Ads for that
product exclaimed, "Have you ever seen a bald Indian?"[1]

At the end of the 1920s, the trade publication *American Druggist* estimated that twenty men used hair tonics to every one woman that did. When
the maker of Vitalis hair tonic conducted its own survey of several thousand

men, two out of three used some sort of tonic. Users of such products were most frequently among higher income groups and among men in their 30s. More city residents used a hair tonic than did country dwellers. There were then about 500 hair preparations for men on the market; 335 of those were placed as dressings, or brilliantines. The remaining 165 products were advertised as hair tonics in ads that claimed health benefits and promised an improvement in appearance. While most of these tonics made vague claims about improving the hair's health, some claimed more directly they could stop or prevent baldness. In 1927, wholesale production value of the tonic industry was $11.6 million. Only a handful of the 165 tonics had any sort of national market, with the rest limited to a local area. The best-known tonics were Lucky Tiger, Jeris, Herpicide, Wildroot, Vitalis, Fitch's Ideal, Kreml, and Vaseline Hair Tonic.[2]

Lucky Tiger was available for sale in 98 percent of all American barber shops and 95 percent of all drugstores. It was claimed that this tonic "will take care of 90 percent of all ailments the human scalp is heir to." Most of these tonic preparations reportedly contained a "dandruff scourge, a strong scent, and a liberal portion of alcohol." Lucky Tiger was started about 1915 in a garage in Kansas City by R. Stephen Harris, who ran a chain of clothing stores. Besides alcohol, it contained salicylates and arsenic. Herpicide was famous for the three little heads it used in its ads with the slogan "Going (Herpicide will save it)... Going (Herpicide will save it) ... Gone (too late for Herpicide!)" Ads for Kreml featured a bald head stamped with the warning "Don't Let This Happen to You." That product's name was said to have come to its German developer one day when he looked out of his hotel room at the Kremlin domes. Later when Kreml was taken over by Americans, it was promoted as the "new German formula" but when Hitler came to power, the slogan was quickly dropped because Jewish drugstores in New York City—75 percent of the total—objected.[3]

Some entrepreneurs developed their own special tonics. New Haven barber John H. Gleason turned more and more to baldness treatment after one elderly patron decided Gleason had made his hair grow. After he spread the word, a group of enthusiastic Yale professors backed Gleason, setting him up in business in New York City. He and his assistants even made house calls to the homes of the wealthy baldies to give treatments. General Pershing was said to be a constant patron. Gleason, who studied the methods of Dr. Sebouraud, treated his clients by subjecting them to much washing of the head for a week or so and then the application of carbon tetrachloride and carbon bisulphide in solution. Another barber turned hair-raiser was George L. George, who had his own independent shop. One of his steady clients for home treatment was reportedly Clifton Webb.[4]

For years Jules Ferond had been a fancier and raiser of long-haired dogs. As some of them suffered from mange, he was prompted to experiment in order to find a mixture to restore their lost hair. It worked on his dogs, he said. Next he tried the formula on his own bald head. It made his hair grow, he said. Then he tried it on his friends. It made their hair grow, he said. Not surprisingly, he established the Jules Ferond Company around 1920 to market the lotion, advertising, "No matter how long the condition of baldness has existed Ferond's hair grower will re-grow hair." That claim led the New York Health Department to haul him into Municipal Court for misrepresentation in advertising. Both sides produced witnesses in court who had used the cure. As to those witnesses from both sides, a reporter covering the trial observed, "It was noticeable that those who testified had no considerable amount of hair." After analysis by the Health Department, the mixture was found to contain Vaseline, alcohol, calicylic acid, and Peruvian balsam—a common recipe in that era. Out of court, Dr. S. Dana Hubbard, director of the Bureau of Public Health Education of the New York City Health Department, commented on male vanity by observing, "A woman knows when her hair is gone it will not return and she goes out and buys more hair. Man, more short-sighted, keeps pouring money on his bald head and spends time looking and hoping. The individual who buys some of these tonics in artistic colors and in attractive containers in order to relieve himself of the embarrassment due to loss of hair defrauds himself and wastes time and money. They are usually blatantly advertised to do the impossible."[5]

For those in that time period who didn't want to use potions and lotions, there was always Emile Coué, an "autosuggestionist" from Nancy, France, whose method of autosuggestion "could cure baldness." After treating many patients successfully in his own country, Coué set up shop in America. It was a simple method. All a patient had to do was to repeat the following: "Day by day in every way I am getting better and better." When the patient repeated this sentence, the unconscious self began to right the things that were wrong in the body. With specific reference to baldness, Coué explained that autosuggestion caused hair follicles to regain their lost elasticity, to secrete normally, and thus to grow hair. Literally, these follicles tightened up under the regime of autosuggestion. When he first started out, Coué had asked his patients to believe in the power of his method to cure them. By the time he reached America, Coué had dropped that requirement. A patient simply had to say the words loud enough to hear them, that was enough. Belief was not necessary. "Doing that gets it written into the subconscious mind, and it is doing that that counts. If it gets there it will work," explained Coué. He then went one step further to make it easier for his patients: "If you are too lazy to say the words, have them put on a phonograph record and hear them regularly that way." Modestly the autosuggestionist added: "I do not work miracles. I am neither a god nor a saint. I am only a man."[6]

In New York City in the 1920s, Maurice Scholder operated the Professor Scholder Institute, which at first offered treatment to baldies only in its clinic. Expanding to include a course of mail-order home treatment to baldies and those thinning on top, the institute advertised over the radio and in the pages of magazines such as *Strength* and *Physical Culture*. Through the mails, Scholder offered individual analysis, diagnosis, and treatment, claiming his method had "uniform success in stopping loss of hair, and eventually growing strong, new hair." A client merely had to send in a few hairs to the institute. In his advertising material, the professor said a learned Dominican friar in Galicia gave him a scientific secret which became the basis of his "great discovery" of a baldness remedy. Claiming to be from Austria where he had many men from Europe's political, social, and scientific circles as patients, Scholder also named Theodore Roosevelt and magician Harry Houdini in his material as satisfied customers.[7]

Determined to test the institute out, a journalist sent in a letter along with a few fox hairs plucked from the fur cuff of a woman's coat. In a reply letter, Scholder stated he had analyzed the hair and "the roots are in a seriously undernourished condition. You are in grave danger of continuous and increasing loss of your hair, but it can still be saved by prompt treatment." Salvation lay in sending Scholder $20, for which the patient would receive by return mail the proper treatment that, wrote Scholder, "will positively restore your hair and scalp to a normal, healthy condition, stop further falling out of your hair, and, if you follow my instructions faithfully, enable you to grow strong, new hair, to replace that which you have already lost." Using another address, the journalist sent in a few hairs from a dog. In response he got the same letter, word for word. Then he sent in a few hairs from a young woman with healthy hair. He got the same reply. For his fourth and last test, the reporter took a two-inch piece of twine, unraveled it and sent in a few strands from that. Despite the fact that those strands bore no relationship to human hair, he got the identical reply.[8]

In his 1928 book *The Story of Hair*, self-styled expert Charles Nessler explained the horrors of baldness when he noted that even the most phlegmatic person "does not fail to become dejected and panicky at the sight of his first combful of fallen hair ... when he sees a vision of himself denuded of his hair, his scalp a skating rink for venturesome flies.... As he sees the covering of his scalp falling off, rapidly and inexorably, like shingles from a neglected roof, he speculates as to when and how it will end and why this calamity has befallen him." Nessler was convinced that men went bald because they cut their hair short. Women grew their hair long, cutting it much less often and not as short as did males. All that long hair exercised the scalp muscles, with each hair falling out at its maximum length, to be immediately replaced by a new one. In boys, the hair was cut at least once a month, never getting longer than one inch and putting no demand on the scalp muscles. As a result no hair ever had to be replaced and none formed. By the time hair started to fall out from baldness, the follicle had "forgotten" what to do because of its long neglect and produced no new hair. That scalp "hesitation" was disastrous since, having no hair, the follicle quickly closed up completely, like the gap after a tooth extraction.[9]

While short hair cuts were the main villains in Nessler's eyes, he also implicated cold water and cold air. A cold shower gave an icy shock to the system, putting it in danger of a shutdown. He advised men to avoid cold water, preferably at all times but especially after heated exercises. Concerning those who had taken cold showers all their lives and still had a full head of hair, Nessler sneered, "These fortunate ones are greatly outnumbered by those who have indulged in this practice only a few times and as a result are now practically bald." He told of a young man in a Swiss mountain resort who enjoyed skating when the temperature was minus 20° C. Although he was dressed warmly, every time he passed a young woman he took off his cap to salute her, shocking his overheated head with a blast of cold air. Nessler warned him of the danger, but the 22-year-old skater just laughed. Just two years later Nessler reported the skater had permanently lost 40 percent of his hair. As to why hair departed only from the top of heads and not the sides or backs, Nessler could only say something about demands being made on the top's "carrying capacity" which was greater than on other head areas and that the top was subject to more erratic treatment—sometimes covered, sometimes not—than the back and sides, which were always exposed to the elements and thus hardened.[10]

Nessler then went on to explain his hair migration theory. When a man noticed the first few hairs appearing on his chest, no matter how young he was, it was a sign that his scalp organization was weakening. Scalp hair was losing its hold. According to Nessler, baldness was "a metamorphosis wherein the hair departs from its accustomed place on top of the head, and appears on another part of the body.... As long as men insist upon implying by cutting and singeing that they do not want hair on their scalps, many scalps will respond by permitting the hairs to migrate to more congenial dwelling places and will refuse to refill the empty follicles." Thus, in this theory, hair was never really lost from the body. It was just somewhere else. The question of why hair never migrated from the chest, say, to the scalp was a point on which he remained mute. If parents allowed their sons to grow their hair five to six inches long, it would help strengthen "the scalp carrying capacity." Going with short hair into manhood, however, and then desiring to wear it longer put a greater demand on the scalp muscles than they had been trained for. As a result, "nearly every man has a good chance to become bald as soon as he demands an addition of an inch or two to his accustomed hair length." For all those men who could not turn back the clock to reverse inappropriate childhood hair cutting, the remedy lay in buying some of Nessler's Hair Milk, which, he insisted, cured baldness, even though his theories seemed to have precluded that possibility.[11]

The 1930s depression and World War II diverted attention away from minor worries such as baldness, with the result that quackery was fairly dormant in that period, or at least drew little media attention. In the late 1940s, a barber by the name of Marinus van Rooijen in the town of Een (population 900) in the northern Netherlands gained attention when he announced he had a secret formula which grew hair. Soon Een became a mecca for hundreds of bald men desperately seeking a cure. Up to 1,500 men reportedly came each week for treatment, among them a man named Derek. He lived 75 miles away in Varsseveld. Once a week he rose early to spend a couple of hours traveling to reach the shop. Van Rooijen charged $132 for a course of treatments, promising to refund the money if after one year there was no "clearly visible" growth of hair. Treatment involved brushing the patient's scalp, applying the secret fluid, then brushing the scalp again. He refused to allow analysis of his formula, telling skeptical Dutch doctors to look at his customers' heads for evidence of his formula's efficacy. Mail poured in for him from abroad. With seven women employed in his Een shop, he hoped to open a ten-chair outlet in Amsterdam. Said one of his Een women employees, "Who would have thought men were so vain?"[12]

Back in the U.S.A. at that time, Patricia M. Stenz ran a hair and scalp treatment center in Hollywood, California. According to her, baldness was caused by a fungus. It ran in families, not through heredity, but because sons caught it from their fathers. "A bald head is something like athlete's foot, at the other end of the body." Among her satisfied clients, she claimed actors Jimmy Stewart, Dick Powell, Gig Young, and Gene Kelly. Her treatment was a lotion applied to the scalp which made it unpalatable to the fungus. Daring Dr. Morris Fishbein, editor of the *Journal of the American Medical Association* to test her lotion scientifically, she boasted, "I will grow hair on any person chosen by the A.M.A. and do it under observation." Declining her challenge, Fishbein repeated an ancient saying, while running a hand over his bald head, "Any ass in Athens can grow more hair than the wisest man. These cells are dead. Anybody who can restore hair in dead cells can restore people from the grave."[13]

So pervasive were baldness treatment clinics and preparations that the American Medical Association's Committee on Cosmetics issued a March 1949 report on baldness and dandruff cures and treatments. Essentially it said none were any good. "Neither massage, mechanical devices, tonics, ultraviolet light, hormones, vitamins, or any other treatment will regenerate hair lost in ordinary baldness" noted the report. Warning against self-designated hair and scalp specialists or trichologists who used fancy names to establish credibility, the AMA observed these people were not doctors: "They have no qualifications other than a full head of hair, a business brain, and an appetite for easy money."[14]

Each year thousands of men paid fees for baldness and dandruff cures equal to those for major surgery. One person paid $200 for 30 treatments of dandruff cure. When there was no change at the end, he was told he had had too few treatments. Another paid $450 for 60 treatments and then was advised more treatments were needed. The Thomas Hair Specialist chain of clinics claimed their 45 offices manned by the "world's leading hair experts" treated an average of 1,800 people each day, 640,800 people a year. At $6 to $10 a visit, the Thomas company grossed $3.8 to $6.4 million yearly. Usually the clinics had a professional aura, with the public invited to have consultation, a free scalp examination, and a diagnosis by a hair expert, specialist, or trichologist. One company stated baldness could be the result of any one of 14 different local causes. They offered to diagnose, in a brief scalp assessment, which of the 14 was responsible in a particular case. Before and after photos often used by such clinics were usually of people who had a specific disease that caused baldness. Once the disease departed, the hair returned.[15]

Dandruff, noted the AMA, was a normal physiologic process which had nothing to do with baldness. Admittedly, seborrhea was a functional disturbance of the oil glands in the skin, whose cause was unknown. However, seborrhea could extend over the entire body, but hair was never lost anywhere except in the classic male pattern. Women with severe, persistent seborrhea never lost hair. Many hair treatment clinics implied that dandruff or seborrhea was the first stage toward baldness. Hair tonics groomed the hair, nothing more. Manufacturers of tonics, said the AMA, "conjure a makeshift adjustment between the pharmacology of these ingredients and pseudoscientific facts about baldness and dandruff…. As soon as a drug is generally accepted by the public as a cure-all it will appear in a hair or scalp preparation. Therefore the sulfonamides are used rather widely for this purpose." With regard to one hair tonic, the AMA report observed, "For some time, people were rinsing their mouths with a hair 'tonic,' since Listerine offered the same formula for its mouth wash and its hair 'tonic.'"[16]

It wasn't just the ordinary man on the street who could succumb to baldness quackery. Scientists who should have known better were equally susceptible. In 1950 some 200 scientists gathered for a symposium conducted by the New York Academy of Sciences at New York City's American Museum of Natural History. Ostensibly the session was to consider the growth of hair as a part of the overall growth pattern of mammals, but the question of baldness in the human male predominated, perhaps because about half of the attending scientists were bald. Late into the night, report after report was read as the science got fuzzier and fuzzier. One report analyzed the chemical composition of the horn of a rhinocerous; like human hair it was a horny tissue. Dr. R. J. Myers, a professor in the Colgate University Department of Zoology, reported the life span and rate of growth of human hair. One scientist challenged his finding, pointing out that Myers's figures "indicated a man could not grow hair over six inches long. And we all know that many wrestlers on television have hair longer than that." Myers responded that the discrepancy was due to "characteristics of the individual studies." Finally, late in the night, session chairman Dr. Marion Sulzberger asked whether any chemical or physical agents had any effect whatever in promoting the growth of hair on baldies. Answering his own question, he stated: "No. Absolutely not. Impossible." As session attendee Dr. James B. Hamilton observed, however, "Many individuals, including scientists who should know better, have a favorite way of 'preserving' their own hair. Don't give up hope is the principle."[17]

That AMA report had little effect in slowing the growth of the baldness curing industry. When asked in 1955 why such cures were so pervasive and popular, Veronica Conley, assistant secretary of the American Medical Association's Committee on Cosmetics, explained that it was because baldness was a "mysterious" condition about which people could be easily fooled and it was the type of problem that bred quackery, she added that "pseudoscientific arguments supporting most baldness cures are frequently so convincing that their unsound basis can be detected only by trained scientists."[18]

Around that time the makers of Hayr scalp treatment were brought before the Federal Trade Commission because they were advertising that their product cured baldness. The examiner recommended that the company be barred from making such claims because, as he declared on February 1, 1956, there "is no cure known to medical science" for 90 to 95 percent of baldness cases. The 5 to 10 percent which could be treated were the result of disease and Hayr would have "no effect whatever" on them stated examiner Earl J. Kolb. Thus, on that date, the United States government more or less officially ruled baldness to be incurable.[19]

Be that as it may, the main Thomas Hair Specialist office in New York City gave over 13,000 scalp treatments in 1958, compared with 9,834 in 1954.[20]

During a 1962 raid on the Basic Remedies, Inc., plant in Monmouth, Oregon, United States marshals seized 750,000 vitamin capsules, along with 250,000 pieces of promotional literature. Food and Drug Administration (FDA) officials said the company's capsules had been "falsely promoted for hair growing." Company literature contained statements suggesting the vitamin pills would promote new hair growth on bald or thin areas, prevent falling hair, promote a feeling of well being, and prevent dandruff. Federal FDA officials declared, however, "Vitamins will not grow hair on a bald head." Another source from that time period reported that "More money is spent annually in the United States on purely cosmetic procedures for the hair than is devoted to all medical research in the country."[21]

Trained dietician and cosmetologist Rita Hartinger was the foremost practitioner of the "hair popping" technique of hair preservation and regrowth; she was working out of New York City in 1968. Eight years earlier she had learned the trade from its originator, hairdresser Marsha Lewis, since retired. Hartinger called herself a "professional hair popper," believing her method of scalp stimulation helped her customers keep whatever hair they had and perhaps sprout a new crop. "I make the hairs healthy.... When you lift up the scalp from the bone structure by popping, it stimulates circulation and nourishes the tissue. Then the hair is strengthened, and it is less likely to fall out," she said. A journalist who watched Rita in action reported that each tug on the scalp did indeed produce a "pop," and he described the sound further by writing it was "as if a kernel of popcorn had exploded on his head." Popped on that occasion was 27-year-old actor Ronnie Hall, who admitted: "Sure it hurts. But I'm in show business, and I want to stay 27 as long as I can." Hartinger charged $45 for each of the first eight treatments and $32 for each of the next eight. She told her customers they could expect improvement after three months if their hair was popped twice a week. In addition, she advised her clients to wash their hair every night in water as hot as they could stand and to perform a five-minute finger massage morning and night. As for the prospects of a baldie recovering all his hair, Rita replied: "If it took 20 years to lose it it will take about 10 years to get it to grow back. A lot of people just aren't interested in spending that much time." Ninety percent of her clients were in the entertainment business, she said, naming Anthony Perkins and Leonard Bernstein as two of her customers. Her two sons, 8 and 11 years old, had each had their hair popped several times by their mother, who noted, "It's best to get a man while he's young." Her husband had refused the treatment, however. "He won't let me near him because it hurts so much," said Rita.[22]

Radio evangelist Curtis Howe Springer was also the founder and operator of the Zzyzx Mineral Springs health spa in Southern California. In 1970 he was convicted on several counts of false advertising concerning two of his products. One of them was Mo-Hair, which Springer claimed would grow hair. He said he got the formula from an unnamed German who had visited his spa. When state officials analyzed Mo-Hair, they found it contained only mud and mineral oils.[23]

A little later that decade, FDA physician Joseph David said the agency hadn't seen much action against baldness cures: "For the last five or six years, I haven't seen very much on this. Maybe the consumer has become sufficiently intelligent to realize you can't grow hair on a billiard ball. In the past we've taken regulatory action about claims in labeling. You can't tell the truth about these products and continue to sell them."[24]

Nomenclature changes were noticed in Britain early in the 1970s when that country suddenly found itself home to around 400 trichologists practicing trichology. One such hair clinic was operated in London by Betty Roney. While her method of treatment was not explained, her belief was that tall men lost their hair more rapidly than short men and that as a man's obesity increased, so did the likelihood of hair loss. "The bigger you are the greater the task of your blood supply to give nourishment to the roots of your hair," explained Roney. When the *Times* of London ran an article on baldness, the paper was swamped with cures for thinning hair. One consisted of a course of pills said to contain no hormones or chemicals, just "pure herbs, vitamins and calcium." A famous London soccer goalkeeper reportedly tried the remedy. He grew no more hair but did develop "wonderful long, strong nails."[25]

Glenn Braswell thought he was going bald in 1972. Five years later he was president of Cosvetic Laboratories of Atlanta, Georgia. At that time, said a reporter, Braswell sported "a healthy head of hair if his picture can be believed." Braswell explained that "I wasn't satisfied five years ago when a doctor told me the only way to keep from losing my hair was to put it in a safe deposit box." Convinced that the right combination of vitamins and minerals, along with good food and exercise, would solve his problem, he experimented until he came up with a vitamin formula which his company sold under the name of Head Start. Being careful not to claim it was offering a baldness cure (strictly illegal in advertising), Cosvetic said that "Head Start is not one of those magical baldness preventatives," but the product "can help keep hair healthy, with a formula that contains seven vitamins and five minerals that hair desperately needs for health." Of course, the implication was that it was a baldness cure. A 30-day supply of Head Start retailed for $7.95. Competition in the area was fierce at the time. Cosvetic had sued Nature Bounty, Inc., of Bohemia, New York, over trademark infringement. The latter marketed Heads Up vitamins. Cosvetic also sued Weider International of Los Angeles over its vitamin product called Head Strong. Weider had to change the name of its product, settling on Vita Hair.[26]

When a reporter visited a New York City trichologist, in 1977, he found a very old theory resurrected. That hair treater argued that bacteria and impaired blood flow in the scalp were responsible for baldness. He claimed his scalp massages and germicides had arrested a number of incipient cases of male pattern baldness. A 45-minute treatment of massage, heat, and germicide cost $10.[27]

America was invaded in 1979 by a 74-year-old Australian woman known as Ma Evans. The Australian Trade Commission turned over its San Francisco office to Evans for her press conference. She was in the United States to promote her $25 a bottle baldness cure. Ma promised that if the first bottle didn't grow hair, the second would. If that failed, try a third. "I don't see how it can possibly hurt," commented Ma. She claimed that thousands of bottles of the stuff had been sold in Australia and that the Ma Evans Company expected to gross $3 million that year. Ma demonstrated her potion by rubbing some on her own scalp, the recommended method. For good measure she took a swig from the bottle and then poured a capful into a nearby potted plant. "We're going to get hair going on that plant, I shouldn't be surprised," she said. The brown potion supposedly contained 15 herbs and tasted a little like Listerine, according to a reporter bold enough to try it. Evans claimed a gypsy gave her the recipe for the tonic back in 1921. The formula lay dormant until 1977, when Ma noticed a friend's thinning hair. "I cried," explained Ma. "I'm a very sensitive person. To think that the Lord could have given people bald heads." FDA officials seized Ma's first shipment to America of 200 bottles because they were labeled as baldness cures, an illegal claim in America. A spokesman for Ma said that shipment was a mistake which contained the broader claims which were not illegal in Australia. The second shipment had more muted claims and finer print. "Is it guaranteed?" read the new label. "No, the only way you can know if it will work for you is to try it yourself."[28]

During that same year, Ernie Terrazas claimed that jojoba grew hair back on his bald head: "I hated being bald. I tried a product, which contained jojoba. Not right away mind you, but in the course of a year, my hair started to grow. That's what made me leave my construction company and get involved with Jojoba. Anyone who uses it becomes a walking billboard." By then Terrazas had set up a company and was marketing a product called Super de Jojoba Energizer, a combination shampoo and hair and scalp treatment. He claimed Senator Edward Kennedy was an admirer of the product. Said Ernie, "The Energizer shampoo will allow hair to grow on a bald or thinning pate only if there are active hair cells on the scalp." The product was also hyped as the answer to just about every conceivable hair problem from dandruff to split ends and was touted as a remedy for skin disorders such as eczema. Ernie predicted his company would gross over $3 million that year. Asked to explain how his product worked, he said: "My Energizer works by breaking up the layers of sebum, a waxy oil brought about by the discharge of the sebecous [*sic*] glands on the scalp. The sebum clogs the hair follicles, eventually destroying the hair root and causing baldness." When asked what specific ingredient in jojoba oil aided hair growth, Ernie only said, "It's a secret formula." At a health food store in San Francisco, a variety of jojoba shampoos were for sale. One was priced at $2.89, while Ernie's Energizer retailed for $21.50. Each contained the same amount of jojoba oil—two percent. When the store manager was asked how the Energizer differed from the other jojoba shampoos, he said, "It really is not any different than all the others, except that perhaps it is marketed in a better way."[29]

By 1980 the nonmedical treatment for Americans worried about hair loss added up to a $150 million a year industry. Thomas Warner, described by a reporter as "a mile-a-minute talker," arrived in Miami to talk about his company, Hair Again, an 11-year-old New York concern about to branch out with franchises. Florida was selected as the first expansion area because, said Warner, "It's easier to get a license in Miami than in California," where he also wanted to set up shop. His own background was said to be in "psychology and lifestyle modification." Hair Again had a "board of medical consultants" headed by a plastic surgeon and a "creative surgery center." That latter division was to do hair transplants if the rest of the program failed. Explained Warner, "If a hair is dead, it's D-E-A-D. But we make the assumption that the hair is there. We don't make it grow. It's not growing for some reason or another. Our treatment rationale creates an environment that will permit the hair to grow if it is there." The company claimed that up to 80 percent of men afflicted with male pattern baldness could regrow hair "through proper trichological therapy." At Hair Again, that involved spending $150 for "hair mineral analysis" leading to a $1,000-or-so program of vitamin and mineral supplements and a "polysorbate detergent (shampoo) to irrigate out the cholesterol in the male pattern baldness areas." Warner asserted, "I am not a snake oil salesman." Carefully staying within the law he pointed out: "We don't promise anyone that he won't be bald. We don't guarantee anything." Although he gave his own hair a permanent wave every 90 days, Warner told a reporter, "I don't want you to put that in the paper because I try to discourage people from having permanents."[30]

A 1981 report in the *Washington Post* said that Americans were spending $10 billion annually on their hair for care, treatment, and replacement. Many of those treatments were expensive. One "herbal cosmetic for baldness" marketed by John Arthur Enterprises consisted of a shampoo and a lotion at $45 a bottle. A three-month treatment which consisted of 12 bottles of each cost a customer $1,000; a six-month supply could be had for $1,860. Customers dissatisfied with their results could get a refund, but only for the cost of their last one month's supply of the products. Pilo-Genic Research Associates stated it rejected around 20 percent of its potential customers after a preliminary interview and exam. According to that company, 13 percent of the clients it accepted were not helped by its "mini-emulsion" cream/lotion shampoo for hair loss, while 40 to 70 percent of its clients reported successful hair regrowth. A three-month course of treatment from Pilo-Genic cost $310; six months cost $600. No refunds and no guarantees were offered by the firm.[31]

Behind the John Arthur Enterprises company was Florida cosmetologist and herbalist Jacqueline Sabal; John Arthur was her son. Sabal claimed to have hit on a secret formula of herbs that converted cleansing agents in lotions and shampoos into smaller molecules. Those molecules then penetrated the scalp, unclogging pores that had been plugged up by natural oils. Male pattern baldness occurred when hairs were trapped under the skin and were unable to get out, explained Sabal. "Think of baldness as 100,000 in-grown hairs." Clients of the John Arthur program had to foreswear all other hair-care products, braiding, permanent waves, and all chemicals. Customers were required to shampoo daily with the special herbal shampoo and had to massage the scalp with a hand vibrator for 20 minutes daily. Hair growth could be seen in 3 to 6 months or up to 1½ years for tough cases, claimed the company. Clients who shampooed and massaged twice a day were, said Sabal, "getting twice as much hair."[32]

Although Sabal agreed baldness was hereditary, she claimed hormones played no part. What a person inherited was overactive sebaceous glands and the shape of the head, explained Sabal. If a man inherited a flat head, the oils secreted by the glands would drip back into the scalp. That explained why people didn't lose the hair from the sides of their heads. A radio personality who used the product said hair was regrowing on his scalp after a few months on the program. John Arthur said that three-inch long black hairs were reemerging on the radio man's scalp, contrasting with the white fringe elsewhere on his head. Because of the coloration and length of this new growth, the company believed those hairs were at least 15 years old. Sabal referred to her hair-liberating product as "Drano of the scalp."[33]

Some treatments were cheaper. None grew hair or preserved existing hair; some were just less brutal on the wallet. Robert E. Murphy of Sacramento, California, sold a hair treatment called New Generation shampoo and conditioner, which he claimed grew hair. Murphy declared his product gave him a 45 percent hair recovery. He claimed only 470 of his 6,000 customers took advantage of his money-back guarantee for the $36 paid for a three-month supply of the product. New Generation promotional material claimed that 80 percent of participants in a test of its products recovered 60 percent of their hair within a year and almost 100 percent reported an end to abnormal fallout within 3 to 4 weeks. Murphy got into the business when he heard that Drs. Illona Schreck-Purola and Kai Setala of the University of Helsinki's Department of Pathology suggested that cholesterol in the hair follicles might inhibit hair growth. Supposedly, Murphy mixed up his product from the Finns' recipe which soon led, he said, to Sacramento baldies regrowing hair and writing him to say his product was doing wonders for their heads. That led the U.S. Postal Service to step in. In October 1981, he was charged with using "a scheme or device to obtain money through the mails ... by means of false representation." Miami dermatologist Dr. Karl Kramer testified that the active ingredient in New Generation was polysorbate 60, an emulsifier commonly used to cut grease. It could do nothing for hair follicles. Several people voluntarily testified for Murphy, including a dentist and a city police captain, who drove from Sacramento to San Francisco to say the product had grown hair. Outside of court, Murphy insisted he wasn't trying to defraud people with his discovery: "My God, we weren't trying to sell anything—we were trying to grow hair."[34]

Speaking of baldness cures in general, dermatologist Dr. Sorrel Resnick thought that "Scrupulous cleanliness, accompanied by the stimulation that goes with daily shampooing, might encourage some growth in the little hairs (lanugo hairs) left behind" even on bald heads after the larger hairs had permanently departed. Yale University's Dr. Ronald Savin said, "Generally, if one fusses with their hair, if they massage it a lot, wash it a lot, they tend to develop an increased amount of fine white hair, what we call vellus.... It never goes on. Resting hairs become stimulated to some extent, but they don't become 'terminal hairs,' the heavy black hairs which you and I recognize as real hair." Whatever dissimilarities existed among hair potions touted to alleviate baldness, all involved a lot of manipulation and massage of the scalp.[35]

Another well-publicized baldness treatment contained polysorbate 60. In late 1978 those two Finnish researchers described their success in treating baldness with polysorbate 60. As a side effect from their cancer research, they discovered it caused a faster regrowth of hair on mice. They went on to test it on humans, using 320 adult volunteers. According to the researchers, new hair growth was seen in 60 percent of the volunteers. No control was used, however. They also admitted that "some of the patients did not come to every biopsy procedure during the trials." Polysorbate was a common ingredient found in many products such as soaps, shampoos, and mayonnaise. It was both an emulsifier and a surfactant. Emulsifiers allow ingredients to blend together; surfactants are found in many cleaning products. Another study done in France purported to find similar results. Soon polysorbate treatment hit the market in Europe, then the United States. Signed testimonials appeared to announce its efficacy. Durk Pearson appeared on the Merv Griffin television show to proclaim it regrew his hair. "There is a cure for baldness.... When you use polysorbate you'll expect to see hair sprouting on someone who's as bald as a billiard ball in about six weeks," he enthusiastically stated. According to Schreck-Purola, polysorbate worked by removing excessive cholesterol from the scalp membranes as well as aiding in cell division. Later she told reporters that the formula grew hair on some scalps that had been bald for many years, but that results were best on those with recent hair loss.[36]

Hal Z. Lederman, president of California-based Pantron I, used the formula in a shampoo, conditioner, and vitamin pills under the trade name the "Helsinki Formula." He did a test in 1984 in which volunteers were treated for three months, and he claimed 60 percent of the subjects "reported some sort of hair growth." Pantron I admitted the test was not scientific; subjects simply completed a questionnaire each month. Years later, after millions of dollars of polysorbate-based products had been sold, the two Finnish researchers were interviewed by a United States postal inspector who was checking out the Helsinki Formula claims. Both said they had never claimed their product would cure baldness. They did believe it might be helpful in decreasing the rate at which a man was becoming bald and that in "certain cases" it might stop excessive hair loss. Both Finns remarked they had been professionally embarrassed by the ads quoting their studies and bearing their alleged endorsements. Commenting on polysorbate treatment, Dr. Norman Orentreich said: "We had some of our patients try this. We took before and after photographs and could see no improvement.... I looked at a couple of patients who had bought the stuff in health food stores and who swore their baldness was better—I compared the photographs and they weren't better. A lot of people find it difficult to be objective about themselves. There's a big difference between growing real hair and growing peach fuzz."[37]

Information about an independent double-blind study of the preparation was reported in 1985. At the time, one writer noted that "polysorbate has been the most popular treatment for hair loss sold in this country over the last five years." Researchers reported there was no difference between the polysorbate treated group of subjects and the control group. Polysorbate was ineffective; neither group produced new hair growth. In terms of subjective reports, 24.8 percent of all subjects who completed the study reported new hair growth—27.9 percent in the polysorbate group, 21.9 percent in the placebo group. Polysorbate preparations cost about $40 for a two- to three-month supply. Other nationally advertised names, besides Helsinki, were New Generation, Bio-Genesis, and Growth Plus.[38]

After 1988 discussions with the National Advertising Division of the Council of Better Business Bureaus, the advertiser for Helsinki Formula announced it was no longer making claims the shampoo could prevent hair loss and promote new hair growth. The advertiser, in fact, had agreed to a consent order with the U.S. Postal Service to permanently discontinue making those claims.[39]

With America awash with hair growth potions, the FDA stepped in to consider excluding such products from the market. Starting in the 1970s, the FDA had been studying the safety and effectiveness of ingredients in a variety of over-the-counter (OTC) products. One group of products touted themselves as able to grow hair or prevent baldness. Legally they were considered OTC drug products subject to FDA regulations because their manufacturers claimed they had the biological effect of causing hair to grow. They were OTC products because they were available without a doctor's prescription. These products were scrutinized by the FDA's OTC Advisory Review Panel on Miscellaneous Drug Products, which consisted of seven panel members who were all medical scientists, including two dermatologists.[40]

When the FDA announced hair products would be reviewed, only three manufacturers submitted information to the panel. One Matawan, New Jersey, maker claimed its hair treatment "activated cellular respiration of the scalp, stimulated blood circulation, and strengthened hair roots." The panel received the formula but no data or actual product. The panel found nothing to support that maker's claim. A Brooklyn, New York, manufacturer offered a laboratory report on its "hair stimulant and grower," which contained lanolin and coconut oil. No data was submitted as to the effectiveness of those ingredients, nor did the panel find any evidence they were effective. The third maker, from Houston, Texas, supplied data on its hair growth stimulator, which was intended to treat "sebum hair loss" supposedly caused by sebum destruction of hair follicles. Sebum is a naturally occurring chemical compound in human skin. Submitted data was from the early 1950s on studies done with rats. While a sebum theory of hair loss had once been postulated in the scientific community, it had been abandoned decades previously by most medical scientists. In its 1980 report, the FDA proposed a ban on the sale of all products which asserted they could grow hair or prevent baldness. The agency's panel concluded that no products sold to grow hair or prevent baldness were effective and stated that "all claimed hair-grower and hair-loss-prevention ingredients reviewed are not effective for OTC external use." Most of those products were sold by mail or by barbers or beauticians. If the FDA proposed ban went into effect, manufacturers who claimed to have discovered a drug which could grow hair or prevent baldness would be required to first provide the FDA with proof of the safety and effectiveness of the drug before it could be sold legally.[41]

While the FDA seemed poised to ban the products in 1980, it did not happen. Five years later the agency surfaced again, apparently ready to finally ban the OTC baldness potions. Agency spokesman Edward R. Nida explained the proposed ban was not because the products were harmful but because they didn't work. "It's not going to hurt anybody except in their pocketbooks. These products do not prevent hair loss or grow hair. How you lose or keep your hair depends on how wisely you chose your parents." No exact figures were available on how much was spent on such products since they were part of the entire OTC drug market, then a $5.5 billion-a-year industry. Nida said those products were produced by "a lot of shady figures on the fringes of the medical profession." At various times the products, he reported, had been advertised in the back pages of *True* magazine, the *Police Gazette*, and *Esquire*. To that list William E. Gilbertson, director of the FDA OTC drug evaluation program, added Sunday newspaper supplements. "We do not know the size of the market. There are probably small companies that make them," he explained. Regarding the announcement of the FDA's proposed ban, *Time* magazine writer Otto Friedrich applauded the move by writing: "Fair enough. It is part of the FDA's job to protect us from snake-oil salesmen." The ban did not materialize, however, and the snake-oil continued to roll.[42]

One FDA spokesman commented that the OTC baldness potions were often nothing more than mixtures of vitamins, minerals, oils, and "stuff that defies analysis." With no blanket ban in place, the FDA had to go after each outfit individually, a costly, slow, time-consuming procedure. Pursuing such activity was a low priority item at the FDA because those duped were not harmed physically. "It's easier to try and keep consumers from being bilked through an education process than going through a series of court cases. If we put handcuffs on one of them we haven't had much impact on the marketplace but if we can get word out to consumers that none works, we'll have greater impact," said the FDA. With limited resources the FDA first went after products that threatened life, then products that threatened health. In a 1984 survey, 58 percent of adults said they had heard of potions to grow hair. Of this group, five percent believed the products to be moderately or very effective. That seemingly small percentage nevertheless represented 8½ million adults in the U.S. Even if the FDA was successful in spreading the word that the products didn't work, the agency realized it might get no thanks. Said an agency spokesman, "One of the most discouraging things that happens here are the complaints we get from people after we try to warn them of frauds. They think we're trying to play Big Brother and prevent them from buying something miraculous."[43]

England's consumer magazine *Which?* sent two bald volunteers to a number of hair clinics in 1973. Prior to those visits a dermatologist had examined each volunteer and confirmed he had ordinary male pattern baldness. Treatments offered the bald men at the clinics included ultraviolet and infrared radiation, electrotherapy, massage, creams, lotions, and shampoos. None would help. Costs of the offered treatments averaged £60, but ranged up to £120. Subjects were pressured by clinic staff to start treatment right away. Sometimes a discount was offered; they were told they could pay on easy terms. On one occasion a subject was asked, "How much have you got on you?" One volunteer was told that if he hesitated even a week or two before taking the advised £80 treatment, it might be too late to save his hair. Follow-up letters were received by the subjects at their homes almost immediately after their visit. While clinics were careful to say their treatment would do no more than stop further hair loss, the idea that hair might grow was implicit. Volunteers were usually told that dandruff or seborrhea was their problem. None of the subjects had those conditions, nor were those conditions involved in baldness, in any case. *Which?* heard from ten of its readers who had gone to hair clinics. Although five believed their rate of hair loss slowed and the other five said treatment had no effect, only one of the ten men thought the treatment was very worthwhile. Ten other readers told the magazine they had purchased lotions and shampoos from clinics that dealt by mail-order. In no case was baldness helped. *Which?* thought the U.K. should impose stricter control over the ads hair treatment clinics were allowed to run. While Britain's Advertising Standards Authority prohibited ads for products claiming to restore hair, it was permissible to claim a product could stop hair loss. Such a claim had never been scientifically demonstrated, however.[44]

Ten years later *Which?* repeated its experiment, this time sending four baldies to the same three clinics. One clinic told three volunteers they were suffering from malfunctioning sebaceous glands and claimed that was responsible for the hair loss. All the clinics agreed the subjects had male pattern baldness. Stating that nothing could bring back the lost hair, the clinics argued that the healthier the scalp, the less likely would future hair loss be. All recommended a series of treatments involving shampoos and massages. The clinics' recommendations were not concurred by the magazine's experts, who had verified the volunteers had ordinary male pattern baldness for which nothing could be done. *Which?* heard from 32 male readers who had used a lotion. Half were dissatisfied, some of the rest thought their hair was in better condition, and some thought there might have been a slowing in the rate of hair loss. Lotions used included Re-Mane, "its function is to regrow lost hair" (£39.50 for a one-month supply); Dercos, "helps strengthen hair roots and activate growth" (£13.75 for a three-month supply); and Banfi, "It's remarkable; it works" (£22 for a nine-week supply). Eleven other men reported on their experiences in visiting a clinic. The majority said it had not affected the rate of hair loss. *Which?*'s verdict on hair treatment clinics was "If you're expecting more hair to grow, save your money." Speaking more generally on its survey of baldness treatments from lotions to clinics to toupees to transplants to flaps, the magazine remarked: "Even some of the satisfied men in our survey said they wished they had never started trying to hide their baldness and would advise others to try to come to terms with theirs. No matter how you try to deal with MPB it will be costly, time consuming and less than satisfactory— no one can give you back your hair."[45]

One hair product that achieved considerable success for a short time was Nutriol, which hit the American market late in 1985. It was made by the Italian company Crinos International, part of Fincrinos, a 39-year-old holding company in Milan with annual sales of about $70 million. Nutriol was a slightly revised version of Foltene, a hair product the company brought out several years earlier and then marketed in nine European nations, Canada, and Kuwait. Crinos's marketing director Antonio Caso told reporters that health ministries in a number of countries, including France, Italy, and Greece, had given the company approval for the marketing of Foltene as a product that stopped hair loss and stimulated hair growth. Foltene's active ingredients were complex organic substances extracted from animal tissues. Those substances, trichosaccharides, were said to be rich in polysaccharides—complex carbohydrates that were claimed to accelerate hair growth. Cleveland Clinic Foundation dermatologist Dr. Wilma Bergfeld was unimpressed with the ingredients, calling them "common conditioners, vitamins and food stuffs, such as sugars and carbohydrates. They've put in everything but the kitchen sink, and this kind of application has never been proven to grow hair." Caso insisted that Foltene spurred hair growth in two or three months, and he claimed that 81 percent of the subjects in Foltene trials showed partial regrowth of normal hair, 11 percent had total regrowth of normal hair, and only 8 percent found the treatment a failure.[46]

Although Caso claimed that Nutriol would also grow hair in two to three months, he noted that the product would be promoted in the United States as a hair fitness preparation with no in-print claims of hair growth properties. Clearly that was done to avoid arousing the wrath of the FDA and possible sanctions. A spokesman for that agency admitted that "off-the-label" claims were made all the time, but it was difficult to establish a case against any product unless those claims were stated on the package. Marketed as a hair fitness "cosmetic," Nutriol needed no FDA approval. Any product that claimed to grow hair was regarded as a drug and couldn't be sold without approval from the FDA which, in 1986, the agency had never granted to any product. Although Nutriol packaging contained no hair-growing claims, it relied on word of mouth for selling and spreading such claims. It was not sold in stores; all sales were direct through multilevel marketing. A distributor bought the product wholesale from the company and then resold it. New buyers signing on with the company solicited more new buyers, with each layer of distributors getting a share of the sales dollars. In its first two months of availability in America, some 4,000 people had signed up to sell Nutriol and wholesale volume reached $700,000.[47]

Each box of Nutriol contained 12 vials of the product. First the purchaser applied the contents of one vial to his scalp every other day for 48 days, the "attack phase." Then there was a follow-up with a refresher treatment one to three times a week for the next six months. Next it was back to the attack phase for another 48 days. Said Caso, "We don't want to promise the moon but we have a product which has been shown to grow hair in two to three months ... and there are absolutely no side effects." Depending on how much product a purchaser used, Nutriol cost between $400 and $700 for a year's supply at the suggested retail price of $49.50 per box. While it wholesaled at $34.97, some distributors retailed the product for as much as $75 per box. Ingredients listed on the box included amino acids, vitamins, deionized water, capsicum extract, caramel, and watercress. NuSkin was the company with the exclusive rights to sell Nutriol in the United States. NuSkin counsel Steven Lund commented, "We're marketing it as a cosmetic product, but we know some people are selling it as a hair grower." One multilevel distributor was Richard Kall of Hauppauge, New York, who claimed to have sold $17,000 worth of the lotion in one month and to have signed up about 200 people to sell it. He observed that some people were showing hair growth in five to six weeks.[48]

Regarding Nutriol ingredients, New Haven surgeon and dermatologist Dr. Ronald Savin noted dryly: "Amino acids are meat. If you think you can cure baldness with amino acids you might just as well walk around with a piece of meat slapped on your head." Six months after its introduction, some 14,000 Americans were said to be selling Nutriol. Although the company said it discouraged the practice, many of those salespeople told customers that the product prevented hair loss and stimulated hair growth. Arthur Bertolino, director of New York University Medical Center's hair consultation unit, commented on how baldness quackery was encouraged by the placebo effect with any special attention to the scalp often having the ability to startle a few hairs into minor and temporary action. "Some studies show that even when the data don't support documentation of any new growth, some twenty percent of the product's users are satisfied that there's been an improvement." Added Savin, "The things you see in ads are usually bull. They're successful for the same reasons witch doctors were."[49]

Most of these potions, while ineffective, were at least harmless, except to the wallet. Some quack remedies, however, could be dangerous. One method reported in the mid–1980s was head filing, a treatment that involved slitting open the scalp and filing the tissue between the skull and hair follicles to thin membranes over the skull. Supposedly that would "wake up the follicles."[50]

After being introduced in Europe in 1981, Foltene went on to become the third largest selling product in all categories of goods sold in French pharmacies within three years.[51]

China got into the baldness curing business in the 1980s with a remedy first formulated by engineer Wu Baoxin, director of the Sanlu Factory in Beijing. Wu had also invented all 15 other varieties of cosmetics produced by Sanlu. According to reporter Yue Haitao, writing in the *Beijing Review*, "All medical textbooks say baldness, which is caused by fatty infiltration, is irreversible." Yue went on to claim the Sanlu product, called the Dabao Trichogen cure, boasted a baldness cure rate of 98.6 percent. Supposedly those rates were from the China Medical Association's Beijing branch, which observed 60 cases in August 1985. By 1986, 300,000 bottles of the product had been sold in China. After experimenting with this cure for one year, the Ohasi Company of Japan signed a contract to become its sole agent in Japan. The cure was reportedly judged effective by "eminent" Japanese medical people.[52]

The Sanlu Factory signed a 1986 agreement with the Super Repute Company of Hong Kong to sell the former's Dabao cure. Before concluding the pact, Super Repute reportedly tested the treatment on 100 baldies for 9 months, with 95 of them reporting some improvement.[53]

A remedy from China which became even more popular was the 101 Hair Regeneration Liniment invented by Dr. Zhao Zhangguang. "I used to be a barefoot doctor. I'm from the mountains in Zhejiang. In the mountains we pay a lot of attention to plants and herbs," he explained. Although not bald himself, he got interested in the condition back in the 1970s when he tried to come up with a cure using traditional herbs. To start with, he mixed herbs and oils traditionally believed to stimulate hair growth. "Those just don't work," he said. "Everybody thinks they do but they don't." After about 40 failures, he was ready to quit, "People said I was mad. They scorned me. They didn't think I'd be successful. That did it. I kept on working." As he continued to experiment, his money ran out. He rented out one of the three rooms in his house; his wife raised pigs and chickens to support the family. Struggling to perfect his formula, he traveled the back country, stopping at rural villages to test his latest creation on baldies. All the while he kept telling himself: "My path is not the wrong one. I would rather die than not find an effective hair tonic." He promised villagers a free lunch if they returned for a second treatment. Finally, after Zhao tried 101 different mixtures, he found the one he claimed regrew hair. Ingredients included ginseng, Chinese Angelica, dried ginger, walnut meat, safflower, and alcohol.[54]

Word of the cure spread. In 1976 a reporter from Hangzhou came by to check out rumors that there were no bald men in Zhao's area. That bald reporter used the potion; supposedly he grew hair. A story was published, and the newspaper invited Zhao to Hangzhou to try his product in the big city. Over several years he treated more than 1,000 patients, with a reported success rate of 90 percent. Officials from Beijing lured Zhao to that city with promises of housing and a factory of his own. Zhao moved there in 1986 and set up a plant to produce his remedy. Average treatment with 101 Liniment took two to three months with daily application of the product and cost $100. Despite the fact that China's per capita income was less than $300, Zhao said he had no shortage of customers willing to spend the money. By 1988, 101 Liniment was available in 18 countries, including Japan, Sweden, and the United States, and Zhao was reported to be working on a second generation of product. Asked why 101 worked, Zhao replied: "101 Liniment invigorates the circulation of the blood, frees the main and collateral channels of the body and thereby makes hair grow. It stimulates the skin in a persistent congestive manner, bringing on the new growth.... It is normal for the scalp to become red or black after using 101. This indicates an improvement in blood circulation resulting from capillary expansion, as well as being a sign of its curative effect." It was an explanation very similar to that given for the blistering treatments in vogue from medical doctors in the 1890s. Such treatments did indeed change the scalp's color through irritation and caused a pooling of blood in the area. That was all that happened, however.[55]

Still on the go in the middle 1990s, 101 Liniment had its praises sung in the Chinese government's English language magazine *Beijing Review*. By then the 101 family of hair products contained four more members, 101A through 101D. One article claimed the original 101 Liniment had treated 2.88 million bald patients around the world with an effective rate of hair regrowth of 95 percent. Among the glowing testimonials to the product was one from Liao Juanshan, who said, "Such fine medicine reflects on the glorious heritage of our Chinese nation!" In late 1990, Greece became the only European Community nation to allow 101 on the market as a medicine. When Zhao Zhangguang visited Athens in 1992, he was reportedly swamped by members of the Greek media as well as long line-ups of bald Greeks wanting to be personally treated.[56]

Pasadena, California, dermatologist Mike B. Corbett remarked that a lot of people from Mexico sent him so-called baldness cures they wanted him to back for 20 or so percent of the action. "I had a patient who was curious and asked me to rub a little of one of these products on his scalp. The main ingredient was a native pepper. His hair didn't grow but he sure did—almost went through the roof," recalled Corbett.[57]

Late in 1983, John Coombs was working on his dairy farm in Wiltshire, England. He was feeding his cow Primrose when dust from the feed settled on his bald head. As he bent to fill the trough, Primrose licked his scalp. Eight weeks later Coombs's wife noticed his hair returning. For a time Coombs remained skeptical, but he finally declared, "My hair is going up like the tide coming in." After he watched a TV program about volunteers who had failed to grow hair using bay rum, bear fat, and herbal concoctions, Coombs decided to go public with his story. "My friends said, 'Good heavens, write in and say you can cure baldness.' So I did. It was like lighting a heap of dynamite," he recalled. Soon swarms of journalists descended on the farm; headlines appeared across Europe. Coombs related that being licked by a cow can be a rough experience. "It feels like a file" was how he described a lick from Primrose's coarse tongue. He said he had been bald for over 25 years. One person to see a commercial opportunity was West German hairdresser Eric Schmitt, who quickly lined up eight patients. These men presented their bald heads once a week to a German cow named Liesel, who licked each head for five minutes, at a cost of $14 per time, per man. After four months of that regimen, Schmitt admitted only one man had grown anything and that was only "peach fuzz." Undaunted, the men faithfully returned each week. Commented Schmitt, "Hairdressers must remain open to new ideas." German and French companies got into the act by marketing a product called Likkit. When he sent his entire dairy herd to the slaughterhouse in December 1986, Coombs exempted Primrose, allowing her to live on the farm. "She's family," he said.[58]

In 1988 a U.S. supermarket tabloid touted a Swiss farmer's baldness cure. It was an ounce of bat milk, selling for $3,500. The following year two Canadians, Philip P. West and Wayne P. Kreklewich, were indicted by the FDA in the U.S. on several counts of mail fraud for selling baldness cures by mail, dating back to 1984. The agency first became aware of the scheme through a letter from the Nashville, Tennessee, Better Business Bureau, which was following up on a customer's inquiry requesting information about the products advertised in a Nashville paper before ordering. For $210 a customer received one four-ounce bottle each of Westmaster Follicle Cleanser, Westmaster Hair and Scalp Lotion, and Westmaster Natural Source Formula Shampoo. After seizure, FDA analysis showed the product to contain a blend of the sunscreen para-aminobenzoic (PABA), aloe vera, protein, vitamin E, jojoba, balsam, water, polysorbate 80, propylene glycol, stearyl alcohol, mineral oil, oleyl alcohol, lechithin, amino acids, and preservatives. All were common ingredients in shampoo and hair conditioners but had no effect as hair restorers, as the Westmaster products were touted. What cost 48 cents to make sold for $12 to $15. During almost four years of peddling this material, the two men were estimated to have made over $3 million.[59]

Foltene was introduced into the U.S. in March 1987. Packaging and advertising made no mention of hair regrowth as they did in Europe, but Crinos planned "a publicity effort to encourage discussion in consumer articles of Foltene's properties of hair regrowth and prevention of further hair loss." Nutriplexx was put on the market in 1981 by Aramis, a subsidiary of Estee Lauder, Inc., of New York. It cost $75 for a 90-day supply. Flowlin came on the American market that same year after being introduced in Japan in 1982 by the Shiseido Company of Tokyo. In Japanese, Flowlin meant "never aging forest." By not making any blatant claims about having a metabolic effect, those marketing Flowlin were able to avoid FDA review. Asked why people spent money on such useless products, Dr. Gerald Weinstein, chairman of the dermatology department at the University of California at Irvine, said, "A lot of people who have lost their hair are extremely vain and will try anything." Products to save the hair were being thrown on the market at a faster and more furious rate than ever at the end of the 1980s because of the publicity given to Upjohn's minoxidil-based Rogaine and ultimate FDA approval of it. UCLA dermatology professor Richard A. Strick commented: "I don't believe they work. If there is an indication they did they would spend the money to get FDA approval, because that's where the real money is." Strick also pointed out: "Those products may have a placebo effect. The mind is a powerful tool." Prior to the minoxidil publicity, investigations of hair-growing potions had dwindled because, said U.S. Postal Service inspection department fraud manager Donald J. Davis, "It was so clear there was no cure, we could shut them down easily." The hype over minoxidil, added Davis, "will cause us real problems." Another lotion was New Genesis Hair Fitness Lotion, which sold for $40 for a one-month supply. Looking at the ingredients list, Weinstein called it "a garbage can of materials. They are safe, but none have anything to do with hair growth."[60]

More products were introduced. In 1989, based in Clifton, New Jersey, Shulton Inc., began to distribute Thrive, a three-step program for thinning hair. Available in food, drug, and mass merchandise outlets, the program included a $4 shampoo, a $6 supplement and a $3 hair spray—all to be used together on a daily basis. All Thrive products were marketed as containing "Hair Vitalizing Proteins … a proprietary blend of keratin and collagen that has been hydrolized or shortened to a more usable form." That same year Revlon introduced Nutrasome therapy, for men's thinning hair. It included an enrichment shampoo, a supplement, and styling gel. Targeted at 30- to 49-year-old males, the product claimed it "builds up the strand from within."[61]

The rash of new hair tonics on the market apparently finally prompted the FDA to take long-promised action. On July 7, 1989, the agency announced it was banning, effective in six months, the sale of nonprescription creams and lotions whose makers asserted they could grow hair or prevent baldness. The ban applied to OTC products used externally. Once the ban was in effect manufacturers of any nonprescription drug said to prevent baldness or grow hair would have to provide the FDA with proof of such claims before the product could be placed on the market. Other products taken by mouth—such as vitamins or food supplements—were equally ineffective in growing hair. While those items were not covered by the ban, the FDA warned they too would be removed from the market on a case-by-case basis if they made such claims.[62]

Upjohn applauded the FDA ruling, saying it served to validate the way the company studied its drug minoxidil. Company executive vice president Mark Novitch said: "The meaning here is clear. FDA does not recognize any existing OTC products as effective treatment for hair loss. We couldn't be more pleased by their issuance of these regulations. What this announcement does is strengthen the FDA's authority over products for which medical claims are made, and that includes OTC products that claim to grow hair or prevent hair loss." Of course, the ban stood to indirectly benefit the sales of Upjohn's Rogaine. Upjohn estimated that $200 million was spent by American men every year on OTC products which claimed or implied effectiveness in treating hair loss. When the ban was announced, the FDA pointed to Upjohn's Rogaine study as a standard for research for other companies seeking FDA approval whether for prescription or OTC status. Said the FDA, "Although that particular product is marketed as a prescription drug ... the methods used to study it would be applicable for an OTC hair grower drug product."[63]

In 1988 the FDA estimated Americans spent annually $100 million on fraudulent baldness remedies. For 1987 the agency estimated Americans spent $24 billion annually for hair care.[64]

In the wake of the FDA approval of Rogaine, there was a rush of announcements of new hair care products. Nutrasome was introduced into department stores by the Revlon Group. Foltene announced plans for several new products in the coming year. Proctor and Gamble was considering a similar product line. Foltene and Aramis's Nutriplexx had combined sales of $55 to $60 million at the manufacturer's level. Sales of Foltene for 1988 were projected at $40 million retail. At $7 retail per bottle (a one-month supply), Nutrasome was much cheaper than Nutriplexx, which retailed for $30 a bottle or $75 for a three-month supply. Foltene retailed for $45 for 10 vials, a 20-day supply. Also available was Recapture at $60 for a 90-day supply. All of these products stuck with cosmetic claims only, thereby avoiding scrutiny by the FDA. They spoke of themselves as enriching shampoos with thickening properties or as products which revitalized the hair, and so on. Full-page color ads regularly appeared in *USA Today* for Foltene. Nutriplexx was touted as a "Thinning Hair Supplement." Although the fine print did admit the product didn't cure baldness or prevent it, the product did proclaim: "At last there is something you can do about your thinning hair. Something more constructive than watching helplessly day by day as your hair becomes thinner, sparser, less vital."[65]

In 1985, Proctor and Gamble gave Drs. Roy Oliver and Colin Jahoda of Scotland's Dundee University £650,000 to study hair growth. That deal was renegotiated in 1988 to ensure the researchers of almost £350,000 per year in funding over the following ten years.[66]

Hair in a can was popular in the 1990s with 30-minute infomercials for the product on late-night cable TV. One such product was GLH Formula #9, which was an aerosol-based dye with some polymers to frizz up the hair and thicken it. With the scalp dyed the same color as the hair, it gave the appearance of making balding men hair-bearing, at least it did on television. GLH quickly sold half a million cans of the stuff at $40 each. A 1994 article estimated American men spent $2 billion yearly dealing with hair loss.[67]

6
WIGS AND WEAVING

A good man goes grey, but a rascal grows bald.
Czech proverb cited by Walter Klenhard,
The Bald Book

Is that your head or is your neck blowing bubble gum?
Dan Carlinsky, "Bald Truths,"
Reader's Digest, June 1983

The word *wig* is short for periwig. That word is a corrupted form of the word *peruke* or the French *perruque*—itself derived from an Italian term meaning "head of hair." A wig covers the entire head, while a toupee covers only part of the head, usually the top. Men's wigs were a European affectation that came into vogue when French king Louis XIII went prematurely bald and had a fiaxen wig made for himself. The custom spread to the rest of Continental Europe and to the United Kingdom. Wearing a wig became a mark of status, denoting a life of leisure or influence. For seventeenth-century men, sporting a hairpiece made a class statement as well as a fashion statement. Initially, it was the senior members of court and society who donned hairpieces. Such was their cultural dominance that the practice of wearing a hairpiece spread to all classes in society, right down to masons and ditch diggers. Even young men with hair followed the fashion. That pattern was repeated in Colonial New England with lawyers, judges, clergymen, and other white collar types bringing their periwigs with them across the Atlantic. Soon all classes of Americans adopted hairpieces. During the seventeenth century, barbershops supplied the wigs. Since wigs fit the best over hairless heads, fashion followers of the period often had their skulls shaved so they could cover them more gracefully. Barbers cut hair, shaved heads, and did wig maintenance. Hairpieces were made by attaching human, bovine, or equine hair to cloth skullcaps, or cauls, sewn to fit the precision-measured contours of the clients' heads. What type of material was found in a wig depended on price and quality, with the cheapest wigs being hair blended with linen or silk. Colonial-era wigs were available in white, black, salt-and-pepper, and various shades of brown. To maintain the wig's color, people often sprinkled powder on them. Those who didn't wear wigs sometimes powdered their own hair to give the impression they were bewigged. Fashionable wigs got in the way, so Colonists, like wig-wearing British soldiers, began using shorter wigs, ultimately devising the tied-back plaited styles with bows usually associated with Colonial dress. Americans wore wigs right up through the War of Independence. Sympathy for the French Revolution of 1789 caused the wigs to fall from favor. By then they were bobbed vestiges of the originals.[1]

During the 1930s, female wig buyers outnumbered male purchasers about three to one. Saul Cohen had manufactured wigs for 30 years, making about 800 wigs in a year, which sold for $35 to $75 each. Hair used in the wigs all came from Europe as American hair—subjected to lotions and waves—was considered useless. Jobbers scoured the rural districts of Europe, buying hair from peasants who cut it about once every two years. A company called Frankle's Inc. sold something called "Frankle's Marvelously Human Deknotted Partings" described as a wig that offered "the perfect and only solution to the age-old problem of baldness." At that time the number one American wig maker was Hepner's which had a Hollywood branch to serve male and female screen stars as well as another branch to serve senators. William Hepner, who died in 1932, first set up shop in 1888 in Manhattan. All his hairpieces were custom made. Ranging in price from $35 up, every Hepner wig was supposedly made from the hair of French children. During Hepner's busiest time, 15 young women were occupied all day in the plant sewing hair into toupee nets. One prominent but unnamed Washington, D.C., man of the 1930s had several wigs of different lengths. Every few weeks he would drop a casual remark about getting a haircut, and then reappear wearing a wig with hair of a shorter length.[2]

Writing in the *Saturday Evening Post* in 1956, Fred Sparks gave an account of how wonderful life was for him after purchasing a toupee. He was a reporter and former war correspondent who often gave lectures for a fee. The agent who booked those tours told him: "I wish you had more hair. We'd get more dates. The public doesn't accept a bald man as a dashing foreign correspondent." Sparks estimated there were then 50,000 male toupee wearers in the U.S. An athletic friend who operated a gym told him: "I sell exercise to retain youthful figures. I am a better advertisement with hair than without." A sales director of a household appliance company was quoted as saying that with all other things being equal; "The man with hair will sell more. I bought toupees for two of my salesmen." Then there was the story of a 29-year-old hotel clerk who was passed over for a desirable promotion. He and his wife decided it was because of his baldness, so he bought a toupee. When his boss next saw him, he exclaimed: "What an improvement! You'll get the next opening. Before you weren't cast for a gladhander's role." As to the response of women to baldies,

Sparks argued: "Many girls are disinclined to start married life with a husband already bald. A toupee can mean acceptance. One girl marched her sweetheart to the toupee shop before exhibiting him to mother, who had a violent dislike of baldness. And many toupees are bought with the wife present to help choose the model." So anxiety provoking could baldness be that wigmakers were said to be not surprised when a customer told them, "My doctor sent me." In the 1950s, wigs were reportedly all produced by hand; human hair was used, with 40,000 to 60,000 hairs in a toupee, 140,000 in a wig. Fifteen tons of hair were imported from Europe into America in 1955. China had been a big exporter of human hair until the Communist revolution of 1949, after which the trade dried up. In New York City in the mid–1950s, human hair was bringing $1 an ounce.[3]

By the end of the 1950s, a designer of men's hairpieces reported a 750 percent increase in his business over the previous four years. Three out of every four sales were accounted for by the new Ivy League crew cut model. At the House of Louis Feder, which made men's wigs, vice president Ben Kaplan commented that "Older men want to look younger, and young men want to look their age." Kaplan said that 76 percent of his customers were under the age of 40; 44 percent were still in their 20s. A decade later a source in the U.K. estimated 100,000 hairpieces were sold in Britain each year, at prices ranging from £100 to £250.[4]

When Herb Yerman bought his first wig in the late 1950s, there was no other hair replacement method. "I'll never forget it. I walked around the building for three days I was so nervous. It was like going to a house of prostitution," he recalled. Two decades later Yerman ran a "hair replacement" business. He felt it was an important euphemism because "A man will buy a hair replacement. He won't buy a rug or toupee." Yerman still found customers who were late for their appointments with him because they were outside circling the block. He understood the man whose wife had never seen him without his toupee; he had such a man working for him. "People come in and they tell you one thing, but deep down, they feel another. I think most men feel the loss of hair is the loss of their masculinity. There are two psychological moments when a man is most likely to buy a hair replacement. Right after he's divorced or before he moves somewhere else," he said. Yerman offered custom hairpieces in the price range of $200 to $900. According to those in the trade, there were two things a man in search of a hairpiece usually thinks of first. Will it come off when it's not supposed to? Will it look natural? Later a customer considered personal convenience and price. Wigs didn't give confidence because the wearers had a deep-seated terror of high winds and intimate embraces.[5]

By the late 1970s the image of wigs was largely negative. Many things from lipstick to capped teeth to deodorant to high heels were also attempts to deceive but were not mocked. Perhaps hairpieces were made pathetic and amusing by the desperation of the complex behind the wig. Wig wearers were no longer cultural trend-setters but were vainly trying to recapture youth and luxuriant locks; they were following fashion creators who were generally young and hirsute. London Institute of Psychiatry lecturer Glen Wilson did research on who wore wigs and why, concluding: "The common factor we discovered was that wearers were usually in social isolation. This meant that the all important fear of discovery was less apparent.... The wearer feels that his social-sexual/career problems will be eased or solved if only it appears to others that he has more hair." Women played an indirect role at least, thought Wilson, in that "It is their association of male hair with youth, energy and attractiveness that is the main motive for wearing false hair." According to journalist Hugh Thomson, about one quarter of those who filled in the "Worried about baldness?" forms were females inquiring for their men. Explained Thomson: "Women have long used the full range of the cosmetic industry to preserve the appearance of youth; some it seems expect men to do likewise. Yet most women feel a toupee demeans a man—it shows that he cannot accept his reality; it shows he is obsessed with what should be peripheral to his personality, interests and career."[6]

At Celebrity House in Beverly Hills, California, owner Bob Roberts provided a custom-made hairpiece for $500 in 1977. Ready-made wigs could be had elsewhere for $100 to $200, and there were even dubious bargains as low as $25. Roberts related that most of his clients had three or four pieces with one client maintaining 15 to 18 hairpieces at all times. He believed a customer could get by with only two pieces if they were careful. Natural hair was attached to a plasticized mesh, weighed less than one ounce, was secured with double-sided adhesive tape, and "breathed" well. A second type was used for sport. That had synthetic hair on a water-repellent silicone base which, while minutely perforated, did not breathe. With the hairpiece held on by the liquid adhesive silicone, the wearer could swim, surf, and shower in the sports model. Roberts advised a hairpiece be brought in to the shop every three to four weeks for a shampoo, color check, and restyling—for $15.[7]

Chicago's hairpiece king was Paul Finamore, who opened Hairline Creations in 1964. Eighteen years later he had sold over one million units. "When I started, it wasn't popular for men to wear hairpieces. Most of the wigs and hairpieces I was seeing were imported and looked phony. I wanted to develop a hairpiece that was comfortable, durable and natural looking," he recalled. At his two locations, he employed 75 people. Finamore offered six different models, ranging from $600 to $2,000. Periodic cleaning here was recommended only every three months and cost $15 to $25. His cheaper models had heavier hair and foundations lasting up to five years with proper care, while the lighter $2,000 model lasted only 1½ years. Among the professional athletes Finamore used to endorse his products were hockey player Dennis Hull, baseball pitcher Gaylord Perry, and football kicker Garo Yepremian.[8]

The president of a candy company in North Carolina ordered all of his bald salesmen to get wigs. Reportedly, sales skyrocketed thereafter.[9]

When the British Consumers' Association surveyed baldness treatments in 1983, it concluded all treatments, including toupees, were better avoided by bald men because all remedies were costly, time-consuming, and less than satisfactory. They heard from 20 men who used wigs and toupees. Only three were dissatisfied, but others had complaints that hairpieces were uncomfortable on hot days and there were too many restrictions on activities if the secret was to be kept. The group's verdict on hairpieces was: "In general you seem to get what you pay for. But at least you can see what you are buying before you pay."[10]

Near the end of the 1980s, American Hair Loss Council president Michael Mahoney reported custom-made wigs ranged in price from $600 to $2,400. In addition, they required cleaning and servicing every three to four weeks, usually at a cost of $50 to $60 each time. With a unit's life expectancy at 9 to 12 months, it could cost $3,000 or more per year to own a hairpiece. The good ones—meaning custom-made—were said to be undetectable, but the cheap, ready-made ones were easy to spot. Mahoney emphasized the items were called "hair replacement units." Los Angeles–based psychotherapist Ashley Siegel, who specialized in emotional problems stemming from hair loss, commented: "We live in a physically oriented culture. The hair replacement unit provides an option. But covering up can lead to a fear of exposure and can cause the person with the hairpiece to push others away to avoid the possibility of exposure."[11]

Houston reporter Clifford Pugh cited the cost of hairpieces at $450 to $1,000 and suggested they should be replaced once a year. Texas actor Woody Watson, 39, bought a hairpiece to help his career after advertising agency representatives told him it would get him more acting work. Watson found he wore his wig for 90 percent of jobs involving commercials but for only 10 percent of his acting jobs—parts that generally emphasized character over image.[12]

Hair Club for Men had locations in 18 American cities, where they made and sold wigs. As the Upjohn minoxidil treatment was strongly hyped in the late 1980s, Hair Club president Sy Sperling remarked: "When Rogaine was introduced last year, I thought I'd have to find another way to make a living. I was wrong. Our business has increased nearly 50 percent, leading me to believe the publicity generated by the drug made every balding guy aware that maybe it was time to do something about it."[13]

Forbes magazine estimated in 1991 that a typical male hairpiece cost $1,000 to $3,500, with maintenance costs running at $40 every two to four weeks. Cheap hairpieces could be had for as little as $325. Human-hair wigs had a life expectancy of about one year, while synthetic wigs, priced at $1,800 to $2,500, lasted up to two years. Maintenance costs for synthetic hairpieces were around $35 to $50 every month or so. Over two million American men reportedly wore hairpieces, spending about $350 million annually.[14]

In 1990, wig sales to Japanese men were running around 120,000 each year. The largest wig company in that country was Aderans. When company spokesman Yoshihiro Kon was asked why so many Japanese men wore ill-fitting wigs, he smiled and replied, "What you don't realize is that there are many people with wigs that are so well matched and fitted that you can't see." Kon said there was no scientific evidence to show whether Japanese men were more prone to baldness than Caucasians, adding: "In 1984 we did our own survey by standing on the street at a higher level than the passersby and counted heads. We concluded that about 18.35 percent of Japan's adult men were bald or going bald." Aderans estimated they had a market of 10 to 15 million Japanese adults. The company opened a U.S. subsidiary in 1979, but the venture failed due to poor sales.[15]

Aderans continued to prosper in Japan, as did a rival company named Artnature. The two wigmakers had about 80 percent of the men's wig business. Together their annual sales in the early 1990s approached $600 billion. Some 25 to 30 percent of their gross went for advertising expenses. With an estimated half million wig-wearers in a nation containing 8.6 million bald men, both firms expected to prosper. Aderans's spokesman Minoru Suzuki commented: "The dread of losing hair is spreading among young people. For the young men of today, who have an intelligent sense of fashion, becoming bald is like the end of their lives."[16]

A variation on the hairpiece method of hiding baldness was hair-weaving, in which the client's remaining hair was used to form a woven base to which were attached wefts of matching human hair. Hair-weaving originated in Harlem in the early 1960s to provide long straight hair for black women whose own hair had been damaged by frequent straightening treatments and who didn't want to wear wigs. Similar techniques were later developed for men. The Beauty Fair by Claire salon in Harlem had a sign proclaiming, "When nature won't, Claire will." Owner Claire Glover said of her weaving: "I've been doing it for six years—but I've never been so busy in my life. I guess it's because all men want to be glamorous these days." Glover did traditional beauty work in her shop as well as hair-weaving for both genders.[17]

Diane's Hair-Weaving Specialists in downtown Manhattan served only males and offered no other beauty services. The shop was opened in January 1968 by Diane and James Jones. The latter remarked: "Most of our customers are white men between 25 and 40 who are not satisfied with hairpieces. They don't like to bother with glue and tape, and they want to wear their hair in swimming. It's not smart to go swimming in a hairpiece." Diane wove the hair into the scalp, and then James, a barber, cut and styled it. Most hair-weavers were secretive about their technique. Glover said, "All I can tell you is that I use a crochet stitch." Usually the technician picked up strands of the customer's remaining hair and wove it around strands of nylon thread to form foundation seams, or bases. From three to six seams might be sewn on a head, but there was no penetration of the skin. Then separate sections of human hair were sewn to the foundation seams, using the same weaving method. Finally the new crop of hair was cut and styled. Prices for hair-weaving ranged up to $500, depending on the shop and the degree of baldness. The Joneses charged $325 for an average three-hour weaving job. Salons in Harlem offered the same service at a much lower price.[18]

Because the foundation seams grew out along with the real hair, clients had to return to the shop about every three months for a $25 "tightening" in which the job was undone and rewoven snugly again. One of Glover's clients was musician Harry Fern, who remarked: "I'm doing this for my girl friends— not for myself. I've tried toupees, but they kept falling off at the most embarrassing moments." Hair-weaver Thelma Davis commented: "Weaving is a psychological thing. A person likes it because he can have a head of new hair— and still feel his scalp when he combs it." At least one dermatologist had no opposition to the technique. Dr. Hillard Pearlstein had recommended the technique to some of his patients for the backs of their heads after they had received hair transplants that formed a natural hair line at the front. He saw no harmful effects but did note, "the only problem is that the foundation seams can make it a bit more difficult to shampoo the head."[19]

During 1968, hair-weaving establishments sprang up suddenly throughout the U.S., with most charging from $250 to $450. Commissioner Gerard Weisberg of New York City's Department of Consumer Affairs worried about this sudden proliferation of establishments. He called on his state to launch an inquiry into the industry, citing the fact that many customers had complained to him and his department about the less than durable nature of hair-weaving. One man complained he looked so bad after swimming that he had to go into hiding because hairs separated and the nylon base became visible. Another said he suffered intense headaches for 72 hours after the procedure. New York Secretary of State John P. Lomenzo received the complaints passed on by Weisberg. Nothing happened in the way of an official investigation, however.[20]

At London's Harvard Hair Centre, a hair-weave cost around £190 in 1975, with a life expectancy of three years. Tightening was recommended every six weeks. This clinic offered an annual service for £70 which entitled the client to return to the center as often as he wanted for a shampoo, haircut, general maintenance and tightening. When the British Consumers' Association surveyed ten of its members, they found six had given their hair-weave up as unsatisfactory. Although the other four claimed to be satisfied with the results, two of them would not recommend the procedure for others. "Expensive and inconvenient" was the consumer group's verdict on hair-weaving.[21]

At a hair replacement business in Los Angeles, Herb Yerman offered customers a variation in hair-weaving which he called a Micro-Lock hair-piece. It was semipermanently anchored to a client's remaining hair with very small compression tubes of lightweight aluminum. The price, at $800 to $1,000, was decidedly macro. There were several such systems available in the late 1970s which featured locking, as opposed to weaving, anchoring systems. In all hair-weaving procedures, there were many problems. First, the unit could not be removed by the wearer, which made it difficult to clean under it. Some wearers developed severe dandruff or other scalp problems. Yerman sold a special scalp brush for his customers to use with their Micro-Lock. Some frustrated wearers resorted to Water-Pics to clean the tops of their heads. Relocking of the piece every two months added a minimum annual maintenance fee of $150 to the cost of the unit.[22]

At the For Men Only hair-weaving shop in New York City, two different weaving methods were employed. In one the hair around the perimeter of a client's baldness was braided tightly against the scalp, and a hairpiece was then bound to the braid by loops of nylon thread. The other method involved tying the customer's hair into small knots at one- to three-inch intervals along the perimeter of baldness and then fixing the knots with a gluelike substance. The hairpiece was attached to the knots by threading. With either method the front of the unit was taped down to the scalp. When asked how a customer cleaned his scalp between maintenance visits, the owner of For Men Only replied it was done with a toothbrush: "You can work it in under the front and through the spaces between the attachments, especially when the unit starts to loosen."[23]

Toward the end of the 1980s, hair-weaves reportedly cost $900 and up, with maintenance running $35 to $50 every six to eight weeks; life expectancy of a weave was two to three years. Hair-weaves seemed less popular at that time because they offered more disadvantages than a wig, at a similar price, while conferring no benefits to a wearer not found in a conventional wig. Basically a hair-weave was a wig which the wearer could not remove. Neither method provided a man with the illusion that he had his own hair back. Both were subject to detection by others, often at embarrassing moments. About the only plus for a weave over a wig was that the former would not come off in a wind.[24]

7

IMPLANTS

God has made very few perfect heads. The rest of them he covered with hair.
                    Senator Jake Garn

Bald: dream symbol of losing ideas or not taking time to think things out. No new ideas growing, barrenness of constructive thought, lack of positive thinking.
                    Wilda Tanner,
                    The Mystical, Magical, Marvelous World of Dreams

Implanting hair and other material into the scalp has often been attempted in the past. Dr. Menahem Hodara of Constantinople tried an experiment in 1898 to cure baldness caused by favus. That was a fungal infection of the scalp more often seen in children than adults. Rarely seen in North America, it was most common in the Middle East and Africa. Hodara simply cut hair from other parts of the patient's head. After trimming these hairs with scissors at both ends he made a series of shallow incisions with a scarifier and then put those hairs into the cuts. Later Hodara checked the results under a microscope and satisfied himself that after a few weeks a new bulb had formed at the base of each implanted hair. The doctor believed there was no reason ordinary baldness couldn't be treated in a similar fashion and asserted, "Clinically there can be no doubt that small bundles of hair stems implanted in incisions made with the scarifier can take root and grow, forming in time long and viable hairs."[1]

Medical journals reporting this method thought it held much promise. Fifteen years later Dr. Jacob H. Parsegan of San Francisco was doing something along those lines, although a little more automated. He punctured the skin with a special instrument which also inserted the dead hair. Capable of operating at up to 60 insertions per minute, the instrument allowed the hair to be cut off at a preset length.[2]

Hodara's method attracted little attention, but one system that did get considerable media play was the "living wig" method developed by Dr. Franz Szekely, a physician at Saint Stephane Hospital in Budapest, Hungary. He came to the attention of the English-speaking world when he gave a demonstration of his method at a Royal Medical Society meeting in London in 1912. A torturer's dream, Franz's method consisted of taking dead hair from women, fixing it in a loop of gold wire, and then inserting the whole affair into the scalp.

Very fine gold wire was used, one five-hundredth of an inch in diameter. One fine long hair from a woman's head was attached in the middle by means of a loop in the gold wire. This wire was then inserted into a hypodermic syringe drawn forward until the threaded loop was just inside the point of the needle. Next the wire was cut to a length of about one tenth of an inch, forming a tiny hook. Several hundred sterilized needles were prepared this way beforehand. The scalp was sterilized and made insensitive by "appropriate treatment." Each needle was then inserted into the scalp, inclined, and twisted through an angle of 180 degrees, which left the loop under the skin anchored by the hook. The two ends of the hair protruded from the hole, giving the appearance of two separate hairs. Skilled technicians could implant up to 500 hairs per hour "without pain." Szekely estimated 15,000 to 20,000 hairs were sufficient to completely cover a bald crown, while 50,000 would be required for a totally bald head. Even in the latter case, a skilled implanter could do the job in 100 hours. Thus in 10 days of 10 working hours, a man could have a "head of hair of his own." Scalp punctures were made one twenty-fifth of an inch apart or about 625 per square inch. So small were the gold wires that the amount used for 50,000 hairs would be one gram, or fifteen grains.

According to Franz, his "living wig" could be brushed, combed, and washed without any annoyance or discomfort. One of his earliest patients still had his hair intact, as good as ever, after seven years. These implanted hairs were dead ones and, of course, didn't grow. Szekely said no one would notice the difference between one's own hair and his implants unless they looked very closely and noticed two hairs instead of one issuing from each point in the skin. Continuous oiling of the implanted hair was recommended by Franz to preserve its softness and delicacy. The procedure, if not entirely painless, caused little discomfort, said the doctor. Inflammation resulting from the treatment disappeared in 12 days or so. Soreness from this inflammation was, reported Franz, "trifling, and is scarcely appreciable after ten or twelve days." The puncture from the needle healed quickly. Scar tissue helped fix the hair better in its place. After a few weeks, Franz said the head of a person treated could be rubbed smartly or slapped "without feeling the least sense of pain." All in all the method was "hygienic, cosmetic, and practical." Szekely insisted to some reporters that he never had a case of intense inflammation or suppuration (pus formation) result from his implanting. To others he grudgingly admitted a few cases of suppuration. A reporter for the *Literary Digest* cynically commented that "It may be objected that the only difference between having hairs sewed separately into one's scalp and wearing a wig is that a wig can be removed when one is tired of it." In the next breath, he scolded himself by remarking "this is hypercritical."[3]

Nothing more was heard of these methods, fortunately. The idea of implanting dead human hair directly into somebody else's scalp fell dormant. It resurfaced in the 1970s in a slightly different form: the implanted hair or synthetic fibers were attached to an implanted base. Some of the 1970s procedures became remarkably similar to the early attempts, however.

Several scientists working on skin research in 1971 at the laboratory of Philadelphia's Franklin Institute came up with a side development by devising hair implants. Drs. William B. Tarpley, Robert A. Erb, and Peter S. Francis were granted a patent that year. Their patent application read, in part, "Each implant may carry one or many hairs. The part that penetrates the scalp has elastic properties similar to those of the living skin. Angular construction enhances the seal between the implant and the skin to minimize infection. To prevent rejection of the implant, it is made of materials compatible with the body, and has an anchoring section in the living structure of the skin made of fine velour or other fibers."[4]

Just one year later rip-off artists had entered the field. The Federal Trade commission (FTC) took action in April 1972 against the Beverly Hills, California, company Medi-Hair International, which surgically implanted a wire mesh in the scalp and then attached hair to it. In that procedure plastic-coated stainless steel wire was stitched into the scalp in individual loops or a weave pattern so that the wire protruded slightly at regular intervals. The effect was that the scalp appeared to have parallel rows of staples end-on-end. Those served as anchors for a meshlike base formed by weaving a synthetic thread back and forth between the anchors. Hanks of hair were attached to the wire loops or the mesh base. That new hair was then cut and styled. FTC authorities ordered Medi-Hair to make it clear to its customers that their procedure involved "a high probability of discomfort and pain, and a risk of infection, skin diseases and scarring." They were also required to tell their clients there was the possibility of other, unknown side effects with continued care necessary after the surgery. Commenting on the method, Chicago dermatologist Paul Lazar said there was "a definite risk of rejection of the anchors through the body's natural rejection process, as well as varying degrees of discomfort and pain .... Scalp disorders may be exaggerated or difficult to treat without removal of the close-fitting mesh base."[5]

Horror stories about implants began to surface in 1976. A man named Harold Crocker went to the Hair Replacement Center in Beverly Hills, California, looking for a wig. Once there Crocker was sold on the idea of having an implant. After paying $1,250 he was introduced to a man called "the doctor" who sewed the toupee to his scalp. It was sutured to the scalp in four places. Performed at the company's offices the procedure was painless and brief. Afterward Crocker had trouble, however; his head constantly ached, especially when he lay down because the weight of the toupee would tug against the sutures in his unhealed scalp. He couldn't sleep, and he couldn't comb his hair. Following one week of agony, he returned to the center demanding the implant be removed. As per the signed agreement, the company replaced the implant with a conventional hairpiece held down with tape or glue. Crocker sued the company but dropped the proceedings when it went out of business.[6]

Billy Bruck had an implant done at Dura-Hair International for $1,425. Besides not being able to sleep at night or comb his hair, he experienced bleeding and swelling of the scalp, headaches, acute infection and relentless scabbing. Over the one and a half years he wore his implant, Bruck paid Dura-Hair another $150 for a series of treatments designed to clear up the problems. When the problems persisted, he sought the help of dermatologist Dr. Edward Frankel, who offered a wide variety of hair replacement alternatives. Frankel didn't encourage implants but would do them if a patient insisted. Ironically, less than one year later, Frankel would be exposed by the state of California in connection with his hair replacement business. He was not a dermatologist nor a certified plastic surgeon as he held himself out to be; he also used false advertising.

Barber Eiler Terkleson at Los Angeles's Century Plaza Hotel dealt in custom hairpieces. Terkleson told of one superstar client for whom he removed a sutured-on hairpiece, "Each place where it was fastened on, it was as if there was a big marble. And each one was terribly infected. I haven't seen any of these that haven't been infected."[7]

At the Encino, California, hair replacement business called Sacha-Michel, a variation was offered. Several rows of hair resembling long strips of eyelashes were attached to the head with several Proline sutures. Cost was a pricey $2,000 to $4,000, plus $350 to the doctor, who normally spent 40 minutes inserting 10 to 20 sutures. Sales tax on the wefts of modacrylic hair added another $120 to $240. Although the modacrylic hair was advertised as being able to withstand heat blasts up to 340 degrees, Sacha-Michel warned that the synthetic hair had been known to "literally fry" under bright studio lights. Thus the company recommended actors choose an implant of 75 percent human hair/25 percent synthetic hair at a cost of $55 more. During the one year it had been open, the company claimed to have done over 200 implants. Acknowledging infection was possible, Sacha-Michel said that since its procedure involved a series of light wefts—as opposed to a heavy hairpiece—it was easier to clean and the weight of the false hair didn't pull on the sutures. "Infection is predicated on cleanliness. The material itself is inert. It cannot of itself create a problem," explained the company.[8]

In 1976 the FTC took action again when it ordered a Boston company to discontinue false and misleading ads about implants and to disclose in its material that the sutures carried a "risk of discomfort and pain, and some risk of infection, scarring and other skin disorders." The FTC ordered the company to disclose that the implant "cannot be cared for like natural hair, but requires special care and handling. Strong pulling on the applied hair, such as may be expected to occur in washing, combing, brushing and shampooing, can cause pain because of the pressure exerted on the sutures in the scalp, may cause bleeding and may cause the sutures to pull out …. The wearer may not engage in physical activities with as much disregard for his applied hair as might a person with natural hair. The wearer must at all times be careful that the applied hair does not pull or get pulled, or become tangled or strained. Discomfort and pain may be caused by common actions, such as rolling the head on a pillow during sleep." By this time, implants permanently anchored wefts of hair to the head by the use of sutures, sutured-down clips, or other types of retaining devices. More and more dermatologists were critical of implants, citing the chances of infection, irritation from the retainers, and irritation from foreign particles. Dr. Joseph Zizmor, chief of dermatology at New York City's St. Vincent Hospital, agreed there were many drawbacks to implants but added, "The implant procedure has several advantages over a transplant—the job can be done considerably faster, usually in one visit; it's more comfortable; when the job is completed, you've got immediate satisfaction." In New York City the cost of an implant then ranged from $1,000 to $2,000.[9]

Implanting of hair became a national media issue in 1977. Most treatment centers were then implanting human hair (not the client's) or synthetic hair directly into the client's scalp; no base retainers were used. The situation resembled that of 1914. The procedure was then under intense attack from medical personnel, but the implant industry claimed it was only being attacked because it was taking business away from doctors. According to medical personnel, the procedure of taking material other than a person's own hair and embedding it, sometimes knotted, into the scalp could not work for long because such a procedure would stimulate powerful allergic reaction and rejection. In the end, customers could end up with less hair than when they started, permanent irritation from broken-off fibers, and possibly serious scarring. A report had recently been done by medical personnel at the Cleveland Clinic Foundation on one implant facility in Cleveland, United Federated Laboratories. Their insertion of synthetic hair caused complications to customers, including facial swelling, infection, scarring, and permanent hair loss. That study also determined the "ultimate futility" of fiber implantation made the procedure unacceptable. Thirty to forty civil suits had been filed against the company by unhappy customers; the state of Ohio was then trying to shut the company down.[10]

At the Cleveland Clinic, Dr. William Hanke described 20 patients who came there for help: 10 had infections, 11 developed ugly scars on their scalps; and all 20 implants eventually failed. Those receiving them had paid an average of $2,427. One patient was a 29-year-old man who had gone to the implant center early in 1977. Every 45 minutes a local anesthetic was injected into his scalp, and fibers were inserted at the rate of 100 to 300 per hour. That went on for 15 hours over a three-day period. For the next four days, the man's head, forehead, and nose were swollen. Three weeks after the final insertion, 90 percent of the fibers came out during a shampoo. Over the following five weeks, the rest of the fibers came out when the man combed or washed his hair. Undaunted, the man went through the entire procedure three more times that year, in July, September, and November. After each procedure the fibers came out. Following the fourth procedure, the client had a severe infection which required treatment at the Cleveland Clinic's Department of Dermatology.[11]

Two such clinics that opened in 1979 in San Francisco did nothing but these implants. While there were then many such establishments in the U.S., those two were the first in San Francisco. One was a branch of United Federated Laboratories. When newspaper reporters visited the newly opened United office, director August Marino flatly said his company's "secret process" had conquered the problem of foreign bodies. United guaranteed its procedure for one year, with any fibers that fell out in that time being replaced for free. Marino said that no more than 10 percent ever fell out. San Francisco's second outlet was the California Cosmetic Clinic, which inserted real human hair (not the client's). Outlet manager Al Rogers said: "Doctors who say it can't work just don't know what they're talking about. We don't use synthetic fibers so don't confuse us with places that do. We use real human hair, and have an anti-rejection formula to keep it there." There had never been a case of rejection, he said, at any other of the company's branches—the Bay area one was the fourteenth. In response to such claims, Dr. Peter Panagotacos commented: "There is no known substance that can go through the skin and remain that way. There is no substance that won't allow bacteria to migrate down there and cause an infection, mild or serious." He called implantation of human hair not one's own "even worse" than synthetic fibers because "A foreign protein is going to kick off quite a rejection and no secret anti-rejection formula will stop it."[12]

San Francisco Chronicle reporter Peter Kuchl went to the California Cosmetic Clinic posing as a potential customer. Manager Rogers told the writer the implanted hair would be coated with a "secret anti-rejection formula," the same stuff used to coat pacemakers implanted into the chests of people with heart problems. It was claimed to be 100 percent effective. Rogers did tell Kuchl that up to 10 percent of the hairs might fall out but would be replaced for just a $35-an-hour labor charge. During the procedure the scalp would be frozen and then a hand-operated needle would insert the hairs ¼ inch into the scalp. A "new follicle" was created by twisting the needle 180 degrees to produce a pull strength 27.8 percent greater than natural hair, explained Rogers. After measuring Kuchl's bald areas, Rogers announced that 36 square inches had to be filled. At $150 per inch, the total cost would be $5,400. When the reporter balked, Rogers said he would reduce the price to $3,200 if Kuchl would allow before and after pictures of himself to be used around town in company ads because they were a new business in the area. When Kuchl replied he wanted to think about it, Rogers said those discount offers were almost all gone and he couldn't guarantee any would be left the next day.[13]

One patient who had a synthetic implant had to go to Dr. Charles Monell of Beverly Hills for help. The client said he looked great for the first three months after the procedure, "But by the fourth month terrible itching set in, infection started and within two months nearly all the fibers broke off." Added Monell, "They had all broken off at the skin. It looks like 3,000 black heads on there, and it's all red and swollen. It's really an ugly looking thing." The man went back to a conventional hairpiece.[14]

Late in 1978, Robert Banks paid $5,400 to have artificial hair implanted at the Underwood Hair Adaption Process office in Mineola, New York. Soon he was hospitalized to recover from chronic infections over his entire scalp. Bills for that hospitalization came to $12,000. Such problems were common. In one implant technique, four to eight strands made of an acrylic fiber usually used in wigs were knotted together and then stitched into the scalp with a curved needle. In another method, the fibers were attached to tiny metal barbs and then shot into the scalp with a pressure gun. Synthetic implants triggered the body's natural defense mechanisms, causing rejection of the artificial hair. Open spaces around the implant were a breeding ground for infection. Dr. Marvin Lepaw, a dermatologist from Hicksville, New York, explained that in some cases the infection became so severe that the patient could end up losing what remained of his hair. "No one has a normal scalp after this procedure," he added. "They wind up looking like trolls." People who worked at the franchises were seldom fully trained skin specialists. Underwood Hair was franchised by founder Donald Underwood, an osteopath who had 17 clinics around the U.S. in 1979. The first of them was set up in Mineola and employed 100 nurses and assistants. Cost of a franchise was $25,000. New York State's attorney general said Underwood earned $1 million from his Long Island clinics in 1978. By the following year, they were closed. Dr. Underwood was then being sought by New York investigators but reportedly had decamped to the Bahamas.[15]

Ivan Rubin opened Syntho-Hair in Rego Park, Queens, New York, in May 1978. Between then and November, when the company closed, an unknown number of men paid $100 per square inch—up to $4,800—for artificial hair implants. Virtually all men lost the fibers, and many still suffered from infections into 1979. One client was Brooklyn transit worker Michael Balsamo, who paid Syntho-Hair $1,000 before he halted the treatment. He still got a "pinchy feeling" and periodic infections on his scalp but had trouble getting a doctor to treat him. "This thing has got so much notoriety nobody wants to touch it," he explained. Ruing the vanity that drove him to do it, he added, "When it comes to ego, intelligence goes right out the window." Balsamo told the state attorney general's fraud office that in his five visits to the clinic, he never once met the supervising physician, Dr. Leo Grant. Instead Rubin, who was not a doctor, instructed the nurses in how to sew the fibers into his scalp.[16]

Another Syntho-Hair patient was tire salesman Randall Lico, who testified that Rubin injected the local anesthetic into his head. Rubin also stitched in some of the fibers (both were illegal procedures in New York State unless done by an authorized medical practitioner such as a nurse or doctor). According to Lico, Dr. Grant inserted a few fibers but then quit, with Rubin taking over. Grant stated that account was "absolutely untrue" but later admitted Rubin "sewed in a handful" of stitches on rare occasions. "He touched very few of the patients, maybe two or one percent, for demonstration." Denying he stood by on those occasions, Grant asserted, "I wouldn't have allowed it," arguing he was often away and was not responsible for what happened in his absence. He did acknowledge that Ivan's wife Joan Rubin "routinely" handed out antibiotics that he, Grant, had authorized and which he "suggested they buy wholesale." Grant obtained the job by answering a newspaper ad. Before he quit the company in opposition to its practices just before it closed, he was paid $15,000. He maintained, "I did not see infection," only cases of rejection. The attorney general's office referred Dr. Grant's conduct to the state's Board of Medical Conduct for review.[17]

Another Syntho-hair patient was Thomas Nasca, who signed up for $3,400 worth of treatments. He told investigators that not long after the procedure, "I noticed that my head was becoming infected." It itched, broke out in sores, and bled. Some of the fibers fell out. All of the remaining implants then had to be pulled out. Back at the company offices, employees began that process using tweezers and no anesthetic, but the pain was so great they finally injected local anesthetic. Not wanting to lose the money he had already put down, Nasca agreed to a new series of implants. Within a month, his head became infected again, and he had to undergo a second removal procedure. "There are still a lot of knots underneath the skin. The hairs broke off when they pulled them out and I still have recurring infections, bleeding, pus pockets, etc.," Nasca reported. Rubin's former partner Larry Goldspiel disclaimed any knowledge of injuries resulting from the business. He complained the company went bankrupt losing him his $30,000 investment. As for the implant Goldspiel himself received from the company, he said, "I got the same problems." He had to have all the fibers removed. While the state attorney general's office was investigating Syntho-Hair in 1979 on a variety of fraud charges, including advertising its implants as "safe, painless and effective," the office was closed. Rubin had fled to Florida.[18]

When the *New York Times* profiled the industry in 1979, it estimated that as many as 10,000 men around the country had received synthetic implants, with infection setting in within six months in 75 percent of the cases. By then the clinics involved had often shut down, and the operators had fled with the money. Costs went as high as $5,000 per patient. When the fibers inserted were knotted, they were particularly difficult to remove. According to Dr. Douglas Lake of Fort Lee, New Jersey, a large part of the scalp sometimes had to be removed. One popular synthetic fiber used was Kanekalon, a modacrylic wig product synthesized from ammonia, natural gas, limestone, petroleum, and acrylonitrile by the Kanegafuchi Company of Japan. That company said the fiber was never intended for such a purpose; it had by then issued warnings against its use in implants. Another modacrylic fiber used was made by the Monsanto Company for wigs. Monsanto said it was only informed of its use in implants after the company ceased active marketing of the fiber.[19]

Another media outlet that issued a warning was *Science Digest*, which stated that preliminary studies suggested that "chronic infection haunts the overwhelming majority of people who've had synthetic fiber implants." After enduring many problems associated with the method one baldie lamented, "It's a shame how they can put a man on the moon, but can't put some permanent stuff that looks like hair in my head."[20]

With so many complaints received, the FDA set up a "synthetic fiber data base" at the end of 1978 to register the victims of implants gone wrong. Quickly the agency received more than 100 reports of injuries associated with synthetic implants. By the end of March that year, the FDA had confirmed 40 of the injuries and was then investigating the others. In the meantime the FDA took the unusual step of issuing a public warning. Agency Commissioner Donald Kennedy said: "Men and women considering synthetic hair implants should consult their physicians before having the process performed. Those who decide to go ahead with implants should consult their physicians immediately should any signs of infection or other problems develop."[21]

Action by the FDA and by various state officials took a toll on the industry, along with all the negative publicity. While the FDA investigators revealed about 90 implant facilities operating around the country early in 1979, by the end of June of that year only about 10 percent remained in operation. United Laboratories of America, the largest of several franchises, with 26 outlets, was no longer in operation. Under court orders granted by FDA initiatives, U.S. marshals hastened the United shutdown by seizing all promotional material and fibers at the firm's main office in Maple Heights, Ohio, and at a franchise outlet in Bellevue, Washington. Marshals also made a seizure at Hairegenics in Atlanta, Georgia. Fibers, considered medical devices when used as implants, were seized on the basis that they were inadequately labeled for their intended use. The state of Ohio charged one implant facility with violating the state's medical licensing laws. One of Underwood's patients described his experience by saying, "Your entire scalp feels spongy, with a layer of pus underneath. The bleeding and itching drive you crazy. You wake up and find the pillow covered with blood." Such damage could take years to correct. Fibers had to be removed and antibiotics taken to control infection. Some patients required scalp removal and skin grafting. *Time* magazine estimated in 1979 that as many as 20,000 people had subjected themselves to synthetic implants.[22]

Also in 1979 the district attorney's office in California won a round in Superior Court against the California Cosmetic Company when a judge signed a restraining order against most of the firm's activities. That order forbade the company from continuing its allegedly false advertising, required the implant procedure to be performed by doctors, and required customers to sign an informed consent document outlining the risk being taken. In addition, the company was ordered to stop claiming professional basketball player Rick Barry was a customer. When the company first started promoting business in San Francisco, Barry was named in promotional material as a satisfied customer. The former Golden State Warrior had nothing to do with the company, however. Earlier the firm had promised to stop using Barry's name, but it was found to be still using it at the time of the court order.[23]

Finally, on June 3, 1983, the FDA banned the use of artificial hair fibers for scalp implantation, saying that no type of hair fibers or synthetic hair implantation technique was safe or effective and that the procedure was dangerous. The ban covered fibers of synthetic materials such as polyester, modacrylic, and polyacrylic, as well as some natural materials like human hair processed for transplantation to someone else's head. From December 1978 through February 1981, the FDA received 166 complaints about the fibers and the FTC received 181 complaints. "These included cases of infection, facial swelling, severe pain, scarring, and permanent loss of remaining real hair. Many cases required extensive medical and surgical treatment," noted the FDA. In seven cases, surgical removal of portions of the scalp was required, while in 21 other cases the fibers could not be removed, so the patients' scalps remained disfigured.[24]

Several years later, in 1987, word came from Japan of a method of inserting thousands of plastic fibers under the scalp and locking them there. A needle pushed each fiber under the skin and tied the strand in a knot. About 20 percent of the fibers fell out each year, however. Japanese doctors reported few of the massive infections experienced a few years earlier in America. Reportedly, the Japanese had used that procedure for a decade or so. Of course, it would be an illegal procedure in the U.S. under the FDA ban. In any event, American doctors were understandably unconvinced.[25]

8

TRANSPLANTS, FLAPS, AND SCALP REDUCTIONS

The best way to save your hair is—in a cigar box.
Journal of the American Medical Association,
February 15, 1965

How ugly is a bald pate! It looks like a face wanting a nose.
Thomas Dekker

The earliest recorded use of taking hair and the underlying follicle structure from a patient's own head and grafting or transplanting it to a bald area of the same person seems to have been in 1890. Dr. R. A. Morrow began using grafts to help a patient who had a scar on his scalp which was exposed due to a scarcity of hair. Morrow took grafts from the other side of the patient's scalp by using a cutaneous punch and then immediately transplanted the grafts into holes of the same size made by the same instrument in the scar tissues. Those grafts included the entire thickness of the derma and subcutaneous tissue beneath. According to Morrow, there was no infection, and the hair grew. He reported the same results with other patients and thought the method had a wide field of application.[1]

Nothing more was reported on that technique until the early 1960s, when the work of Dr. Norman Orentreich, an assistant clinical professor of dermatology at New York University came to the public's attention. Around 1954 he began to punch out small patches of hair and scalp from an area of heavy hair growth, such as the back of the head, and transplant them into the bald spots. Adjoining hair easily covered the vacant spaces at the donor sites. Implants were obtained with a sharp circular punch something like a cookie cutter. Each patch was about 3.5 millimeters (⅛ inch) in diameter. Under local anesthetic, 10 to 12 patches were transplanted on each visit, placed about ¼ inch apart. Orentreich took care to see that the growing angle of the hair on all the implants pointed in the same direction. Initially the patches encrusted and the transplanted hair fell out, but in two to three months the patches regrew hair. Orentreich got the idea for his technique from the fact that plastic surgeons had to select skin grafts carefully to avoid covering parts of the body with unwanted hair, he noted. "I apply the principle in reverse." By 1961, Orentreich had done transplants on 200 men and reported that virtually all were successful. "It doesn't seem to matter whether a man has been bald for five years or 20 years. Hair is still growing on my first patients, treated seven years ago." Of course, no new hair was grown using this procedure; existing hair was simply redistributed. Having a full head of hair himself, Orentreich commented, "If I were bald I wouldn't have the nerve to treat baldness."[2]

Transplanting was a technique that quickly caught on. By 1966 one estimate was that the punch graft technique had been performed on about 10,000 men. Orentreich and his associates had done some 3,000 of the total, and their clients included actor Jack Nicholson. An estimated 100 to 200 dermatologists around the country were then using the technique. As evidence that the transplanted hair survived, Orentreich explained, "In several patients grafts growing hair were implanted at the edge of a receding hairline. In two years following the grafting, the hairline continued to recede. The grafts, however, continued to show hair growth, greater and greater distances being manifest between the hair of the graft and the hairline." Each plug of hair contained 6 to 20 hairs. The patient usually applied gentle pressure with his fingers to keep the graft in place for a few minutes until a clot formed to anchor it. Some men required 300 to 500 grafts to give the illusion of a full head of hair. Up to 25 plugs were transplanted in each session. As each graft needed time to heal before a new one could be placed next to it, 75 grafts a week, in three sessions, was the maximum rate at which the work could be done.[3]

Another practitioner was Dr. James W. Burks, clinical professor of dermatology at New Orleans's Tulane University Medical School. Burks had done punch grafts on 500 patients in 2½ years and called the procedure, "the most successful thing I have ever done in dermatology." Limitations to the technique were that the patient needed time, money, and enough hair somewhere on the head to be relocated. If baldness was still progressing, odd patterns could develop, with more and more grafts needed to cover newly emergent denuded areas. There might not be enough hair on the sides and back to go around. When the procedure was done, the head looked terrible for the two- to three-week healing period; it was scabby and crusty. The price ranged from $5 to $25 per graft. Supposedly, it was impossible to detect any scarring once the transplants had sprouted.[4]

More modest in its assessment of the number of American men who had received transplants was the *New York Times*, which put the figure at 5,000. University of Arkansas dermatologist Dr. D. Bluford Stough explained the increasing popularity of the procedure by saying: "Acceptance of hair transplantation is gradually increasing primarily because physicians are recognizing this technique as a proved and acceptable procedure. …Thousands of people have overcome the false belief that a desire for their original appearance is a form of vanity. This devise is not limited to any social stratum … but a great majority of my patients are physicians." A second dermatologist who performed the procedure reported, "Forty-nine of my first 50 patients were doctors." Both men attributed the high ratio of doctors as patients to the fact that "doctors first read about the technique in medical journals."[5]

Stough, who himself underwent transplants, reported in a survey he conducted that 90 percent of the cases were successful, with most patients stating they were satisfied with the results. In Stough's own practice, an average treatment consisted of 10 sessions of 90 minutes each. A total of 200 plugs would be relocated—20 per session. At $5 per plug the cost came to a total of $1,000. With about 15 hairs per plug, a total of 3,000 hairs were resettled in the average bald head. Admitting the procedure could be painful, Stough commented: "It's no fun. Sort of like going to the dentist, but it is tolerable. If the patient is treated by specialists skilled in transplantation, assisted by good nurses, the procedure will be neither bloody nor painful. But it can be pretty gory if used by those not well versed in the technique." Of the 100 or so doctors then doing punch grafts, Stough estimated that only a dozen did it frequently. A second dermatologist who had performed grafts on 800 men said the degree of the patient's satisfaction "depends on his motivation in the first place. If a person simply wants hair where he doesn't have it, he can be completely satisfied. But if he wants hair to gain a new wife or girl friend or a promotion, the chances are that he is going to consider the transplantation a failure."[6]

Hair transplants became popular in the early 1970s. Some of those who had undergone the procedure by then were hockey superstar Bobby Hull, Frank Sinatra, television personality Hugh Downs, comedian Joey Bishop, and U.S. Senator William Proxmire. Sinatra reportedly paid $25,000 to Beverly Hills celebrity transplanter Dr. Samuel Ayres III. It was a lengthy, painstaking procedure involving months of time and constant care. It was also expensive, which was why many men preferred hair weaving. Hugh Downs freely talked about his transplant on television, but Bishop did not want to talk about his at all. Proxmire's was done in Washington, D.C., by plastic surgeon Ronald Cameron. When he had it done, the senator appeared before newscameras with his scab-encrusted scalp. Most of the procedures were done by dermatologists and plastic surgeons. An estimated 50,000 men had by this point received transplants in the U.S. since Orentreich did the first modern one in the 1950s. Orentreich's office then employed 14 surgeons to do the grafts. That office did about 10 percent of the estimated 35,000 transplants then being done in the U.S. annually. Orentreich no longer did any himself. Waxing eloquent about having hair, he commented: "We are no longer a frontier culture. As a culture matures and becomes more sophisticated, there is free time to look at the aesthetics of life. Hair is beautiful—furs are attractive aren't they?—and hair is nothing but fur. It's sensual. Each hair is an exaggeration of sensation, acting as a lever to multiply the sensations of touch…. If the average head is shaven—some may be beautifully round, but some are ghoulish. Hair covers sculptural defects."[7]

At that time Dr. George A. Farber of New Orleans mailed 1,034 questionnaires to people who had undergone transplants. Of those who replied, 37.7 percent reported being fully satisfied, with another 62.3 percent reporting they were partly satisfied. While the number of replies received was 442, only 176 were from patients who had fully completed their transplant procedure. The greatest source of dissatisfaction was the lack of enough available hair for relocating. Scars and hairline problems were also reported, but Faber was very positive and upbeat about the procedure. One executive who received a transplant at Orentreich's clinic commented, "Of course, I can't prove it but I don't think I would have gotten my last promotion if I didn't have the transplants."[8]

Transplant reality was, however, somewhat different. Dr. Charles M. Monell, chief of surgery at the Beverly Glen Hospital in Los Angeles, averaged three transplants a week in private practice. He believed one problem was that the technique appeared deceptively simple, and as a result, almost any doctor thought himself qualified to do it as an office procedure. Admitting it was a technique of great promise, Monell stated: "Much of the promise is not being realized…. The blame must be directed at the people doing the job." Common errors made by physicians in grafts included, said Monell, too few grafts, punching out grafts larger than 4 mm in diameter, and the removal of fat and follicles from the bottom of the grafts. Many of the results were calamitous, with the patients looking like zombies. One man got an unnaturally inverted hairline that came to a sharp point low in the center of the forehead. Monell said the only thing comparable was the hairline created for actor Bela Lugosi when he played Count Dracula in various films. Another patient received a "grotesquely" arched forehead, high in the center and low at the sides. Another practitioner used large, haphazardly placed grafts to produce a straight line located almost half way down a patient's forehead. Other mistakes were grafts too large, plugs allowed to dehydrate, and grafts put in backwards so the hair grew in the wrong direction.[9]

Outright scam artists set up shop. The National Hair and Scalp Clinic was set up in Washington, D.C., in 1973 by a Philadelphia firm. Virgil Ginyard was hired to run the operation. Using television commercials, the clinic attracted customers for a year, promising a fuller head of hair. Customers paid up to $1,300 for treatments that did not work. Finally Ginyard and another employee, Maryland Nance, were convicted in federal court of fraud and false pretenses. Both men represented themselves as doctors specially trained in hair and scalp problems. In addition, they made extravagant promises to customers about results from hair and scalp treatment and refused to refund money to customers who had been defrauded. When one dissatisfied customer threatened to go to court to get a refund, Ginyard responded: "To hell with the judge, to hell with the jury.... I'll run my clinics the way I want." James R. Chaney showed the jury the bald spot on his head, saying he had paid $940 for the firm's unsuccessful attempt to cover the spot. Chaney and other witnesses testified they were taken to Philadelphia ostensibly to get transplants done, but the work was never done and their money was never refunded. One witness who testified for the defense as a supposedly satisfied customer finally, after pressed by the state prosecutor, admitted to the jury that on the stand he was wearing a $15 wig purchased at a local store.[10]

In the Los Angeles area, Edward B. Frankel operated hair replacement centers under several different names. These were shut down in 1977 after a civil suit was filed against the companies by the California attorney general, Evelle J. Younger, who charged misleading advertisement. Frankel held himself out to be both a dermatologist and a board-certified plastic surgeon, but he was neither. Advertisements claimed that members of the royal family had been to his clinics, as well as movie producers. None had, except one person who barely qualified as a producer. In his ads Frankel used a picture of a bald man who, in fact, was not bald and never had been. Those ads implied that a full head of hair could be obtained in one session, while in truth it took many sessions. Readers of his ads were further misled by his claims that the procedure was as easy "as 1-2-3," when in reality it required anesthesia and surgery and carried elements of risk.[11]

Chicago dermatologist James Bernard Pinski performed the most transplants in the Windy City in the mid–1970s, doing four men—two hours each— on Fridays. He only did them on Fridays because he found it a monotonous job and didn't want to abandon his more challenging work. With his limited schedule, he had a two-month waiting list. Pinski had himself received over 500 transplants. "If it weren't for the chance of hitting a bleeder or an allergic reaction," he admitted a competent technician could do the job. Patient selection was his biggest problem because, as he stated, "You have to be careful and screen out the nuts. If you feel you can't satisfy a guy, you don't want to do him because you can never please him. I never promise them the world. The hair almost always grows well but you can't guarantee it. We're not God." While he found the work monotonous, he conceded, "It's a lucrative thing." The going rate at that time was said to be $10 to $15 per plug, except in California, where it was $25 to $35. A very bald man could need up to 600 plugs for adequate coverage, which would still not reestablish the luxuriant growth of youth.[12]

Usually Pinski transplanted 50 plugs per two-hour session, but he could do as many as 100. While the patient sat in a chair, Pinski administered a local anesthetic, sticking the needle 15 to 25 times into the donor area on the back of the head and a similar number of times into the receptor site. Virtually nothing was felt by the patient after the initial prick. During the week of healing little pain was reportedly caused by the grafts. Having clipped the hair in the donor area, Pinski punched out 50 plugs, using a miniature cookie cutter. "It takes a lot of practice to direct the punch so you're not cutting off hair follicles," he said. Next he punched out 50 holes in the receptor site from a premarked area to accommodate the desires of the patient "and sometimes of the patient's wife as well." Ten plugs per square inch provided a sketchy job, and twenty plugs per square inch gave the best coverage. Thick, dark hair concealed better than thin, blond hair. At that point in the procedure, Pinski left the room while an assistant went to work pulling the plugs from the donor area with forceps. Some came free with a slight tug, but some had to be snipped with scissors. Hairy plugs were trimmed, cleaned, and lined up in rows in a petri dish containing a saline solution. After the patient's head stopped bleeding, Pinski returned to insert the plugs, taking care to point them in the appropriate direction. On the brow they were pointed down, faceward, the way the original hair grew. As soon as the blood clotted, the plugs were fairly well stuck, although a patient could knock them out with rough treatment. Pinski applied a bandage wrapped tightly around the head to control the bleeding. In two or three days, each plug became crusted with a hideous clot that stayed about a week. Although the plugs would not hurt, the donor site might sting for a few days; blood would ooze onto the pillow at night for a time. The top of the head would feel numb for several months until the nerves became reestablished where the punch severed them. Because the follicles in the plugs went into the resting phase when relocated, all the hair fell out, but it started to grow again in two to three months. At a growth rate of ½ inch per month, it took a year for the plugs to blend in.[13]

Commenting on the difference between transplants and toupees, Los Angeles plastic surgeon Dr. George Semel said: "A man who swears by a toupee is running, but the man with hair plugs is dealing with the problem. When you change your body, it becomes part of your body image and you accept it. A toupee is an appliance. It's taken off. It's never assimilated as part of a person." He added: "There are people who are very happy with wigs who won't be happy with transplants. Hair plugs aren't as luxuriant as a good hairpiece. They are a compromise."

With more practitioners in the field, there were more botched jobs. "I've had quite a few patients come to me for correction," said Dr. Samuel Ayres. He had done transplants since 1961 and virtually no other dermatological work since 1963. Unnatural hairlines were one of the more common mistakes Ayres came across. It was possible to have 200 grafts but only 100 of the plugs functioning. Then the patient didn't get the expected coverage and lost permanently the donor hair.[14]

Pop singer Elton John made his official bow with a transplant in October 1978. He had had his first session done in Paris a year earlier, when he was nearly bald. Later he had a second session. A third session was foreseen, but he considered the procedure so successful after only two sessions that he went public with it, agreeing to be photographed. Prior to that time, John had always been seen wearing a cap or other headgear. He explained: "I had the operation because I did not like being bald. I admit it is 100 percent vanity—and I am thrilled with the result."[15]

Transplants were also big business in the U.K. Freddie Martin, manager of a London clinic that did transplants, said, "A large percentage of our patients are disillusioned toupee wearers." At Martin's about 80 grafts were done per session. They recommended patients stay overnight at the clinic as a safety precaution. Two hundred grafts done over three sessions would cost £400 to £450 in 1975.[16]

London's Harley Hair Transplant Clinics instituted a home service in 1976, offering transplants for those too inhibited to be seen entering a hair clinic. Owner Neagle Cathcart took a team of a surgeon, two nurses, and a porter with him. If required, they were even prepared to fly to a client by a private plane. Three visits were usually needed to complete the job, with an in-home cost of £2,500, which was £500 more than in the clinic. Saying the home service was very popular, Cathcart would not name specific clients in the first three months of operation but they included a prominent government official in Brussels, three MPs, nine footballers, and four television personalities.[17]

John Terry owned Biograft International, a transplant clinic in Bradford, England, which opened in 1971. After a slow start, the company had treated 1,000 patients by 1976; about 40 percent came from the Continent. Cost for transplants at Biograft ran from £300 to £2,000. Most of the clients were young men worried about their sexual attractiveness to women. Terry estimated 70 percent of his patients wanted hair for sex, with the other 30 percent being middle management men feeling threatened by younger competition at work.[18]

The British Consumers' Association magazine *Which?* did a survey of baldness treatments in 1983 and concluded that lotions, potions, toupees, and transplants were better avoided by bald men. All treatments were found to be costly, time-consuming, and less than satisfactory. The magazine charged that transplants, which cost from £430 to £4,680, were often carried out by unqualified people in clinics that were not carefully controlled. Calling the graft procedure "risky business," the magazine added, "There were complaints of bleeding, pain, swelling and scarring; unnaturally severe hairlines that had to be covered with long strands of hair; hair that was impossible to style or comb and 'doll scalp'—tufts of hair in neat rows." Some of the men would need more transplants in the future as they continued to go bald. *Which?*

concluded about transplants: "Until the clinics are more strictly controlled you'd be unwise to risk your money or your remaining hair. It is difficult to ensure that you will get the best treatment." The magazine noted that, unfortunately, "No one can give you back your hair."[19]

Dr. Richard Dobson, a professor in the Medical College of South Carolina Department of Dermatology remarked: "Since I think a person's problem usually has nothing to do with being bald I don't advocate hair transplants at all, and I try to dissuade anyone from it. I regard baldness as quite normal and, in fact, I think it makes very little difference in anybody's lifestyle." He stressed that skill of the operator was crucial in transplants. Although he considered the procedure expensive, Dobson said it did involve little risk, "Except one, as with any cosmetic procedure, it is unusual for hair transplants to meet the individual's expectations. Most individuals have extremely high expectations, and after they are disappointed with the results." So botched were some of the transplants that the telltale hairline became described as a "picket-fence." Perth, Australia, surgeon Dr. Wayne W. Bradshaw claimed, however, that he gave his patients a smoother, more attractive hairline by reducing the size of the plug from 4.5 millimeters to about 1 millimeter.[20]

Another surgeon who claimed to have a better method was Dr. Constantine P. Chambers, who had been doing 3,500 patients a year for about 20 years. He had clinics in nine states. In the late 1980s, he developed a small electrical surgical blade that reportedly cut the microstrips of skin and hair without destroying the blood supply and eliminated the scarring that led to a corn-row effect. Dale Duffel was a partner in one of his clinics. Initially Duffel was reluctant to get involved in transplants, but he was impressed by the results of Chambers' method. "Most of the procedures I had seen used the old punch method which gave a cobblestone effect." he explained. Duffel invented the Derma-Vak, a hair replacement that fitted like a suction cup with water, as does a contact lens on the eye. For years he had been against transplants, saying he covered many of them with a hairpiece. Then Duffel himself had a transplant by Chambers and concluded: "There is no bumpiness with Chambers' methods. The instruments are so fine and the work is so exact."[21]

Generally, by the late 1980s, reports on transplants were not very positive. Washington, D.C. dermatologist Dr. David Green said, "There is a lot of deception and misinformation about hair transplants and a lot of people have conned the public into thinking that because they perform hair transplants faster, they must do them better." Green thought most transplants looked like transplants; the hair grew in corn rows, if it grew at all. Houston dermatologist Roy Knowles had done them for 20 years. He found the most willing candidates for grafts were men who dealt with the public—salesmen, professional athletes, attorneys, and actors—and men who worked out regularly. Said Knowles, "They have wonderful bodies, but hair is one thing beyond their control." About 60 percent of the men who came to Knowles for transplants were turned down by him because their goals were unrealistic. They wanted the hairline of a 20 year old, or they didn't have enough hair for a transplant. Baylor College of Medicine Dermatology Department chairman John Wolf remarked, "It's expensive, it's painful and you might not like the end results." A third dermatologist said that most transplants, even the best ones, looked unreal. In an informal survey, he added, "Most women we talked with said they like men with little or no hair better anyway." Houston dermatologist Paul DesRuisseaux commented: "You have to be motivated and if someone isn't motivated, I won't do them. I don't know if they will finish the job and then I will look bad. Those who don't finish look like the hair on a doll."[22]

When *Consumer Reports* assessed transplants, it said they could cost as much as $15,000 and take a year or two to complete. Dr. Robert Stern was quoted as saying many patients didn't get enough coverage to look natural. Another major problem was finding a surgeon who could produce good cosmetic results. Dr. Stern concluded: "For many people, I don't think the cosmetic benefits justify the costs and discomfort."[23]

In the early 1990s, *Forbes* magazine reported transplants could cost upwards of $10,000, with an estimated 30,000 American men annually spending $250 million on such treatments. Over a two-year period, one man spent $30,000 to undergo eight transplants and four scalp reductions. Another big-spending client explained, "I figured that, well, I could have a fancy sports car or I could get my hair fixed." Another source estimated 35,000 transplants were performed annually, up from 7,000 a decade earlier. American Hair Loss Council spokesperson Mike Mahoney thought more doctors were performing more transplants and that in some cases this was an attempt to make up for lost income resulting from a decline in demand for cosmetic breast surgery.[24]

Dr. Dow Stough of the University of Arkansas School of Medicine's Dermatology Department refined the transplant technique down to the single-hair graft. He said it helped to eliminate the ugly "baby doll" or "picket-fence" hairline look so common on transplant recipients. Stough averaged 250 micrografts in a three-hour period but sometimes did as many as 700 in a session. His method of course, also cut down on the size of the "wound" at the donor site. His largest graft contained just three hairs. "But I have not been able to achieve the density of hair of an unbalding male," he conceded.[25]

A variation on the punch graft technique called the bi-lobe flap operation was developed in the mid–1960s by Dr. Louis J. Felt, associate professor of plastic surgery at the Polyclinic Hospital and Post-Graduate Medical School in New York. He cut a Y-shaped piece of hair-growing scalp from behind each ear and swung it to the front of the bald head to form a new hairline. Donor sites were then filled in with small pieces of hair skin taken from other areas. Punch grafts were used to fill in any remaining bare patches. Felt had performed 50 flap operations by 1966 but still regarded the procedure as experimental.[26]

A decade later Los Angeles hair replacement business operator Herb Yerman offered customers his variation of the flap method. In his process a small piece of skin was cut from behind each ear and grafted to the head, usually one piece at the front and one at the back. A depression was then created in the scalp between the grafts along the top of the head. The result was a tunnel of skin to which a hairpiece could be securely attached to cover the rest of the bald head. That provided the wearer security because the unit would not come off unexpectedly, and it also could be removed to allow cleaning underneath. A major problem was that when the toupee was removed, the unsightly, permanent ridge remained. If a client changed his mind, ridges could be removed but the procedure was expensive. Yerman offered this flap technique for a price of $1,900 to $2,500 and estimated about 300 customers had undergone the procedure. "It's a lot of money for a hairpiece, but men will pay any price psychologically," he said.[27]

By the end of the 1970s, the technique had been further refined. An inch-wide swath of hairy scalp was cut from over and behind the ear. Leaving one end attached, the flap was brought around up over the forehead and then sewn into an opening cut along the intended new hairline. As at least the one end remained attached, the flap retained its own blood supply. Thus failure of the flap to take in its new site was reportedly unlikely. The patient, of course, acquired his new hair instantly. Normally two such operations were performed, with an interval between. One flap was taken from each side and placed one behind the other on the forehead. Donor sites near the ears were stitched closed, leaving no hairless gap to show.[28]

The size of the flap taken out could vary considerably. At least one practitioner took a slice of scalp 6 to 9 inches long and 3 to 4 inches wide. Another surgeon took a flap 10 inches long and 1½ inches wide. At first the flap was cut and loosened, but not resited, allowing a few weeks wait for the attached end of the flap to develop a blood supply adequate for the entire flap. By the early 1980s, the cost was around $5,000 per single flap. Problems with the technique had also surfaced by then. Scarring was inevitable and while normally not visible, there was a risk of disfigurement. Often the frontal hairline had an abrupt, unnatural appearance. The flap of hair grew in the wrong direction, backward instead of forward as the original hair had. That necessitated careful styling with varying degrees of success.[29]

Near the end of the 1980s the cost of the procedure ranged from $5,000 to $7,000 per single flap. By that time the procedure had waned in popularity as its drawbacks became obvious. *Consumer Reports* termed the technique controversial, noted the above mentioned disadvantages, and pointed out that in some cases the flaps didn't take, meaning the client lost all of the resited hair from the flap. In the 1990s the cost was about $9,500 for a flap.[30]

Then there was the scalp reduction method, which was developed around 1980. One practitioner was Baton Rouge surgeon Dr. Martin L. Bell. In this treatment the hairless part of the head was simply cut away and the rest of the scalp was stitched together to create a fuller looking head of hair. Said Bell: "You can stretch the permanent fringe to three times its initial size and it won't look appreciably thinner if a man has a suitable fringe. If you can take out the bad and stretch out the good to cover it, hair will grow over it to cover what remains." Scalp reduction generally required two operations performed about two months apart, giving the scalp time to stretch after the first surgery. Each operation was done under local anesthetic in Bell's office, at a cost of about $800 each. It took around 35 minutes, and the patient was able to return to work in a few days. The only side effects were said to be a headache and a tendency "to look like a conehead" for a few days until the stretched skin began to relax. For some patients with receding hairlines, transplants were needed to augment scalp reduction. Bell tried to avoid them, however, because he said, "they give a seedy, patchy appearance and give hair-replacement a bad name." On one patient Bell removed a five-inch long oval on the crown of the head while an anesthesiologist was present in the office. The 29-year-old patient had started to lose his hair at the age of 21. Referring to the scalp reduction procedure, he commented: "It took guts to do this, but I'm think-ing there's going to be a big difference once this is through. I don't think my wife's real excited about this. She couldn't care less if I looked like Yul Bryn-ner, but it was something I decided I had to do."[31]

British scalp reduction patient Arthur Needham had his procedure go bad when a swab was inadvertently left under the skin. He lamented: "I should have listened to my wife. She did not want me to have the operation." Beryl Needham added, "You should leave as nature intended and not mess about."[32]

In scalp reduction, the scalp could be stretched only an inch or two at a time, necessitating several such operations to completely close, or consider-ably lessen, the bald spot. By the mid–1980s, this procedure was modified to involve scalp enlargement before the reduction took place. Dr. Richard D. Anderson of the University of Michigan described how he enlarged the scalp first by inserting a balloon under the scalp which was kept inflated by weekly injections of saline water. After a month or so, the scalp had expanded enough so that more of it could be pulled across more of the bare region. Anderson remarked, "It is not a mere stretching of the skin but an increase in tissue."[33]

One of the better-known practitioners of the scalp expansion/reduction technique was Dr. Sheldon S. Kabaker, a surgeon who taught at the Univer-sity of California at San Francisco. He inserted balloonlike devices called tis-sue expanders beneath the hairy part of the scalp on the sides. Then he slowly filled the balloons with sterile water over a period of several weeks. As the bal-loons expanded, they stretched the skin, enlarging the area of scalp that still had hair. When the expansion ended, the surgeon cut away the hairless part of the scalp and filled the area with stretched, hair-covered skin. While the hair was thinner, Kabaker said that if it was kept at least two to three inches long, the thinness was invisible. Hospitalization was not required, but most patients kept their heads covered because their scalps were temporarily deformed. The technique took up to six weeks and cost up to $4,500. It was only considered a supplement to other surgical methods such as transplants. Dr. Kabaker remarked: "It certainly isn't a cure for baldness, and it's not for people who are looking for simple answers like rubbing something on their heads. But it can be important for men who are psychologically and physically motivated."[34]

Kabaker found the greatest problem he had in treating his patients was their reluctance to appear in public with the scalp deformity created by the expanders; he called it "the most negative aspect of the procedure." To lessen the problem, symmetrical expansion was performed, growth of long hair was encouraged, and a beret or cap was worn when the patient appeared in public. The principle behind tissue expansion was similar to what happened naturally during pregnancy, when the skin stretched considerably. The largest bald area treated by Kabaker to that point was about 3½ inches by 6 inches. The procedure was limited only by the amount of hair the patient had remaining. It created no more hair; it merely stretched it out over a larger area. Many of Kabaker's patients had previously had hair transplants. He said: "It's more psychologically uncomfortable than physically uncomfortable because the greater the deformity we create, the better the results are going to be. So these people begin to look like Cone Heads or the Elephant Man, if you will, and they get very anxious about that. But when you take six to eight weeks of discomfort and measure it against a lifetime of hair coverage, most say it's worth it." Nonetheless, Kabaker knew scalp enlargement was not a therapy of first choice among baldies: "Most men who are bald don't want to be, but they also want some sort of simple, nonsurgical procedure, and there just aren't very many viable alternatives in that area."[35]

Plastic surgeon Ernest Manders of the Milton S. Hershey Medical Center in Hershey, Pennsylvania, was performing the procedure in 1990. Depending on the size of the area to be covered, he charged $3,000 to $7,000 and took two to four months to enlarge the scalp. Reportedly some film and television actors had undergone the procedure by then, although no names were mentioned. Scalp reduction was a technique that had relatively few takers, however. One reason was that while reduction was used to form a smaller bald area to which grafts were applied, subsequent grafts did not always take hold. Then there was the worry that if too much scalp was removed, one's ears might be relocated closer to the top of one's head.[36]

9

CELEBRITIES AND POLITICIANS

There's one thing about baldness; it's neat.
Don Herold

Now see here! I cut my own hair. I got sick of barbers
because they talk too much. And too much of their talk was
about my hair coming out.
Robert Frost

Some of the Hollywood celebrities who hid their baldness in the 1950s by wearing a wig included Charles Boyer, Fred Astaire, Gene Kelly, Bing Crosby, and Jack Benny. A mid–1950s Hollywood survey indicated that one out of every ten male actors over the age of 35 wore some kind of toupee.[1]

After Yul Brynner shaved his balding head for his role in *The King and I*, his image as a chrome dome was firmly established. For a following film, *The Buccaneer*, he donned a wig but decided he looked so absurd he quickly returned to the shaved head style, which he maintained until his death. Actor Ray Milland threw away his toupee after 15 years, revealing his baldness in the film *Love Story*. Milland, then 67, explained: "For the past 15 years in movies I had to wear a toupee. I hated the damn thing. Yes, I suppose people were shocked to see me bald in *Love Story*. It didn't bother me. Now when people ask me what happened to my hair I tell them that it's in a box in the south of France." U.K. film director Richard Lester, who began to go bald at 18, commented it began "just at a time when I wanted to look older so in fact it didn't worry me at all. You could say that it's helped my career in that I'm not often mistaken for Anna Neagle." Telly Savalas first shaved his head for the role of Pontius Pilate in the movie *The Greatest Story Ever Told*. He just kept it like that, explaining, "I would not wear a wig for a role—after all, if they wanted someone with hair, they would not ask me." Rock singer Erroll Brown of the group Hot Chocolate, who was then 27, remarked: "I shaved my head

121

two years ago—my hair was dropping out anyway, and I was beginning to recede. If you're receding it makes you look much older."[2]

By 1980, celebrities reported to have undergone transplants included Frank Sinatra, Jack Nicholson, Elton John, Roy Clark, Joey Bishop, Hugh Downs, Tom Smothers, and his brother Dick Smothers. Sinatra was quite sparse on top in 1966 when he was about 50. That year Beverly Hills dermatologist Dr. Samuel Ayres III began the singer's grafts. Hugh Downs, host of ABC TV's *20/20* program, who received his transplants in 1966 from the Orentreich clinic, remarked that the hair was still growing some time later: "I'm very satisfied. I've had no regrets."[3]

Other screen idols who wore wigs included Gary Cooper, Humphrey Bogart, Jimmy Stewart, Brian Donlevy, Lorne Greene, William Shatner, Burt Reynolds, John Wayne, and Sean Connery. One article argued that while Reynolds, Wayne, and Connery were all bald, they were still macho. None of them ever appeared bald in public, however, or in their film roles, except for Connery in recent roles.[4]

Dallas Cowboys all-star defensive back Mel Renfro began going bald in his senior year at high school. During his first year in professional football, he took to wearing a toupee but discarded it shortly after he entered his 30s. "When I was in my 20s it bothered me because not very many men in their 20s are bald. But there are a lot of men who are bald in their 30s. The hassle of putting on and taking off the toupee wasn't worth it. And it became too much of a conversation piece." Granville Waiters, a 22-year-old Ohio State University basketball player in the early 1980s, was already bald. While he never seriously considered a hairpiece or a transplant, he was deluged with home remedy suggestions from friends. One suggestion was that he rub Indian sage on his head. He never tried it.[5]

NBC weatherman Willard Scott of the *Today Show* wears a $700 lace-front hairpiece for his *Today* program appearances. He began to go bald at 19. Using the wig mainly as a prop, Scott once shocked network officials by ripping it off his head during a *David Letterman Show* appearance. Scott had to dye what remained of his own hair to match the color of the wig, which changed due to age and exposure to sunlight. Claiming he would discard it if he wasn't a performer, he added, "Anyone who has ever cared about me in my life hasn't liked my hairpiece." Although his wife Mary Ellen reportedly hated the wig, when she once saw him on television without it, she chastised him, "Don't you ever go on without it again."[6]

Chicago's famed curmudgeonly columnist Mike Royko reported in a humorous column on baldness that people who felt insulted by what he wrote about them sometimes responded in kind. Said Royko, "I sort of keep track of the variety and quality of these insults, and in recent years, one of their favorites begins something like this: 'Look you baldheaded ...' etc., etc."[7]

During the mid–1980s, Sean Connery asked to do the latest James Bond film without his hairpiece, but producers denied the request. Since that time Connery has made some of his films without the hairpiece but was denied that option in others. Obviously, he was never allowed to appear bald in any of his Bond films. In the media the bald were rarely portrayed as sex symbols but instead got roles like that of Mel Cooley on the old *Dick Van Dyke Show*, where Richard Deacon was the continual butt of bald jokes. Other roles were those of Fred Mertz on *I Love Lucy*, Ensign Parker on *McHale's Navy*, and Lou Grant on the *Mary Tyler Moore Show*. In television commercials, bald characters tended to be nonthreatening avuncular types such as the Shake 'N Bake butcher, kindly Mr. Goodwrench, or the meek and mild Mr. Whipple, who politely advised housewives not to squeeze the Charmin. Exceptions did exist with balding stars like Nicholson, Bruce Willis, Robert Duvall, and Clint Eastwood essaying sexual characters. In those cases the baldness was less severe than in most bald men or came later in their careers, well after the establishment of their screen personas. Willis was said to be so distraught by the look of his thinning hair in his movie *Hudson Hawk* that he had every offensive frame retouched. Film officials denied the story, citing the high cost of such an undertaking.[8]

Women did sometimes have positive things to say about bald men. *Cosmopolitan* editor Helen Gurley Brown commented: "I think it's good to say, to hell with it. Why not be bald? The men who do, indeed just let it rip, are so attractive." Suzy Mallery, president of the Los Angeles-based Man Watchers, Inc., said: "Burt Reynolds was our first Most Watchable Man. He's Numero Uno. And everyone knows he doesn't have any hair." True enough, but he never appeared that way. Mallery estimated that about 6 percent of her group's 10,000 members preferred bald men. Such statements had little apparent effect, however, on making baldness more acceptable to bald men.[9]

Actor Alan Rachins, who played lawyer Douglas Brackman on the television series *L.A. Law*, blamed baldness for a career crisis in the early 1980s when he abandoned the toupee he had worn since he was 20. Suddenly roles stopped coming his way because he was considered too young to be a character actor and too bald to be a romantic lead. He said: "You've never seen a bald Hamlet and you probably never will. Superman is not bald. Baldness has an avuncular image, more negative than positive." One episode of the series revolved around the Brackman character's new wig which he discarded after enduring taunts and cruel comments. Rachins said he had no plans to return to a wig: "I'm comfortable being what I am." His wife on the show and in real life, Joanna Frank, remarked that Rachins once modeled his toupee for her after they married and she was "totally revolted." Frank thought bald men were more vulnerable than hirsute males.[10]

Politicians were another group that were quick to cover-up. There were exceptions, however. Senator Alan Cranston, a California Democrat, refused to wear a toupee, saying, "If I went to all that trouble to cover up my head,

editorial writers might theorize that I was covering up something else as well."
Senator Jake Garn, a Utah Republican, plastered his state with billboards read-
ing: "Garn-candid. Garn-decisive. Garn-aware. Garn-bald." He won. Said
Garn: "God has made very few perfect heads. The rest of them he covered with
hair." On another occasion Garn commented, "Every man is given a certain
amount of hormones and if some want to waste theirs growing hair, that's
their business." Two other senators who made the best of their baldness were
John Glenn and Alan Simpson. The latter called his head "a solar collector for
a sex machine." Simpson added, "I've been living with the same chick for 32
years. I don't mind being bald, and she says she likes it." He counseled, however, "Before you lose your hair, marry a beautiful woman."[11]

Senators William Proxmire and Strom Thurmond both had transplants
performed by Dr. Ronald Cameron of Bethesda, Maryland. Thurmond had
his procedure done in 1973, when he was around 70. "It helps your appearance," he explained. "It is just like going out and buying a new suit." Cameron
commented: "Men in Washington feel the competition more. We're talking
about a lot of people who have to go back home every two years and get re-
elected. Whether it's good or not, appearance does play a part." Added Washington, D.C., dermatologist David Green, "Most men who have hair loss are
so self-conscious that if a doctor gives them five hairs on their head, they
think he is a miracle worker." Senator Joe Biden also had grafts.[12]

One of the cheapest ways to conceal hair loss, albeit a very obvious one,
is to use the always unsuccessful illusion styling. To observers, however, there
is little illusion. Writing about former Boston mayor Kevin White, a *Boston
Globe* reporter related that his "part moved an inch or so down every few
years as he searched for strands to comb across the top." Reporter Vera Glaser
had this to say about the Senate Select Committee on Intelligence chairman:
"David Boren appears to be wearing a coonskin cap—the result of an ardu-
ous rearrangement of hair to give the impression of thatch were semi-nudity
exists." Senator Bennett Johnston of Louisiana parted his remaining hair low
over the left ear and then swept long strands over to the right to try and cover
his baldness. This styling was referred to as the "Douglas MacArthur Returns"
look. Mentioning examples of political heads that would be better without illusion styling, another reporter cited Senator Sam Nunn, a Georgia Democrat,
and Bennett Johnston. This reporter added, "As for bad toupees, they're all
over Washington, D.C." During the nationally televised Iran-Contra committee hearings in the summer of 1987, Arthur Liman, the chief counsel for
the Senate committee probing the scandal, was mocked for his hair styling as
his "plastered spaghetti slithering along his thinning pate did more than provide acerbic relief." The mere sight of him was said to be enough to make
"women across America shudder and turn to their mates with, 'Darling, don't
ever wear your hair that way.'" Reporter Iris Krasnow of the *Los Angeles Times*
considered the crowning sin in male grooming to be "covering up baldness

by inching the part toward the ear and stretching the hair across the Great Plains of skin. Worse yet is flipping the locks over from the back. These camouflage tricks seem to be especially prominent in image-obsessed Washington."[13]

According to journalist Glaser's 1987 article, over 100 members of Congress were bald or gray and many attempted to hide those facts. She attributed the cover-ups to the role of campaign consultants and the growing impact of television; televising from the House began in 1979 and from the Senate in 1986. Thurmond may have been pleased with his transplant, but Glaser observed, "From the Senate gallery one views Strom Thurmond's fringe of hair, dyed strawberry blond, and his patch of transplant plugs sprouting like zoysia on a summer day." Claude Pepper wore a hairpiece for a while but discarded it after he apparently realized that it resembled "dried crabgrass." Senator William Roth, Jr., wore a toupee "which has been compared to a rug from Levitz."[14]

Several congressmen and one senator reportedly bought toupees from Antonio Trapaini in Bogota, New Jersey, where he sold $800 custom hairpieces made of synthetic material designed to withstand tennis and swimming. Trapaini remarked: "We don't use the word hairpiece. We call it a unit." When House Republican John T. Myers wore a toupee while dancing at a party, it flopped in time to the music. George McGovern appeared on the Senate floor in a toupee when he was seeking the Democratic presidential nomination. An aide recalled, "He only wore it for two weeks, then chickened out." During that period McGovern carried the hairpiece in a paper bag to a beauty shop to be washed one day, but he met a campaign official in the shop. Embarrassed, McGovern dropped the bag and departed. A popular hairstyle on Capitol Hill was the long-bang cut in which the hair covered most of the forehead. It lent a slightly Cro-Magnon look to around 35 members of the House, including Jack Kemp, Trent Lott, Carl Perkins, and Tom Daschle, who adorned his look with a row of forehead ringlets. While that style was said to recall the youth and vitality of John F. Kennedy, beauticians noted that it was also one of the best styles for disguising a unit.[15]

G. Vance Noble published *The Hirsute Tradition in American Politics* in 1978. He argued that while baldies could be elected as mayors, governors, congressmen, and senators, it was rare for a bald man to be elected to the presidency. According to Noble, 26.5 percent of all men 35 and older (the minimum age to be eligible to be president) were bald, yet he pointed out that only two bald men had ever been elected president. "All other things being equal, a bald man cannot be elected President of the United States," he asserted. "Given a choice between two bald presidential candidates, the American people will vote for the less bald of the two." That fact, thought Noble, is "a rather vivid indication that something in the American psyche rejects the idea that a candidate who has lost his hair is capable of national leadership." That prejudice could be traced "to the latent anti-intellectual macho streak that runs through our history, baldness being associated in the popular mind with ivory-tower academics and for some reason, the absence of aggressive attributes Americans subconsciously seek in a President and commander-in-chief."[16]

Martin Van Buren was the first bald president, according to Noble. Van Buren was called names such as "Old Skinhead" and "His Royal Balderdash." He was described in his era as "a fop, with indulgent and high-falutin tastes." Although he considered the public relations value of wearing a wig, Van Buren rejected the idea, fearing it would only add to his image as a dandy. Dwight Eisenhower ran against party rival Robert Taft and Democrat Adlai Stevenson. While Ike was bald, Taft and Stevenson were balder still, argued Noble. Stevenson had particular image difficulties because he was depicted as an egghead, an ivory-tower professor. Noble described two other presidents, Washington and Garfield, as "highforeheaded but not bald." Balding Gerald Ford was, of course, never elected to the presidency. Since Noble's book came out, the only new presidents have been the hirsute Ronald Reagan, George Bush, and Bill Clinton. Noble speculated that George McGovern might have had better success in 1972 against Richard Nixon if he had "only bent a little in principle by going the Bill Proxmire transplant route or wearing a well-styled wig." Other hair styles have come and gone; there have been short-haired and long-haired presidents, as well as some with a moustache or beard. Those types were electable, depending on the fashion of the day. The bald look, however, has never been in for presidents, argued Noble.[17]

Apparently Noble made his theory work by defining the number of bald U.S. presidents in a very narrow fashion. In his book, Dr. Garard Aldhizer argued that six of the first eight presidents were bald or balding: George Washington, John Adams, James Madison, James Monroe, John Quincy Adams, and Martin Van Buren. Journalist Albert Vorspan described Herbert Hoover as being bald. In 1988, reporter Stephen Chapman surveyed the last ten presidential elections. He found that when candidates with unequal manes competed, the hairier man won nearly every time: JFK over Nixon in 1960, Nixon over Humphrey and McGovern in 1968 and 1972, Carter over Ford in 1976. The only exception was in 1964, when LBJ beat Barry Goldwater. In the 1988 primaries, the Iowa caucus featured seven Democrats and six Republicans; none were bald. The 1984 campaign featured baldies like Alan Cranston, John Glenn, and George McGovern. These men, said Chapman, were "about as competitive as a pot-bellied sprinter."[18]

Lee Sigelman conducted his own study of baldness in a political context. His thesis was that since visible hair loss detracted from a positive personal image, candidates so afflicted should find themselves at a significant electoral disadvantage. Sigelman mentioned one observer who noted that "President Reagan's campaign was certainly not hurt by possessing the full hairline of an eighteen-year old. Those that were worried about his advanced years were reassured by his vigorous hairline." For his first study, Sigelman used O. T. Norwood's typology of seven categories to classify every "Anglo" male governor, U.S. senator, and member of the U.S. House of Representatives, as of 1988. Excluded were all female officeholders, blacks, Hispanics, Asians, and American Indians. A total of 522 men were typed. Of that number 328 (62.8 percent) were classed as Type I or II (falling below the minimum baldness threshold, i.e., not bald), while 194 (37.2 percent) were rated Types III through VII, that is, bald or balding. Using the more stringent criterion of "advanced" baldness, Sigelman found only 31 officeholders (5.9 percent) were rated as belonging to Type V, VI, or VII. He concluded that significant hair loss was the exception rather than the rule, with advanced hair loss being rare. According to Norwood's normative tables for the general population, if the officeholders were randomly drawn from the appropriate age cohort, only 249 of them (47.7 percent) would be expected to display no significant hair loss, compared to Sigelman's 62.8 percent, and 273 (52.3 percent) would be expected to fall into Types III through VII, compared to Sigelman's 37.2 percent. Norwood's age norms led one to expect 118 men (22.6 percent) to be rated as having the advanced baldness of Types V through VII; Sigelman found only 31 such officeholders, 5.9 percent.[19]

From that study Sigelman concluded there was a bias against bald and balding men in high executive office. To test that assumption, he selected and interviewed 500 adults in a large city who were summoned for jury duty. Each subject got an election campaign package for Allen Jordan, a mythical candidate. Six different models were used, ranging from Type III to VII. As controls, each of the six was photographed as well with a hairpiece which allowed each to be classified as not bald. Thus a total of twelve different brochures depicted the six models, all as Jordan. Donning the hairpiece lowered the perceived age of each model by at least three years and as much as five or six years in the case of two models. No significant differences were found for perceived character traits or for physical attractiveness. Jordan was considered neither more nor less masculine with a hairpiece than without. Also there was no difference in the desire to vote for the bald Jordan or the hair-bearing one. These results did not support Sigelman's hypothesis. He concluded that if the bias against baldies in high public office did not reflect discrimination on the part of the voters, it must stem from other factors. He speculated that if hair loss diminished one's sense of attractiveness, self-worth, and personal efficacy, one could expect baldies to be less aggressive about putting themselves forward as candidates. If potential candidates, party professionals, financial donors, and others involved in candidate selection believed bald men to be less effective, regardless of the truth of that image, then bald men would have a harder time winning political nomination.[20]

Writing tongue-in-cheek, Vladimir Voinovich suggested Soviet politicians should be divided not into hawks and doves, but into the Bald and the Hairy. The two types alternated in the Kremlin with amazing regularity: Lenin was bald, Stalin was hairy, Krushchev was bald, Brezhnev was hairy, Andropov was bald, Chernenko was hairy, Gorbachov was bald. "All the bald leaders have been revolutionaries or, at least, reformers. All the hairy ones have been reactionaries. All the Bald ones have had utopian goals and ultimately suffered defeat," explained Voinovich. "The Hairy, on the other hand, have always achieved what they wanted.... The Bald ones left behind them nothing but problems." Since that article appeared, the bald Gorbachov was succeeded by the hairy Yeltsin.[21]

A different slant on bald leaders came from U.K. journalist Philip Purser in an article complaining about the lack of able political leadership in Britain. Purser argued that the height of British achievement this century was between 1940 and 1955, when the nation won a war, withdrew from an empire, set up a viable welfare state and created an efficient education system under the premiership of two bald men—Winston Churchill and Clement Attlee. After 1955, when Purser saw the decline start, there was a succession of leaders with luxuriant locks: Anthony Eden, Harold Macmillan, Harold Wilson, Edward Heath, Wilson again, and James Callaghan. The only exception was Alex Douglas-Home, whose tenure, thought Purser, was "too brief" to mean anything. "Can anyone doubt this correlation?" wondered the writer. Then Purser cited Germany as being rebuilt from scratch by the bald Conrad Adenauer and then stagnating under the hairy Erhart and Schmidt. Also cited was France, which was "inspired" under the hairless de Gaulle and nearly bald Giscard d'Estaing. "Britain and Germany are both countries given over to television; in France it has never become quite the same national institution. So in France a bald coot can still be elected, here it has to be someone hirsute. Vanity rules," explained Purser. Since the publication of Purser's article Britain has been ruled by Margaret Thatcher and the hirsute John Major.[22]

Perhaps a "bald coot" could get elected in France, but that doesn't make the condition any easier for the afflicted to live with. Valery Giscard d'Estaing, president of France for seven years, wrote in his memoirs that he first noticed he was losing his hair in the bathroom of a hotel in a small German town. With the light coming in through a skylight in a certain way, he saw how in the mirror the light went through the crown of his head, allowing him to see each strand of hair separately. He wrote, "It filled me with a kind of terror."[23]

10
BALD ATTITUDE

He used to cut his hair, but now his hair has cut him.
Theodore Hook

Baldness: A symbol found by Freud for castration. Castration stands for losing something you value.
Susan Gottenberg,
Make Sense of Your Dreams

Attitudes toward baldness have been overwhelmingly negative. Writing at the beginning of this century, Dr. Woods Hutchinson argued there was no question "that from a very early stage of civilization, certainly from the dawn of literature, the term 'baldhead' has been in common use as an expression of scorn and derision. Moreover, the condition is referred to in the earliest proverbs of many literatures and races, always as an undesirable, but by no means unusual consummation." Over half a century later Dr. Christopher Papa remarked: "It's almost impossible to exaggerate the significance that scalp hair has for the human psyche. Historically it has been a woman's crown of beauty and man's symbol of strength and vigor."[1]

The belief that hair expressed physical strength, virility, and manliness is typified in the biblical Samson legend, but variations of the story can be found in folk tales around the world. Primitive people believed that hair contained a sacred spirit. Among such tribes there was often a strict taboo against hair cutting. One journalist argued that "This superstitious regard for hair is evident in every race and every age." Julius Caesar made the Gauls cut their hair as a token of submission. Indians scalped their victims to deprive them of their spirit so the ghosts would not walk. During World War II, the French shaved the heads of women who had consorted with the Germans. More recently the Irish Republican Army has meted out the same punishment to Irish females believed to have consorted with British troops occupying Ireland. Men inducted into the military have their heads shaved nearly bald. While there may have once been hygienic reasons for that practice, today it can only be seen as rendering the recruit submissive and impotent.[2]

Back in 1893 medical doctor Condict Cutler believed that baldies were held in such low regard that "even ballet dancers are apt to look down upon them.... That a bald head is not a desirable possession is evidenced by the enormous sale of nostrums warranted to restore the natural covering to the scalp." A second physician described the condition as "the deformity of youth, and scarcely to be borne with equanimity in old age." A few years later the magazine *Independent* remarked that no affliction that runs its course without pain or danger to general health "causes so much acute discomfort and even positive suffering as advancing baldness." Harlem Hospital dermatologist William Cunningham noted that bald heads and gray hair were regarded as evidence of the degenerative changes coming with advancing age: "Viewed in this light they are a detriment to the seeker of employment.... The possession of a bald or whitening head is in most of the paths of industry a very undesirable asset." During the times of World War I, journalist Lester Reynolds stated, "It is very evident that men hate to be bald." Yet he believed baldness was not a drawback to men in either business or social life. That left only one reason to hate baldness, "vanity—the very best reason."[3]

When the *New Statesman and Nation* asked in 1934, "Are bald heads advantageous?" writer Albert Griffin stated the first answer to suggest itself was a "direct negative." Baldies did not like their condition: "Witness their frantic efforts to keep among the ranks of the bethatched. When the skull begins to show through there is consternation.... Each hair from that time is cherished with deep affection." Yet Griffin was one of the few writers with positive things to say about being bald. According to him, a bald head was worth £1,000 a year in extra income to a medical doctor. "Many a practitioner without a practice worth the name would part with a fairly round sum for a good, cheerful, amiable bald head." One could not get by with a shaved head since one could not make money out of counterfeit baldness: "There is an honesty and truthfulness about a genuine bald head that a razor can never produce." More generally, Griffin argued that a bald head stood for wisdom in many businesses, thus drawing customers. He also believed it stood for mature philosophy. The father in a family gained from his bald head since it "gives him the character of a jolly, hearty, generous man which he enjoys." In conclusion, Griffin wrote, "The world would be the loser by the extermination of all those whose character is boldly proclaimed by the graceful protuberances and gentle depressions of a bare skull."[4]

Half a century later Dr. Barrett Hays, a 27-year-old bald resident physician at Breckenridge Hospital in Austin, Texas, thought the condition had won him some patients: "Several patients look at my colleagues who are 30 or 32 and tell me 'I don't want that younger doctor; I want you.'" He admitted, however, that a lot of young women in their early 20s refused to date him, thinking he was much older. Hays exclaimed: "It's basically lamentable that one would lose one's hair or hairline. It just looks better having them."[5]

When the *New York Times* editorialized about hair in 1868, it argued that no one should complain about the value humankind placed on abundant and beautiful hair "if we reflect what a difference there is between the appearance of a bald-headed unfortunate and that of a person with a head well thatched by nature. The one bears some resemblance to a Winter-stricken tree; while the other looks like the same tree in its Summer luxuriance of foliage."[6]

Such scorn directed to baldies has led to a number of ways to attempt to hide the condition, short of resorting to plugs, rugs, or drugs. Washington, D.C., dermatologist David Green commented: "Men would rather lose their wallets or their children in White Flint Mall than lose their hair. Even in the back hills of West Virginia, you may not see any hair transplants, but you will see bald men wearing baseball caps during the winter, summer, spring and fall."[7]

Perhaps the most popular of all covering techniques was the unusual hair style, often pathetically obvious. Caesar favored that technique himself. Ancient coins depicting that leader showed a hair style in which hair from the back is combed forward to hide the baldness. Former Canadian prime minister Pierre Trudeau favored that styling during his days in the limelight. Back in 1915, Dr. Cunningham remarked that a man going bald "notes with marked anxiety the thinning at the top, and ingenuously manipulates the more resistant filaments to hide the shining scalp. This artifice is usually futile. No eye is deceived by it except his own." A generation later a journalist observed of the cover-up styling that "As the locks become thinner, the parting creeps down the side, and finds a resting-place just above the ear, prior to vanishing altogether. When at last the scalp is innocent of garnish, every available side is requisitioned, and carried over the top in strings with geometrical regularity, like so many lines of latitude on a globe. Seen from above the skull in this state is an interesting study." Some modern day barbers specialize in "illusion styling," which means they brush and arrange what hair remains artfully flopping it over the bald spots so the head doesn't look bald—at least until the customer sneezes, or until the first wind.[8]

That styling, also called a comb-over, has been regularly mocked. *San Francisco Chronicle* columnist Jon Carroll described it as "letting the hair on one side of the head just above the ear grow unnaturally long. These lengthy tresses are then taken by oxen across the broad prairie of the top scalp and secured above the other ear." He wondered about the level of self-deception involved. "Do men with comb-overs look in their mirror and say: 'My, what a darned fine mane of hair I have now'? Or do they say: 'This should be pathetic enough for even the most demanding sadist.'" Los Angeles writer Preston Lerner noted, "The combed-over hair is secured by mammoth applications of heavy-duty mousse or hairspray." When asked for his opinion, Beverly Hills, California, hair salon owner Giuseppe Franco remarked: "The first thing a good stylist will tell you is that taking one strand of hair and wrapping it across and spraying it with cement looks ridiculous. When you go to the comb-over look, you're not just losing your hair; you're losing your mind."[9]

Special barber shops for baldies have existed for as long as a century. In 1891 a Brooklyn, New York, barber made a specialty of polishing bald heads. Situated near City Hall, his shop was much patronized by politicians. Over the door a sign read, "Bald-Head BURNISHING 25 cents extra." The barber copied the idea from Philadelphia, where several "burnishing parlors" were in operation. After a bald customer was seated in a special rear room of the shop, a bucket-shaped contrivance was placed on his head. Then an attendant pulled out any superfluous hair with a pair of tweezers. Next the scalp was sponged with alcohol, then rubbed vigorously with glycerine, then a coat of something like varnish was applied with a brush. The barber then arrived with a chamois and several brushes of varying sizes. After he rubbed the scalp vigorously, said the *New York Times*, "the scalp is too slippery even for flies to tread upon."[10]

During the 1980s, Tommaso Foresta operated a barbershop for bald men in Manhattan. From the outside it looked like an old fashioned shop, complete with striped pole and copies of men's magazines. Foresta had enough steady customers that he took his ad out of the Yellow Pages. Inside the shop he cut hair, did toupee maintenance, performed hair weaving, etc. Customers came by appointment and only seldom encountered each other. Particularly shy clients were served behind a closed curtain. One of his customers believed his wife of 25 years didn't know he was bald because he had never taken off his hair weave in front of her. Foresta wore a wig himself but not all the time. "I never approached a single woman without the hairpiece. But once I got married, it didn't seem so important," he explained. Another customer told Foresta that some women recoiled in horror when they discovered that he was wearing a toupee. He had a blind date with a woman who said to him over the phone in an initial conversation: "You sound bald. I'd rather go out with guys with hair." After the date the woman said she wanted to see him again. His reply was to yank off his toupee, smile broadly, and bid a quick farewell. What his customers wanted most was what nobody could give. "They want their own hair back," said Foresta.[11]

So touchy was the subject that at a Washington, D.C. hair treatment center, the owner said he tried never to use the word bald, "I just say hair loss. I try to stay away from bald. Bald is a harsh word. You have tooth loss. You have hair loss. Hair loss is soft. Hairdressing is diplomacy." Jane Leahy, who reported the above story, noted, "Going bald is the closest a man will ever come to feeling like a woman.... Baldness is an affront [*sic*] to their expectations; a public acknowledgment that control is an illusion. Baldness contradicts [*sic*] the powerlessness they seek to deny."[12]

Whenever a study was launched on some new baldness treatment, the center was usually flooded with contacts from men wanting to volunteer. In 1983 when the Stanford University dermatology department announced a call for volunteers for a new baldness treatment, "Within hours of the announcement, the university had been bombarded with calls from hundreds of baldies (as well as some of their wives)," reported the *Los Angeles Times*. Yet psychologists agreed that anyone who measured his self-esteem by the amount of hair on his head wouldn't benefit much by covering the naked spots. Yale University dermatologist Ronald Savin who, despite hair transplants and minoxidil treatments, described himself as "moderately bald," stated that hair "is terribly important to self-esteem. A full head of hair has always implied youth, confidence and vitality."[13]

University of Chicago skin specialist Dr. Stephen Rothman advised his patients to forget their vanity and grow bald gracefully. "A patient's vanity is often the most difficult part of baldness to deal with," he said. "It is responsible for much of the money spent on hair restorers, massages and tonics. Bald men can be quite good looking.... So forget your vanity."[14]

Many men couldn't or wouldn't forget, however. A London dermatologist remarked: "I get a lot of young men coming to see me. It is, in its own way, a tragic procession. Many of them are pathetic. They come to tell me they fear they are going bald. Many of them have become neurotic about it. They are all in an anxiety state. They tell me they have failed in life; failed with girls; failed with jobs. They believe their baldness is the cause of their failure. But they have failed because they are inadequate."[15]

When Upjohn was busy touting its minoxidil treatment, the company issued a press release which mentioned a study that confirmed the psychological effects of hair loss and spoke of the "genuine worry and distress" caused by baldness. Writing in the *Saturday Evening Post*, Fred Sparks commented: "Psychiatrists recognize the masculine distaste for premature baldness as a source of inferiority complexes, and, in extreme cases, depressive mania. Some bald young men have been known to isolate themselves from all social contacts." Then there was the man who kept his hat by his bedside so he could put it on the minute he woke up. He even jilted his bride-to-be when he realized that walking down the aisle would mean removing his protective headgear.[16]

Anxiety over baldness reached such an extreme level in Barry Palmer of Bristol, England, that he committed suicide, reported the *Times* of London, without details. According to Dr. Thomas Stuttaford, anxiety about baldness could become so great that those afflicted could start to display symptoms of dysmorphophobia, an obsessive dislike and preoccupation with some part of their anatomy—in this case, their balding scalp. Other doctors dismissed dysmorphophobia as a symptom of a disturbed personality, suggesting that if the patients were not worried about their hair it would be their nose or teeth, or something else. As to baldness, Stuttaford thought that "few women find it attractive, and men tend to view it as a sign of vanishing youth."[17]

During the 1980s a couple of doctors who should have known better mentioned the idea of hair loss as a sign of virility. Ronald Savin called the condition a male secondary sex characteristic, arguing that "Baldness is just like the red comb on a rooster. It means he's the male king of the barnyard." Medical College of South Carolina dermatology professor Richard Dobson said: "In effect what the bald man is saying to the world is that his male hormones are working. With a man who has a full head of hair, you can't be sure." At least one of the two, Savin, was bald.[18]

Also attempting to be upbeat about hair loss was New York City's deputy mayor, Henry H. Curran. In 1938 a Bronx woman named Margaret McKenzie wrote to the politician explaining she had a cure for baldness and requesting Curran's help in informing the citizenry in order that they might keep their hair. She noted that even if aesthetic considerations were not a sufficient reason, a good head of hair also protected the skull against assaults and injuries. In his reply, Curran wrote, "I don't see why 'for the good of mankind' I should aid you in your 'drive on baldness.' Why not be bald? Nobody ever made a nickel out of his hair. We cannot sell it, or use it, or rent it, or put it in a show window." He had no objection to people wishing to seek her out for treatment, but as for the baldie who asked for no change, he said, "Don't put on a 'drive' against him. He is happy as he is. With a high degree of intelligence within his polished pate, he is kindlier to his fellows than the ordinary man, more tolerant of their foibles, more resigned to his own. He chuckles and beams, in or out of the front row. A ray of sunshine in an anxious land, a rollicking bald-headed Santa Claus." Curran was bald.[19]

Generally, however, the image was negative and was associated with loss of virility and aging. Miami psychiatrist Ronald Shellow remarked that many men saw hair as a symbol of virility or masculine beauty and became upset and frightened when they lost their hair. Jane Capps, wife of Bald-Headed Men of America president John Capps, commented that "From our letters, we have found that many men consider baldness to be a sign of growing old, and it's not." Even though women often were quoted as saying they found bald men attractive, it was not enough to ease the anxiety of one unnamed congressional aide, who worried, "When women say that bald heads are sexy, you don't know if they're patronizing you or if they mean it." Author Walter Klenhard noted that baldness had never been in fashion because a full head of hair signified youth, strength, energy, and physical attractiveness, while baldness symbolized mortality and aging. He pointed out that evidence for the fact that men didn't like being bald could be found in the money spent on remedies and treatments. Advertisements, magazines, and television did not feature baldies, commented Klenhard, who also observed there were no bald newscasters, although some bald weathermen were on the air. In a mid–1980s piece in the *New York Times Magazine*, the journalist noted that while it may be true that women frequently find bald men attractive, "wherever I look, I see our culture offering up evidence to the contrary. The ideal image of masculine good looks is seldom a bald one. Look at the male models appearing in advertisements, the movie stars with their hair transplants.... Given the choice, would any man go bald?" Cited as evidence of hair worshipping culture were the Beatles, Elvis Presley, John F. Kennedy, and the musical play *Hair*. This reporter also equated baldness with aging and mortality, points often made in the media.[20]

Sometimes it was reported that the female was the main force driving her man to seek hair replacement treatments. One account explained that the woman, "with her proverbial intuition, has a feeling of inferiority in the presence of a bald man. Throughout the course of history, woman has pretty much had her own way with men—hairy men, that is—and she lives in dread of the day of the baldhead, a superior being she no longer will be able to outsmart." A second account offered the opinion that most men who bought hairpieces did so because they had been "motivated" by their women.[21]

When dermatologist Philip Eisenberg studied 200 men in 1959, he found that a man's first reaction to the discovery that he was losing his hair was normally one of "shock, personal loss and a feeling of disfigurement." He believed that men over the age of 35 or 40 "became truly resigned" to the condition, while for younger men the resignation was only "apparent." A New York psychologist thought baldness was most disturbing in its early stages, when the sufferer was forced to revise his self-image. Once the hair was gone, however, the man usually found it was not as bad as he feared. Washington, D.C., dermatologist Naomi Kanof thought a full head of hair was a critical need for entertainers, but she advised others to accept the fact that baldness was normal. She conceded everyone would rather have hair, but recognized that most bald men didn't have a choice except for expensive and time-consuming procedures. Relief at any price wasn't something she thought bald men wanted. Kanof cited three types of reactions to baldness: First, there was a small percentage of men who didn't care. At the other end of the spectrum, there was a small percentage of men who were emotionally devastated, and Kanof believed "these are the people who have devastating problems of which this simply becomes a symptom." In the middle were most men, who were mildly unhappy about their hair loss. That last group, thought Kanof, might or might not decide on a wig or some other treatment. The reporter who interviewed Kanof summed up his article with the comment: "All bald men may not be rich, but have you ever noticed how many rich men are bald?" You get the same result by changing the word bald to the word old.[22]

Mike Mahoney edited the *Hair Loss Journal* out of Tyler, Texas. That publication was put out by an organization of toupee makers, hair transplanters, plastic surgeons, and dermatologists. According to Mahoney, hair-replacement clients tended to be college-educated, upscale, 30- to 50-year-old men, who would not respond favorably to transparently foolish claims or to the large number of quacks in the industry who drove potential customers away by insulting their intelligence. Yet he conceded such quacks who sold creams and lotions "guaranteed to grow hair" operated a multimillion dollar industry. "They can well-afford those guarantees because most of their customers are too embarrassed to complain," he added. There was also the placebo effect, which led desperate baldies to think they detected hair growth where none existed. As to the nonquack hair-replacement industry for which Mahoney spoke, he estimated it had penetrated only three to four percent of the bald and thinning marketplace in 1988.[23]

Illustrating the lengths to which a man would go to regain his hair was a supposedly true story published in the *Washingtonian* in 1983. Reporter John Sansing related the tale of an 18 year old who went to see a Washington, D.C., doctor about his hair loss, which left him depressed and in anguish over the thought he would be bald on top by his early 20s. Trying to shake the young man out of his depression, the doctor told him there was one way to stop his hair from falling out. After telling the patient it was a pretty drastic method, the doctor paused and then said, "castration. We'd have to cut off your testicles." For a moment the grim-faced patient sat stunned, before he sighed and replied, "Well, okay." The story was probably false.[24]

Attempts by the media to put a less negative spin on baldness appeared on rare occasions, but were uniformly woeful. In the 1950s, Ruth Scott tried to help baldies accept their condition by writing banalities such as "Practice happiness," "Don't be so sensitive about your hair," and "Don't be vain." Around the same time, Dr. Eugen J. Van Scott, head of the dermatology service of the National Cancer Institute at Bethesda, Maryland, presumably tried to comfort the hairless when he uttered the following inanity: "Baldness is not a loss of hair. The hair just becomes shorter, thinner and finer. Finally you can't see it at all, even under a microscope. But there's hair there.... Even the totally bald have hair. You just can't see it."[25]

In 1975, *Time* magazine attempted to declare that bald was in, that bald was beautiful. The magazine had precious little to cite to support that idea, chiefly Yul Brynner, Telly Savalas, and a few others. According to *Time*, bald was indeed beautiful in the eyes of "a bevy of female beholders." In this case the bevy was precisely three, two of which were unknown to the general public: Soprano Beverly Sills was the third. A decade later *Newsweek* made a similar declaration, citing a few bald actors and celebrities and arguing that men were more accepting of baldness than they had been in past decades. Half of the article commented, however, on the clamor as thousands of men desperately tried to enroll themselves with Upjohn as guinea pigs for minoxidil studies; the article noted the amount the share price of Upjohn stock had soared in one year. Perhaps the weakest of all the "bald is in" articles was a 1990 piece published in the newspaper *USA Today*, whose evidence to support the ideas that "bald is becoming beautiful" and "thinning hair is in" was limited to citing film actor/director Ron Howard, who wouldn't wear his hairpiece offscreen, and actor Ted Danson, who appeared at the Emmy awards without the toupee he wore on the *Cheers* television series as Sam the bartender. The character Sam typified the importance and image of hair in our society. Sam was an excessive womanizer with a full head of hair. He was also obsessed with his hair, constantly tending to it.[26]

Sometimes the shaved head look was mentioned as an example of virile, macho men, from circus strongmen to Mr. Clean to Yul Brynner to football player Otis Sistrunk. As a style, it became even more popular in the early 1990s, with many more athletes adopting it, particularly in the NBA, where it was seen on such luminaries as Michael Jordan and Charles Barkley. The shaved head is not male pattern baldness, although some have adopted it in response to their MPB. Shaving the head bald is a voluntary act, an assertive act, which can be reversed at any time; MPB cannot be reversed. Shaved heads are assertive, macho, active, and nonconformist while regular bald heads are reactive, passive, and powerless.[27]

If the shaved head look was bald and proud for some, Manhattan's Ed Liebowitz thought others should be bald and proud even if they didn't feel that way. He went around New York City posting up pictures which were computer-generated photos of bald men who appeared usually in public as hair-bearing. The Liebowitz tactic was similar to the campaign of "outing" gays. Bald photos of public figures such as Charles Bronson, Ted Danson, and William Shatner were posted over a caption that read "Absolutely Bald." Bronson responded: "I am not bald. If I don't get a retraction, I am going to take legal action." Liebowitz promised to put up no more Bronson photos. Danson explained that he did wear a partial toupee, but only professionally. Shatner refused to comment. Asked how he knew which celebrities were bald, Liebowitz explained: "We compared earlier publicity shots with later shots. And we could pretty much figure it out." All the photos bore the slogan: "Because shinier pates today mean a sunnier tomorrow." Other celebrities targeted and postered were Larry Hagman and Joe Namath. A spokeswoman for Namath exclaimed: "He's not bald. Definitely not. I don't know where they got that." Liebowitz gave no motive for his campaign except that baldness was nothing to be ashamed of. He denied he was just seeking publicity.[28]

Commenting on Nora Ephron's remark that height is to men what breasts are to women, *Chicago Tribune* writer Karen Heller remarked: "I disagree. I think it's baldness. I think men are more concerned about their hair than about anything else. No one wants to be bald. They don't want to look like Sean Connery unless they can have all the rest that goes with being Sean Connery."[29]

Surveys done on attitudes towards baldness have yielded unpleasant results for baldies. A 1983 survey questioned women aged 21 to 35 in New York, Boston, Houston, and Los Angeles. Of those questioned, 65 percent

said they did not think bald men were more virile than hirsute ones; 77 percent responded that they did not think bald men had more sex appeal, 75
percent said they did not think baldies were more intelligent; and 75 percent
replied they thought bald men looked older than their ages.[30]

In the early 1990s, a major Japanese cosmetic company surveyed 733
men between the ages of 15 and 59 on the streets of Tokyo. Respondents were
queried about their habits and personalities and were asked whether their
hair was thin, receding, or abundant. Results indicated that men who were pessimistic, methodical, and irritable were more likely to have thin hair. From
this survey the typical balding man was a person who "is a little overweight,
a heavy smoker, sweats easily, often drinks alcohol and has a thick beard and
body hair."[31]

One of the earliest psychological studies was reported in 1971. Sixty male
and female college students were shown 15 slides of male faces varied by
amount of hair. Respondents were to evaluate the faces on various aspects.
Prior to the experiment, researcher Samuel Roll theorized that bald heads
would be rated the least valued, while heads with full hair would be most valued. Results found heads with full hair were rated as valued, were high on several potency scales, and were viewed as most active. Balding heads were judged
as the most valued, least potent, and least active, while bald heads were viewed
as the least valued, but were high on one potency scale, and were viewed as
active. That balding and bald heads were seen as less potent than full-hair
heads caused Roll to comment, "This brings into question the generality of
the fantasy that 'bald men make good lovers.'" He thought, however, that his
finding was in accord with several psychoanalytic writers who had proposed
that there was a strong association between hair and potency.[32]

Grimmer still was the study done by Old Dominion University psychologist Thomas Cash, who compared balding men to those with a full head of
hair. Cash found balding to be a stressful event for his subjects, with stress
greatest among young men and those who were single and not dating. "The
greater the hair loss, the greater the psychological cost," he explained. In his
study Cash found that "both men and women rated bald men as less attractive, less confident, less successful and less likeable than hairier men. The
greater the hair loss, the more negative the impression." Baldies looked considerably older than hair-bearing men of similar age, said the report.[33]

Cash was back shortly with another study on the topic. He used 18 pairs
of balding and nonbalding men's photos matched on other physical attributes. Half the pairs of photos were of men under 35, half of older men. Those
photos were shown to males and females for evaluation. Overall Cash found,
results indicated that "hair loss had a nearly uniform, adverse impact on how
the men were initially perceived by others." Compared to their nonbalding
counterparts, the balding men were perceived as significantly less physically
attractive, less self-assertive in their personalities, less socially attractive, less

likely to experience success in personal/career life, and less personally liked by the evaluators themselves. Younger nonbalding men were judged two years younger than their real age, baldies 3.6 years older. Among the older men, nonbalding men were rated 3 years younger, baldies 1.4 years older. Presence or absence of hair loss did not affect perceptions of intellectual capabilities. Both genders of raters rated the balding men equally negatively. The one exception was in the area of personal likability. While both sexes expected balding men to be less personally likeable than the nonbalding, that rating was stronger among male raters than among females. Essentially, the genders viewed baldies in a very similar fashion. Cash concluded, "In sum ... visible baldness has a modest yet reliable and largely negative influence on how men are initially perceived by others."[34]

In the Netherlands a researcher did a follow-up on 201 men who had tried to enroll in a minoxidil study at a Rotterdam hospital but were rejected because there were too many volunteers. Two years after being rejected, 68 of the men (34 percent) had consulted one or more medical professionals about their hair loss. The consulting men were found to be more anxious and worried by their hair loss than the men who did not consult anyone in those two years. The consulting group agreed more often with statements such as "feels less attractive," "discomfort in the presence of women," and "feels ashamed" than the nonconsulters.[35] A different Netherlands researcher sent a questionnaire to medical doctors in that country requesting information on bald patients. According to the 80 responding physicians, 47 percent of their bald male patients had psychological problems in addition to hair loss. Most frequently mentioned were "low self-esteem" and depression.[36]

Stephen Franzoi gave questionnaires to 91 men to have them rate themselves on a four-point hair amount scale and a public self-consciousness scale. He found that men with thinning hair judged themselves less attractive than nonbalding men judged themselves. Additionally, he determined that men with high public self-consciousness were more likely than those with low public self-consciousness to believe that balding men would be judged as less attractive and that females would be less likely to date them.[37]

When University of Louisville psychologist Michael Cunningham surveyed 204 students to see how they perceived bald men, he found they rated them as less attractive than nonbalding men. They also perceived them to be five to seven years older than their actual age. He concluded that people associated hair with attractiveness and youth. New York psychologist Stanley Teitelbaum agreed, saying, "Men with little or no hair are seen as less desirable." Thomas Cash commented that bald men were considered more likely to bomb at romance and in their personal lives. They were also believed to have a harder time making a good first impression. "Society definitely discriminates against bald and balding men.... It's little wonder balding men are trying to stop going bald, especially with a bad economy," added Cash.[38]

Researchers who surveyed 145 balding men in 1994 found that 84 percent were preoccupied with hair loss. To compensate for the stress and lowered self-esteem, many of the bald men increased their amount of exercise.[39]

If baldies didn't have enough to worry about, consider the recent results reported on the link between baldness and coronary artery disease (CAD). Researchers in Malmo, Sweden, reported in the mid–1980s on a long-term study of 464 men. Among the bald men, 25.5 percent had CAD, compared to 19.7 percent of the men who weren't bald. Besides the usual factors considered responsible for heart disease, this study concluded, "In addition to the common risk factors, baldness seems to be of importance."[40]

Another long-term study was started in 1975 at the University of Naples Medical School in Italy. Men were divided into three groups: those with no signs of hair loss, those with just a receding hairline, and those with fronto-occipital baldness (male pattern baldness). Blood pressure and cholesterol readings increased for all three groups from 1975 to 1987. Although those differences were not significant, the increases were steeper in men with fronto-occipital baldness than in the other groups. Researcher Dr. Maurizio Trevisan remarked: "Baldness isn't a risk factor for heart disease. But it is associated with other risk factors." He added, "We can't say that if you exhibit typical male pattern baldness you're going to have a heart attack."[41]

Clinician Carlos Herrera reported in 1990 on eight articles that contained data on both baldness and coronary artery disease. He found that three showed a link between baldness and CAD when controlling for the CAD risk factors, two were inconclusive, and three others showed no relationship, but the latter didn't control for CAD risk factors. Herrera concluded, "Overall, the data reviewed suggest that a small risk of CAD due to baldness may exist, but this risk is smaller than that of well-known CAD risk factors such as smoking and hypertension."[42]

Unpublished data from a long-term study of risk factors for heart disease in Framingham, Massachusetts, have shown a similar statistical link between baldness and heart attacks. The study which got the most media coverage was released in 1993 by Dr. Samuel Lesko, lead author of the Boston University report. Five years earlier Upjohn approached the institution seeking information about the relationship between baldness and heart disease. With its drug Rogaine just officially on the market, the company was worried about the possibility of reports of adverse effects like heart attacks among minoxidil users. Upjohn wanted to determine whether such cardiac problems reflected use of the medication or a general risk factor. If baldness in men itself was a risk factor for heart disease, a higher incidence of such complications among minoxidil users compared to nonusers might be attributed to the drug when, in fact, baldness accounted for the difference. Upjohn funded the study which looked at 1,437 men aged 21 to 54 who were admitted to Boston area hospitals from 1989 to 1991. Of the patients admitted to the hospitals for noncardiac conditions, 23 percent had vertex baldness. Of the men with no history of heart disease, who were admitted for a first heart attack, 32 percent had vertex baldness. Reportedly the link held in all three age subgroups independently of other well-known risk factors for heart attacks. The link did not hold for frontal-only baldness, however. In addition, the greater the amount of vertex baldness, the greater the risk of increased incidence of heart disease. Lesko noted, however, that the risk of developing heart disease for men with severe vertex baldness was slightly lower than the risks from smoking and untreated high blood pressure. Researchers speculated the male hormone dihydrotestosterone was involved.[43]

Yet another study was released by Professor Peter Schnohr and his University of Copenhagen colleagues in 1993. For a twelve-year period, they studied 20,000 men and women living in Copenhagen. At the end of that time, 9 percent of the men and 3 percent of the women had experienced myocardial infarction. Regarding women, they found what was already known—"most women keep their hair for a lifetime and never become bald." For the few women who did lose some of their hair, this condition did not increase the risk of coronary attack. Schnohr found, however, that bald males had significantly more heart attacks than men who kept their hair.[44]

Given the number of negative factors they face, it is not surprising that baldies often band together. Over the past century, there have been several clubs for baldies. All have involved more than a little humorous self-depreciation. The earliest and most informal was New York's Bald Head Club, which was formed in February 1896 by R. H. Halstead of the New York Stock Exchange. That month Halstead enrolled 28 men in the club. All were brokers who traded on the floor of the Wall Street exchange. On February 8, when the exchange chairman was absent, Halstead seized the opportunity for a public display by the Bald Head Club. Sixteen of the members answered his call. Arranged in company order, the group paraded around the floor. At the front was William French, who removed his brown wig for the occasion. A messenger boy was commanded to lead the procession, holding aloft French's wig, the club's emblem, and carrying a placard which read "THE NORTHERLAND BROS.: No relation to the Sutherland Sisters: Use Our Preparation: BALDY & CO." Obviously, the statement meant something in its day, but these words are inexplicable today. This little parade drew cheers and applause from other brokers and spectators in the visitors' gallery. After a couple of circuits of the floor, most of the club members disappeared to execute stock orders they had received as they marched. When French discovered he was almost alone, he grabbed his wig, slapped it on his head, and also left to transact business. Without his wig French was described as "displaying a glossy surface of scalp, embossed at the neck and over each ear with patches of hair about the size of half-dollar pieces." Henry Clews was one member who didn't answer Halstead's appeal to march. Clews sent word that after considerable reflection he had concluded he was not eligible for club membership on account of the fringe of hair around the side of his head. There was too much of it, he thought. The Bald Head Club disappeared as suddenly as it appeared.[45]

Longer lived was the Bald Head Club of America. This group became a formal and official organization in 1920, when it filed articles of association in Hartford, Connecticut, with the secretary of state. Founder and president of the club was John Rodemeyer, editor of the Greenwich *Weekly News and Graphic.* One of the organization's objectives, set forth in its articles, was, "to promote and foster a sentiment of fraternity among those whose domes of thought protrude through and tower above the foliage that affords shade and adornment." The following year the club applied to the Connecticut State Legislature to extend its incorporation charter so that the Bald Head Club of America would have the authority to set up branch chapters anywhere in the world. The group claimed to have already received hundreds of applications for such branch clubs.

In due course the legislature granted such power to the club but not before having a lot of fun at a hearing on the issue. One member of the House suggested the hearing should go to the Committee on Agriculture. This was ruled out by Senator Kenealy, who decided it was not a crop-raising project. Another suggestion was made to send the hearing to Public Health and Safety. This was vetoed on the ground that baldies weren't a menace to the peace of the community. The hearing was left with the Incorporation Committee. At the hearing Rodemeyer contended a bald man "being as radiantly happy as a fat man, was a blessing to the community" and that his club contained "the merriest band of good fellows who ever got together." Rodemeyer replied in the negative when legislators asked if he planned to establish a junior organization for prematurely bald men or a cradle roll for infants slow in growing hair.[46]

The Conley Inn at Torrington, Connecticut, was the site of the Bald Head Club of America's first annual banquet on May 9, 1921. An estimated 350 baldies turned out to have their domes inspected. Excess hair was cause for expulsion from the club. All members passed muster that year. One member had a rabbit painted on his scalp for the occasion. He was calling it a hare. During his address Rodemeyer remarked, "This is the season of bud and blossom when mother nature confers on every limb a rejuvenating baptism of youthful vigor and fresh foliage and in her lavish bestowal on the limbs leaves us out." Area manufacturers supplied several novelty souvenirs, including special egg beaters labeled "hair-oil mixer." Beverage bottles were draped with mourning bands and pictures of bald heads that were marked "gone, but not forgotten."[47]

Five years later this group was still going strong. Members responded in mock horror early in 1926, when plans were announced to locate in Connecticut a college of hair research to study the causes of baldness and find a cure. Rodemeyer immediately enlisted two high-ranking state politicians, one Republican, one Democrat, both members of his group, to lead a bipartisan revolt against the planned college. Rodemeyer promised formal resolutions against the college would be passed at the club's upcoming annual banquet because, he said, "The future of the Bald Head Club of America is seriously threatened."[48]

In 1933 the Bald Head Club of America had chapters in 37 states. Members of the "Jolliest Club in America" included William Howard Taft, William Jennings Bryan, and politician Nicholas Longworth. This group seems to have suddenly expired, however, as no more references to it surfaced.[49]

Other countries also organized clubs and activities for the hair-challenged. Achille Scagni was head of Italy's 1,000-member Baldheaded Association. In 1956 that group, whose motto was "Baldheaded men of the world unite," named President Dwight Eisenhower and Russian leader Nikita Khrushchev honorary members of the club. Several years later what was billed as the first world rally of bald men was held at the seaside resort of La Baule in Brittany, France. A mere 50 baldies turned up to discuss such issues as whether baldness was an obstacle to a professional career and whether it hindered marital happiness. They also enjoyed the friendship and good humor provided by the common link of baldness. A female panel selected a "Mr. Bald Head." When a suggestion was made to the Wrockwardine Wood Bald Headed Men's Club in Shropshire, England, in 1968 that its members should test a herbal remedy said to cure baldness, club secretary V. Hinds declined. Worried that it might work, Hinds explained, "It would destroy the spirit and atmosphere of our club, which we formed to help people lose their shyness about being bald." During the early 1980s, the annual Bright Head Contest was held in Japan, a beauty pageant for bald men.[50]

One American special event was announced in 1989 when Lew Wilson, president of Regal Retreats, a Tallahassee, Florida, company that organized golf outings, announced the first Bald Golfers of America Tournament to take place later that year. It was to be a two-day, 36-hole event in Palm Beach, Florida. Participants had to be at least half bald, and borderline cases were required to wear rubberized, flesh-tone skullcaps. Entry fee was to be $3,000 per person, which covered three nights lodging, food, and golf fees. It is unclear whether this event ever took place. Joe Amiel owned the Old Mill Inn in Basking Ridge, New Jersey, where he held "Bald Is Beautiful" nights at which bald men ate in his restaurant for half price. Amiel wore no hairpiece himself, saying of his baldness, "It's not just that it's beautiful—it's different."[51]

Perhaps the best-known and longest-lived group for baldies is the still existing Bald-Headed Men of America (BHMA) which was formed in September 1973 by John T. Capps III in Dunn, North Carolina. Not too long thereafter it moved headquarters to the appropriately named Morehead City in that same state. A year or so after formation, the club claimed 1,000 members in 42 states and 5 foreign countries. Capps remains the BHMA executive director and also runs a printing business in Morehead City. Asked about the group's formation, Capps explained: "I applied for a job selling stationery and forms to financial institutions, but was turned down because I didn't look young enough. I was only 21 at the time, but was rapidly losing hair. That rejection really burned me." He brooded for a decade before forming BHMA "to instill pride in having bald heads." Capps made a list of all the bald and balding men he knew through the Rotary Club, the 4-H Club, and his church. He then sent them all letters inviting them to join the club. "I did it inch by inch, bald head by bald head," he explained. Believing that everyone was too serious, Capps formed the group in 1973 "to do something that would put a smile on people's faces. We wanted to try to make people enjoy life a little bit more."[52]

By the beginning of the 1980s, BHMA had some 9,500 members in 50 states and 10 foreign nations, including former president Gerald Ford, Senator Henry Jackson, actors Telly Savalas, Phil Silvers, Scatman Crothers, weatherman Willard Scott, sportscaster Joe Garagiola, and Utah Senator Jake Garn. Members, said the club, had "learned to cultivate a sense of pride in their condition." Capps said: "What's important is what's underneath, not what's on top. We want to promote a positive mental attitude about baldness." He claimed his group didn't know or care how many bald men there were, what caused the condition, or how to get rid of it. Headquartered in a converted service station, the BHMA had as its motto: "If you don't have it, flaunt it." To qualify for membership, all that was needed was a bald spot. Members ranged in age from 11 to 93. For $5 annual dues, the joiner got a membership card, a certificate, and the quarterly publication *Chrome Dome*. The group's only activity was an annual convention held in Morehead City in September, which featured events such as bald fishing, a bald ball, a bald banquet, and contests for the sexiest, smallest, and shiniest bald heads. The convention was "the most topless thing in America," quipped Capps.[53]

Most of the club members, Capps believed, were "pretty well-adjusted to their baldness." The group thought that "Skin is in," and they liked to say "we're proud of every hair we don't have." BHMA regularly received mail from psychologists and physicians requesting information on how it might help patients having trouble adjusting to baldness. A lot of mail came from wives, girl friends, and secretaries, telling BHMA their husband, boy friend, or boss was concerned about losing his hair but that they found it attractive. Remarked Capps, "It's a pity that people spend thousands to try to regain hair. The serious part of the club is we believe it's more important what's inside the head and heart than what's on top of the head. We're not 100 percent against toupees, hairpieces or transplants if it makes that one individual feel better. On the other hand, we feel as though America has had enough coverups."[54]

At the September 1982 convention, about 200 attendees competed for the Sexiest Bald Head, Best All Round Bald Head, Prettiest Bald Head, Smoothest Bald Head, and the Most Kissable Bald Head. Four female judges selected the winners. A pamphlet outlining membership benefits stated, "the Lord is just, the Lord is fair, He gave some brains and the others hair." Coinciding with the convention was the end of the "Rub a Bald Head Week." Capps gave out 300 to 400 certificates to women who rubbed different bald heads in town for good luck. After the one-day convention, bald Mayor Rod Dixon declared the following seven days "Bald Is Beautiful Week" in Morehead City. Capps was a member of the fourth generation in his family to go bald.[55]

At the end of the 1980s, BHMA membership had grown to 18,000 in 28 nations, although convention attendance had declined to between 50 and 100. The 1987 get-together was held in the "Bald Room" of Mrs. Willis's seafood restaurant. Dues were then $10 a year, which entitled the recipient to a "Bald Is Beautiful" lapel pin and bumper sticker and a subscription to *Chrome Dome*, then published twice a year. Members could also purchase imprinted T-shirts, special chrome dome combs (they had no teeth in the center), and hairbrushes that were more polishing cloth than bristles. By then the club had an official poem that included these lines:

On the head of us men who are bald, there's heaped a lot of abuse.
But as age advances our hair turns gray or else it turns loose.
It's a mark of distinction if upon our head we haven't any hair.
It sets us apart from all those fuzzy folks; makes us suave and debonair.[56]

Capps ran the club from a room in his company, Capps Printing and Copies, where could be found the Bald Boutique, which was jammed with caps, mugs, buttons, T-shirts, and sweatshirts. The 1988 convention was held in the Holiday Inn "Baldroom." It featured a Bald-as-a-Golf Ball Tournament as well as group sessions where baldies could talk about hair loss and how it had affected them.[57]

A journalist who attended the 1989 convention described it as "a semi-serious paen to baldness consciousness-raising. It is also the John Capps show: part evangelical revival, part cornball comedy act, part power-of-positive thinking seminar." A year earlier the company that manufactured the Helsinki Formula, which purportedly rejuvenated hair growth, wanted to set up a display at the BHMA convention site. When Capps declined, the company rented an airplane to drag a banner across the sky which read; "Real Men Don't Go Topless. Use the Formula." Morehead City officials posted a "Welcome Baldies" sign. Contests were the same as in past years, with a newer one being "Best Tanned Solar Dome." Asked if he would use a miracle cure which gave hair without pain if one were discovered, Capps said, "I wouldn't use it and I don't think the guys in our organization would do it. I don't think people want to look like everybody else, even if it's what the economy and the media want." Capps' philosophy and humor included the slogans mentioned above as well as "We don't have time for plugs, rugs, or drugs" and "Baldness is just mind over matter. It doesn't matter if the person doesn't mind."[58]

11
THIS IS NOT SNAKE OIL

You manufacture, with the aid of unguents, a false head of
hair, and your bald and dirty scalp is covered with painted
locks. There is no need to call a hairdresser for your head.
A sponge, Phoebus, would do the business better.
Martial

In the history of baldness treatments and "cures," probably none has
generated as much publicity as has the drug minoxidil. During the mid–1960s,
researchers for the pharmaceutical company Upjohn were studying antacid
compounds when they discovered that one, minoxidil, reduced the heart rate
of laboratory animals. Upjohn patented minoxidil in 1968. That same year
company researcher Dr. Charles A. Chidsey began testing minoxidil on human
subjects as a remedy for high blood pressure. In 1979, after receiving FDA
approval, Upjohn began marketing the drug under the trade name Loniten as
a prescription drug for easing severe high blood pressure. Minoxidil is a potent
vasodilator. Its principal effect is to make the arteries more elastic so they will
dilate, reducing blood pressure. Used only in severe cases of high blood pressure when other treatments such as low-sodium diet or other drugs have
failed, Loniten was reportedly given a "low-key sendoff" by Upjohn. Minoxidil has many side effects; if uncontrolled, it could raise a person's blood pressure, cause the heart to beat faster, and cause the kidneys to retain water and
salt. Patients using Loniten usually had to take other drugs, including diuret-
ics, to counter those effects. It was those serious side effects that quickly made
Loniten only a third-line defense in the treatment of hypertension. As it was
not apparently destined to be a big money-maker for the company, Upjohn
researchers began looking at one of the less serious side effects noticed during clinical trials.[1]

Researchers stumbled on to the hair-growing properties of minoxidil
accidentally. When one bald patient developed new hair on the top of his
head in 1973, Upjohn took notice. Experimenting further, they discovered that
when the drug was applied to the skin surface around the shoulders, it caused

147

significant hair growth in three of the four volunteers it was tried on. A marked increase in hair growth was noted at the site of application, whereas no change occurred at control sites. One of the researchers who announced that finding was Dr. Gunther Kahn, director of resident training at Miami's Mount Sinai Hospital. Noting the entire body was covered with hair with most of it being practically invisible, Kahn enthusiastically stated: "The drug caused this hair to grow into the thicker, luxuriant kind.... The exciting thing is that even a bald person has this small hair on his scalp and it might be stimulated to grow with vasodilators." Patients who had taken minoxidil orally sprouted hair in unusual places. Hair follicles that had been producing pale little vellus hairs suddenly started producing dark, strong terminal hairs on the forehead, arms, legs, back, and on the scalp, a result that became known as the "werewolf" effect. "All these people with high blood pressure started looking like little monkeys," recalled one dermatologist connected with the Loniten research.[2]

Hypertension specialist Dr. Harold Schnaper from the University of Alabama Medical Center told Upjohn it had a gold mine on its hands if it could get the hair to grow just on the head. Upjohn was way ahead of him and was already trying to do just that. By 1980, company researchers were rubbing a minoxidil lotion on the heads of 40 bald inmates at the state prison in Jackson, Michigan, where the company maintained a clinic for drug testing that was not far from its headquarters in Kalamazoo, Michigan. Results from that study were described by the company as "inconclusive." Some inmates grew a little fuzz on their heads, some did not. The company was encouraged enough, however, to finance two more investigations. Two of the researchers involved in separate preliminary research were Harvard Medical School professor Dr. Howard Baden and New York City's Dr. Norman Orentreich, the hair transplant pioneer. A Baden associate said that it wasn't even necessary to advertise for volunteers, "All you have to do is whisper in the corridors that you're doing a study of male baldness and you get all the volunteers you want."[3]

Any attempt to study minoxidil in relative obscurity ended in December 1980, when the *New England Journal of Medicine* published a letter from Dr. Anthony Zappacosta. Based on just one patient he had treated for kidney failure and hypertension, Zappacosta praised minoxidil for its hair-growing properties. According to the letter, the 38-year-old patient, balding since the age of 20, regrew hair on bald areas as thick and as dense as that on nonbald parts of his head. After 8 weeks, the new hair was ½ inch long. Many years later *U.S. News & World Report* claimed that Zappacosta's letter to the medical journal "inspired Upjohn to concoct a lotion for the scalp and test it widely." The company was already doing just that before the letter appeared. According to one account, an anonymous caller telephoned the *Detroit News* to tip the paper to Zappacosta's letter. That account also noted that Zappacosta stated that when the patient stopped taking the medication, his hair reverted to what it had been—the baldness recommenced. In fact Zappacosta's letter said nothing about what happened if treatment was discontinued. After the *Detroit News* ran the story, it was picked up by the Associated Press and distributed to other newspapers around the country. Upjohn got a lot of publicity. At that time no one knew just how minoxidil supposedly grew hair. It did not grow hair on all bald heads. Doctors who had observed test subjects disagreed about the quality of the hair grown. Some physicians reported it was so fine it was "barely visible." Asked about the possibilities of minoxidil being a baldness cure, Upjohn president William N. Hubbard cautiously said, "There's a big difference between being able to grow some hair and curing baldness." Company spokesman Joseph Heywood observed, "We're not optimistic about this." Another spokesman said: "We really don't take this very seriously. We just feel we owe it to the bald men of the world to give it a shot."[4]

For 1980, Upjohn earned $170 million on sales of $1.8 billion—up 14 percent from 1979—making it the tenth largest pharmaceutical maker in the U.S. In the first few months of 1981, the price of the company's stock moved from $61 to $69 a share. Nevertheless, analysts considered Upjohn's prospects for the coming few years only moderately good in an industry where the outlook was excellent because an aging population was good for the drug business. Minoxidil's sales were then estimated at $1 to $5 million a year, a tiny fraction of Upjohn's total. Obviously though, its potential was enormous.[5]

Soon Upjohn had around 20 separate, full-fledged studies underway around the country, at a total cost estimated at $3 million. Each of these studies used about 100 volunteers. The leader of one study was Washington Hospital Center dermatology department chairman Dr. Thomas Nigra. The number of bald men desperate for hair could be seen from the response Nigra got when he first put out a call for volunteers. He recalled: "All of the trunk lines—40 lines coming into the institution—were blocked for two or three days. Even emergency calls couldn't get through.... I was not a popular man around here." His office also received around 5,000 written inquiries. That was at the beginning of 1981. Five months later he was still getting three or four calls a day on a special line. In an enthusiastic statement about the drug, Nigra said: "Unquestionably there is promise in that it works. The question is, 'How often does it work, and who will really get a good result?' We're seeing successful hair regrowth." Volunteers were required to apply solutions of minoxidil to their scalp twice a day. They also had to report to the hospital on a regular basis. Groundwork had by this point been well laid for Upjohn. Already it had been noted that minoxidil would not work on everybody, but nobody could tell who would and would not possibly benefit. It would be expensive, and you had to apply the drug for the rest of your life or the baldness returned. Minoxidil had all the makings of a wonder drug, except that it was not then available over-the-counter or even as a prescription drug for baldness treatment. In a moment of candor, Nigra added: "A decision has already been made by

Upjohn to manufacture the drug. We're doing the study, but they already know it works. We know it works. They wouldn't be spending all this money if they didn't feel they had something successful. I think we're going to end up saying that almost everybody that's bald probably deserves a trial on this before they give up. That's a little bit premature, but that's my impression." So much for the idea that something had to be proved scientifically and so much for the idea of objective researchers.[6]

Another study was done at Stanford University. It was led by dermatologists David Wilkinson and Elaine Orenberg. When they put out the call for volunteers, they received 6,000 applicants, either in person or in writing. One was from an airplane pilot who volunteered to fly in every month from anywhere in the country. A secretary phoned to see if her boss qualified. One man wrote, "I have been bald for six years and am having problems getting work because people think I'm in some crazy kind of cult." Wilkinson observed: "Perhaps we should have foreseen the response. We seemed to have touched a nerve." Another man hoping to be selected as a volunteer was 80 years old. Yet another man, who lived at 7,000 foot-high Lake Tahoe, wrote to suggest the study be expanded to investigate the effects of high altitude on hair fall-out. Of course, he thought the subject for that aspect should be himself. One letter arrived addressed only to the "Stanford Hair Growing Department." It said, "Please send that special ointment for people getting bald on top. Hurry!" Included as subjects were men aged 19 to 49, but only those whose bald spot could be covered with a silver dollar were eligible to be included.[7]

A third study was headed by Dr. James Storer of Tulane University. When his study was announced, he was also swamped with calls and letters. He said: "I arranged the letters into piles, interesting, normal and kinky! I've had lots of parents write for their children, lots of women whose fiancés or husbands are thinning, men of every age. I've had hundreds of letters from servicemen. I've even started to get Christmas cards from these people." Patients at all centers were divided into three groups for the year-long studies. One group received a three percent minoxidil solution, the second group was on a two percent solution, while the third group received a placebo for four months before being switched to the three percent minoxidil for the final eight months. To determine hair growth, hairs were counted in a 1-inch diameter circle at the crown of the head. Those in the study were promised that they would be kept supplied with minoxidil after the study ended and until FDA approval was granted. Cost of the minoxidil solution used in the study was reported to be $27.50 for a bottle that lasted three to four weeks. Of his early results, Storer commented: "The majority of patients have had some change in hair count. But in terms of cosmetically acceptable results, I'd say Minoxidil will work for 40 to 60 percent of patients. It depends on age, degree of baldness, duration of baldness, overall health. I think long term baldness will be hard to correct. I doubt this will be a solution for everybody." One patient in the study, Stephen Willey, who had 268 hairs on his 1-inch circle at the start of the experiment, reportedly had 558 hairs after 12 months. Storer was also using minoxidil on his own head.[8]

Nigra released the results of his study in December 1984. Of the 91 men and 5 women in his group, 9 people developed allergic side effects such as redness or burning of the scalp and had to drop out. According to Nigra the treatment had no effect on 6 subjects, but the hair count at least doubled on 27 people. Of that latter number 6 people had excellent results, 14 had good results, and 7 had modest results. No one in the study lost any hair, reportedly. Commented Nigra, who called the results "cosmetically acceptable": "This is only a progress report at one year. One has to think in terms of five years before one can make a significant statement." That is the length of time a hair grows. Overall, 81 of the subjects showed an increase in the hair count for the one-inch circle. There were no side effects. Nigra regarded minoxidil as therapy, not a cure, noting "You must continue to use it or your hair will fall out." Baldness treatment, he thought, had "been left to charlatans and quacks and these people have preyed on the emotional needs and hopes of patients. But we really haven't had anything to offer.... Perhaps in the near future we will." Upjohn then had about 2,200 volunteers participating in experiments at 27 centers. Company spokesperson Jan Aufderheide said, "the company remains cautiously optimistic." Minoxidil was used in two and three percent solutions because Upjohn had determined that strengths of five percent or less had no effect on blood pressure. While Norman Orentreich was involved in early, preliminary Upjohn research, by December 1984 he had withdrawn because he found the minoxidil results in hair-growing to be "generally disappointing."[9]

During 1985, Upjohn received thousands of calls and letters from people who had heard of minoxidil. "They want to know if there really is such a drug, does it really work, where they can get it," explained a spokesperson. Analysts were then predicting minoxidil could produce $1 billion in gross yearly sales for Upjohn in the early 1990s. It was a projection based on a 24 percent incidence of baldness, giving a potential market of 40 million Americans with 8.5 percent of that target group expected to purchase the drug. During the experiments, 85 percent of the subjects indicated they would remain on the drug even if they had to pay for it. At an estimated cost then of $85 a month for the drug therapy, the yearly cost would exceed $1,000. Wall Street was unanimous in believing the product would be important for Upjohn. Oppenheimer and Company analyst Ronald M. Nordmann stated that "Topical minoxidil for male pattern baldness could become one of the largest selling drugs in the world and transform Upjohn into one of the fastest growing major domestic drug companies." Total sales for Upjohn in 1984 were $2.18 billion, with net earnings of $173.3 million. Upjohn stock started 1985 trading at slightly under $70, by mid–April it was $80, and one month later it stood at $110. Nordmann believed that once minoxidil was approved by the FDA it could generate $500 million in annual sales for Upjohn, with a net income of $204 million. In the summer of 1985, Upjohn announced it was investing $23 million in a plant to manufacture minoxidil.[10]

The company composition patent on minoxidil expired in 1984. That year Upjohn obtained a use patent for grinding up minoxidil tablets and applying the drug topically in a liquid or paste form to restore hair. This gave the company another 17 years of patent protection. Upjohn vice president Lawrence C. Hoff warned in June 1985 that his company was prepared to sue pharmacists who decided to use a generic form of minoxidil to prepare their own antibaldness drug, pending approval of Regaine by the FDA. Regaine was the name Upjohn had by then chosen to call its product. With the expiration of the Loniten patent, any company could manufacture its own minoxidil-based hypertension drug and market it thusly. At that time minoxidil had not been approved as a baldness treatment and could not be marketed as such. Upjohn, however, had no objection to pharmacists recommending Loniten for use by bald men; it just didn't want any other company's antihypertension product used in such a fashion. The use of Loniten to treat baldness was then widespread.[11]

During a June 1984 meeting of the International Congress for Hair Replacement Surgery in Manhattan, minoxidil was mentioned because a number of doctors had been prescribing it for use on the scalp. One doctor mentioned he was getting hair growth from minoxidil; another said his tests had failed. The latter physician asked for a show of hands by those who had tried the method "and several dozen arms went up." Then he asked for a show of hands by those who had observed hair improvement "and only one hand was raised," reported the *New York Times*. None of these doctors were associated with Upjohn or its official studies. All were independently prescribing recompounded Loniten. Another reporter claimed that although minoxidil had not yet been approved for treating baldness and could not be marketed for that purpose, it was nevertheless being widely used everywhere. Every dermatologist she spoke to either prescribed it or knew of others who did. Said Columbia Presbyterian Medical Center dermatologist Vincent DeLeo, "It is widely available and physicians are using it." When a physician prescribed an approved drug, such as Loniten, what the doctor, pharmacist, and patient did with it was their business. It was not illegal for a physician to instruct a pharmacist to grind up the tablets, extract the active drug, and make up a lotion to apply to the scalp. Some New York physicians were providing supplies to patients for $150 to $200 a month. Dr. Michael Lorin Reed, assistant clinical professor of dermatology at the New York University Medical Center, remarked he had "at least several hundred people on the drug right now" and there were a "zillion people prescribing minoxidil for hair growth.[12]

Upjohn spokespeople were quick to point out that the company did not promote topical application of the drug. The company must have liked the sales figures, however. In 1983, sales of minoxidil were $7 million; the next year they were $15 million. Estimates were that 1985 sales would be $30 million. Stock analyst Ronald Nordmann remarked, "The growth is clearly not coming from the hypertension market." Dr. Reed explained that to convert Loniten to a baldness remedy, 180 tablets were crushed and mixed with water, alcohol, and propylene glycol. That produced 2 ounces of hair lotion, enough for a one-month supply. The price through Reed was $100 for those two ounces.[13]

Dr. Robert Stern randomly selected members of the American Academy of Dermatology and sent 900 of them (1 in 6) a questionnaire to see how many were prescribing minoxidil during the March to August 1985 period. Of the 552 responses he received, 400 doctors (72 percent) indicated they prescribed topical minoxidil for hair loss during that period. Overall, 9 percent of the responding dermatologists were responsible for over half of the patients treated during the period. Extrapolating his findings, Stern estimated American dermatologists were prescribing topical minoxidil to over 100,000 patients per year. While he asked no specific questions about the drug's effectiveness or cost, 21 respondents provided spontaneous comments. Fifteen of them expressed a belief that the drug didn't work, four indicated the main difficulty was its high cost, and two indicated that both high cost and limited effectiveness made the use of the drug questionable.[14]

Late in 1985 the FDA stepped in to warn that the antihypertension drug minoxidil should not be used to treat baldness, except in controlled studies. The agency asked the cooperation of medical professionals in not supplying patients with recompounded versions of the drug before controlled studies by Upjohn were done and evaluated by the FDA. Labeling on Loniten warned of potentially adverse side effects, including increased heart rate, difficulty in breathing, upper body pains, dizziness, fainting, nausea and vomiting, and hair growth. Due to those side effects, the baldness trials run by Upjohn excluded anyone with hypertension, heart, kidney, liver, or endocrine disease and anyone over 49 years of age. The agency asked Upjohn to change Loniten's labeling to specifically warn against recompounding for hair regeneration. Although the FDA warned that commercialization of the recompounded drug could be illegal, it was all bluff. There were no effective legal steps which could be taken. Upjohn did put a warning label on Loniten cautioning against its use on the skin. The company had been testing ads in 1985 to appear nationally offering to sell topical minoxidil that had been recompounded from Loniten tablets as a baldness treatment, but after the FDA complaints, the company dropped the idea. Upjohn still had to face the FDA to get its approval to market Regaine.[15]

Some companies did cash in on minoxidil publicity by marketing it themselves. Upjohn claimed they infringed on its patent, while the FDA charged they made drug claims under the guise of cosmetic usage. One firm took out a full-page ad in *Playboy* advertising its product. Upjohn filed suit against Riahom, which was marketing a minoxidil-based product called Rivixil.[16]

In the twelve-month Upjohn study conducted at Duke University that was led by Dr. Elise A. Olsen and involved 126 subjects, 72 thought they had achieved moderate hair growth and two thought they had complete hair regrowth. Dermatologists conducting the test, however, rated only 29 of the subjects as having moderate hair growth. As with all the other studies, no reason was given for the failure to continue the control group for the full 12 months—a flagrant violation of the basic principles of experimental design. Twenty-seven subjects dropped out for various reasons. Of the 16 who quit due to lack of interest or from a perceived lack of efficacy, 12 were receiving an active solution. Their data, of course, was not included in the final results. During the monthly hair count in the one-inch circle, a count was taken of vellus hairs, terminal hairs, and all hairs combined. It was supposedly a double-blind experiment. Concerning this one study, the experimenters concluded, "The results indicate that topical minoxidil can increase terminal hair growth in early male pattern baldness." However, they also admitted, "The placebo group had a slightly longer average duration of hair loss relative to the active medication groups which corresponds to a larger number of subjects with a more advanced pattern baldness relative to the 2% and 3% topical minoxidil groups." In other words, the control group members had more baldness and had been that way for a longer period of time than the treatment groups. The researchers did add that those differences were "compensated" for in statistical analysis. After four months the placebo group was not significantly different in hair count from the two percent group, and the latter group was not significantly different from the three percent group. The three percent group had a significantly greater increase in hair count than the placebo group after those four months, however. The placebo group had a greater increase in vellus hairs than the two active groups, while it had a lower increase in terminal hair count than both of the active groups. All of these were reasons to continue, not abort, the placebo group. Its members were growing hair. While there was on average a twofold increase in the total hair count in the two active groups, the researchers commented, "Even a doubling in the number of vellus, intermediate, or short terminal hairs in an area of pronounced hair loss may not lead to a cosmetically acceptable degree of hair growth." Nonetheless, Olsen stated: "We can affirm that topical minoxidil does stimulate hair growth in male pattern baldness…. Topical minoxidil is the first medication proved to have a positive effect on the course of early male pattern baldness."[17]

Upjohn vice president Lawrence Hoff stated that the Duke study showed "a majority" of those who did not grow hair after using minoxidil nevertheless stopped losing their hair after they started using the drug. He added that of the studies completed till then, results showed one third of the volunteers grew normal hair, a third grew hair like that of a baby, and one third showed no growth. Hoff noted that men had cried and offered bribes in an effort to be included in one of Upjohn's trials: "We always thought the female was vain. They can't hold a candle to bald men." In December 1985, Upjohn formally asked the FDA to approve the sale of Regaine Topical Solution.[18]

Upjohn released more complete results in April 1986. At the 27 centers where minoxidil was tested, 1,833 of the 2,236 subjects completed the experiment. All but 50 were men. The company decided the two percent solution was optimum to balance benefits with risks. In that group, 619 finished the study. Upjohn spokesman Bruce Berger said 32 percent of the patients grew new nonvellus hair at four months, 61 percent at 8 months, 76 percent at 12 months. Biopsies of skin samples showed "A significant increase in number of hair follicles and growth of additional hair," said the company. Twice daily treatments of Regaine were then estimated to cost potential users $1,200 per year.[19]

Late in April 1986, Upjohn issued a press release in which it said that minoxidil had been found in tests on humans to help reverse male baldness without major side effects. Company officials allowed the FDA to screen that statement at a meeting a few days before it was released. Upjohn failed to respond fully to agency concerns expressed at that meeting, however. As a result, after the release was issued, the FDA publicly attacked Upjohn for exaggerating the safety and effectiveness of minoxidil. The agency also charged the press release violated federal drug law by making false and misleading statements about minoxidil. It asked Upjohn to stop distributing the news release but took no other action against the company. FDA executive William Purvis argued the press release "exaggerates the efficacy of the topical use of minoxidil solution through selective data reporting, omission of certain efficacy results and minimization of adverse information about the drug." As to the issue of safety, the agency argued that "full safety and toxicity issues for chronic topical use have not yet been fully evaluated or elucidated." Also attacked was Upjohn's failure to disclose that studies of the drug produced conflicting results. Some studies, said the FDA, found minoxidil about as effective as a placebo in treating baldness, whole others found the placebo "to have better results than the drug itself in clinical trials." When Upjohn issued its press release, company stock rose $8.50 in a single day. When the FDA released its accusations, the stock fell $9 in one day, rebounding a little to close off $6.50 on that day. In response to the FDA, Upjohn defended its claims but said it would comply with the agency request to cease distribution of the press release. Defending itself, the company claimed it issued the release because it feared failure to do so would run afoul of federal securities law intended to lessen insider trading. Those laws encouraged companies to make public as quickly as possible any information that might be considered material to investors, to prevent insiders from having an edge in the stock market.[20]

In conjunction with questioning dermatologists to see how many were prescribing Loniten for baldness, Robert Stern assessed some of the Upjohn studies. In one he considered, only 14 percent of the subjects had an increase of more than 130 terminal hairs per square inch in bald areas. While that was clinically substantial improvement, it was still only about 5 percent of the density of terminal hair in a normal scalp. The average adult scalp had around 3,000 hair follicles per square inch. As for the Olsen study, Stern noted her best group averaged no more than a two percent regrowth of lost hair. He concluded, "When only patients who continue therapy for at least one year are considered response rates for cosmetically acceptable hair regrowth for patients with androgenic alopecia is almost certainly less than 25%, and probably 15% or less."[21]

Free publicity accrued to Upjohn from more and more sources. The comic strips "Cathy" and "Doonesbury" both took note of minoxidil in the summer of 1986. ABC's television program *Nightline* gave it a more serious look.[22]

Elaine Orenberg was one of the researchers who conducted the minoxidil test at Stanford. To attract volunteers, she asked the Stanford Medical Center News Bureau to place a request for volunteers in the student newspaper. That request was also released to the local media. Remarked Orenberg, "Within one hour, every phone line into Dermatology was jammed. We received more than a thousand calls within two weeks." It was a similar experience for Dr. Ronald Savin, who conducted a study at Yale. He noted: "My phone went absolutely crazy. My regular patients couldn't get through for about a month. Men called from all over the country dying to volunteer." One man who was accepted into the Yale study was John Varrone of New Haven, who said: "Losing my hair was sort of like cancer. Once it started, it wouldn't stop." After he started to go bald at 17, he tried everything: "I'd drive all the way to New York once a week to get injections in my scalp. Nothing worked."[23]

Norman Orentreich remarked in 1986: "I prescribe minoxidil.... But I'm not a fan of it. It's not a 'breakthrough.' At best it's a 'mini-breakthrough.' My results have not been as good as some other researchers."[24]

Business analysts continued to see a rosy future for Upjohn, whose stock price moved from $70 to $133 a share in 1985 before settling back to $90 in 1986. After the Canadian government approved the sale of the product in 1986, the stock price jumped up again. Journalist Adam Smith explained that Wall Street loved Regaine because it didn't work on everybody but nobody knew who was in the chosen group until they used it. It was to be a prescription drug after approval, which meant it would have the authority of the medical profession behind it. In addition, customers had to use it forever. If they stopped, any gain would be lost. Regaine would be expensive and very profitable. Concluded Smith, "We are on the cusp of a revolution that, in crude dollar terms, is going to rank somewhere between the Pill and the hair-coloring revolution for women." One of the few cautious business analysts was David Saks, a vice president of the Wall Street firm Morgan, Olmstead, Kennedy & Garner, Inc., who said, "The test results mean that it's not snake oil, but it's not a wonder drug either."[25]

The FDA misgivings about the original name Upjohn picked—Regaine—caused the firm to rename it Rogaine in 1986. The product remains known as Rogaine in the U.S. and Canada. Everywhere else, however, Upjohn continued to call the product Regaine. One FDA official thought the original name implied a promise of total efficacy. When he threatened to make an issue of it, Upjohn backed down. Explained a spokesman, "We wanted the FDA to concentrate on efficacy and safety and not get hung up on the name."[26]

Doubts about the product and attacks on Upjohn tactics were prominent early in 1987 as the time for an FDA approval decision neared. From the U.K., the staunchly probusiness publication the *Economist* was surprisingly against the product receiving approval, claiming, "it will be setting a dangerous precedent." It feared it would be the first of a breed of cosmetics that worked not by merely coating the skin but by attacking the body's chemistry. "Until now, people who were not ill but who took drugs were either hypochondriacs or addicts. Regaine is a drug for people who have nothing wrong with them." Oral contraceptives were conceded to be in the same category, but in that case the magazine believed health and social benefits outweighed any possible side effects. The *Economist* worried approval for the product would open the way for many more "life-enhancers" to hit the market, such as new slimming pills and memory pills. Although the idea to sell Regaine by prescription only seemed like a "wise precaution" at first glance, the *Economist* explained it meant the product would not have to meet the far stricter safety demanded of products available over-the-counter. If it had to be approved, along with other "life-enhancers," the magazine urged these products should be sold for what they really were: "cosmetics. And, as powerful drugs, they should meet the more stringent tests set for over-the-counter markets."[27]

Upjohn's tactics were attacked by the Public Citizen Health Research Group, a consumer organization which accused the company of trying to "make bald people feel insecure." Dr. Sidney Wolfe, head of the organization, claimed Upjohn had been paving the way for the sale of Rogaine to the public by issuing press releases under the letterhead of an organization it had formed, Hair Awareness Information and Research (HAIR). One such release was titled "Psychological Aspects of Hair Loss." It asked, "Can an emerging bald spot or even a noticeably receding hairline, damage your ability to get along with others, influence your chances of obtaining a job or even interfere with your job performance?" Quoted in the release was H. Hugh Floyd, Jr., a sociology professor at the University of New Orleans, who said, "Losing one's hair can have tremendous psychological influence and definitely affect self-confidence and self-assurance." Wolfe argued that Upjohn was engaged in a "sleazy, shameless pre-promotional campaign to make bald people feel as bad as possible" to encourage them to use Rogaine. Company spokeswoman Jan Aufderheide said the campaign was not negative. "It was informational, not promotional," she said. "This is a common practice to inform and educate the public." Judged by letters and phone calls Upjohn received, Rogaine generated more consumer interest than any other product in the 101-year company history.[28]

On March 16, 1987, the FDA's Dermatologic Drugs Advisory Committee held a four-hour hearing on Rogaine at the agency's Rockville, Maryland, headquarters. Described as having a circuslike atmosphere, the hearing was attended by several hundred people including as many as 40 financial analysts. Seven TV cameras were present. It was perhaps the largest turnout the FDA ever had for a drug hearing. At its conclusion the five doctors on the advisory panel unanimously recommended approval of Rogaine as "safe and effective," while warning the drug was not a cure-all and that it had been shown to be effective for only a small percentage of those tested. Additionally, the panel members urged the FDA to require the company to rewrite labeling for Rogaine that they thought overstated its effectiveness. Panel chairman Robert Stern commented, "I really don't consider it a panacea or a major medical break-through." While the FDA was not bound by the recommendation, an FDA official, Dr. Carnot C. Evans, conceded, "It's unusual that we wouldn't go along with" the committee recommendation.[29]

Upjohn testified that their studies "indicated that 40 percent of those surveyed believed they had 'moderate or dense' new hair growth since beginning treatment." Note the use of the word *believe*. Stern argued that when the placebo effect was discounted, "We're talking about 10% to 15% difference" between the two groups. It was that percentage that Stern then believed might benefit. The panel heavily criticized Upjohn for switching all the placebo groups to an active treatment after four months, leaving the experiment with no control group. The panel noted that the four-month stage was "a point at which the difference for 'moderate-to-dense' hair growth was not statistically significant between treated and placebo groups." Trying to defend the company's action, Dr. Richard L. De Villez, Upjohn's clinical research associate manager, said the company switched the men to minoxidil because it thought it would be unfair to keep them on a placebo "while they continued to lose hair and while others who were taking the drug were experiencing hair growth." De Villez added these were "ethical and practical reasons." As Stern and others pointed out, however, the placebo groups were growing hair at that stage, as much as the active groups in some cases. Although the FDA panel voted for approval, it was less than enthusiastic. When Stern asked his colleagues if they could agree that there was a consensus that Rogaine caused hair growth, even if the amount was uncertain, one panel member replied, "moderate. Or infrequent, I don't know which." Another responded, "I don't know the answer to that. Minimum." Upjohn admitted the product worked best on younger men, those with a briefer duration of baldness, and those with a smaller area of baldness. Admitting it had no idea how or why minoxidil worked, Upjohn also conceded that it worked only on the crown of the head; it had no effect on baldness at the front of the head.[30]

Perhaps the main reason for recommending approval was the fact that Rogaine was widely available both on the black market in the U.S. and abroad, where it had been approved in 13 countries and was on the shelves in 7 of those nations. Many American baldies were buying Rogaine in Canada. Panel member Dr. Neal S. Penneys said that "one of the strongest arguments for approval of this medication" was its then wide availability. As a whole the panel said, "Part of the reason for recommending approval of the drug was to shut off this underground market." Stern said he would prefer the drug, no matter how effective or ineffective it was, to be administered in "well-formulated doses." He worried that excessive doses could cause serious side effects for people with heart problems. Rogaine had no serious side effects, declared the panel. Business analysts were still enthusiastic. Merrill Lynch & Co. analyst Richard Vietor said Rogaine could be "one of the biggest drug introductions in pharmaceutical history." Paine Webber Inc. analyst Ronald Nordmann optimistically estimated worldwide sales of $1.5 billion by 1990 for Rogaine.[31]

When the *New York Times* editorialized about the approval recommendation, it noted Stern's estimate that only about 15 percent of users would benefit, compared to Upjohn's estimate of 40 percent. The editor then urged the FDA, if it was to approve Rogaine, to "insist the low chances of success be clearly stated" on the product's packaging. "Otherwise millions of bald Americans will be scalped again," he wrote.[32]

Even more pessimistic was the British medical journal the *Lancet*. Writer Anton DeGroot looked at several of the Upjohn studies in his article. In the study by De Villez, who was by then an Upjohn employee, 10 percent of the subjects were judged "excellent" by the number of hairs on the target area, although the length of hairs was not reported. That "excellent" group had an average of only 31 more hairs per square cm. Since the mean density of hair follicles in the adult scalp is around 500 per square cm, the De Villez increase amounted to only 6 percent of the normal hair density. In the Olsen study, the group listed as having at least "moderate" improvement went from 29 hairs per square cm up to 84 hairs after 12 months on three percent minoxidil. That was about 17 percent of normal density. Counts were lower for the group on a two percent solution of the drug. In the placebo group, the increase in hair count was 16, compared to the two percent group, which had an increase of 36 hairs per square cm.[33]

None of the Upjohn studies lasted over one year. One independent study done in Italy found that 78 of 430 men had a "good" result after six months of treatment. One year later, 52 of the 78 men had lost the hair they had gained, leaving only 26 of the 430 men (six percent) still showing hair growth which the researchers considered cosmetically acceptable. Those researchers thought increased hair growth, such as it was, continued for eight to ten months, but that longer treatment yielded little further improvement. Terminal hairs became fewer between 12 and 33 months in 14 of 20 men who after 24 months switched from three percent minoxidil twice daily to once daily for the last nine months and in nine of 21 who continued twice daily applications. *Lancet* noted that in Upjohn's tests, "although the pooled data showed significant efficacy, statistical significance could not be shown in 19 centres for the mean terminal hair count and in 21 for the physicians' assessments." Although Upjohn claimed 31 percent of its subjects showed "moderate" growth and eight percent had "dense" growth, *Lancet* pointed out that dense was not defined, while moderate growth might be "mostly fluff." This magazine believed that the drug would induce a cosmetically satisfactory growth of terminal hairs in only a small percentage of users, "probably less than 10%." Elise Olsen was cited as saying "with time both patient and investigator became less optimistic about the change in hair growth over baseline." While he was not enthusiastic about seeing Rogaine on the market at all, De Groot thought if it was to be available it should only be a prescription drug because "The only way of preventing exploitation of consumers may be to control promotion of the product prescriptively, and more strictly than has so far been envisaged for any prescription drug."[34]

Around the time of the FDA hearing, bootleg minoxidil was indeed widely available. Upjohn appealed to the International Trade Commission in Washington to stop imports of minoxidil by 20 American companies and six firms in foreign nations. Upjohn argued its patent rights were being violated because it was convinced this imported minoxidil was being sold for the treatment of baldness. Brainerd Chemical company of Tulsa acknowledged selling minoxidil. Brainerd president Tom Kaye said the company bought it overseas as a powder and then repackaged it in small quantities. "We have sold the product with no intended use," Kaye explained. "The raw minoxidil powder is not covered by any patent whatsoever. They do have a valid patent for the hair growth, depending upon who you talk to. But nobody has really challenged that substantially." In a separate action, Upjohn filed a lawsuit in Dallas to stop the treatment of baldness by a Dallas clinic that was allegedly using minoxidil.[35]

In April 1986, FDA officials collected samples of products and literature from J. Coburn, Inc., in West Palm Beach, Florida. The company made a product called Rivixil for the Riahom Corporation, based in Jupiter, Florida. Analysis showed the product, which contained minoxidil, claimed to stimulate hair growth. Brochures included statements such as "For a Fuller, Thicker Head of Hair" and "See Your Hair Reborn." Rivixil was described as a

European antibaldness cosmetic. At the request of the FDA, U.S. marshals seized 608 kits and 97 bottles of Rivixil at J. Coburn and made seizures at other hair-treatment facilities around the country. In all, 2,355 kits with a value of $353,200 were seized. All were destroyed.[36]

Another company cashing in was Future Marketing & Associates of Canoga Park, California, which was selling a hair restoration product called Minox-a-gro. Distributed in California and Texas, each kit contained one bottle of shampoo and one bottle labeled "MINOX-A-GRO action plus +++ Homeopathic Alopecia and Thinning Hair." FDA officials learned of this outfit when an inspector received some Minox-a-gro literature anonymously. A pharmacist reported the company told him the product contained two percent minoxidil. On analysis the product was found to contain 0.6 percent minoxidil. The FDA charged the company with marketing a new drug which had not been approved by the agency. On November 7, 1986, U.S. marshals seized 29 kits, which were later destroyed.[37]

Washington, D.C., journalist John Sansing noted that in his city the names of doctors willing to provide the drug were passed along. Sansing visited an area dermatologist who was willing to supply it at $75 for a two-week supply. Of his 17 patients who had tried it, the doctor detected some fuzz on six men, nothing else. He was not enthusiastic about it and did not encourage Sansing to try it. At the Cleveland Hair Center, which specialized in transplants, there were about 40 patients in programs using minoxidil, at a cost of $430 for three months. Additionally, the Washington Hospital Center had 300 patients paying $1,500 a year for the drug and check-ups.[38]

Upjohn was exploring foreign markets as early as 1983, when company officials had discussions in England with the Committee on Safety of Medicines, a group which determined whether a product required a prescription or was available over-the-counter as a cosmetic. The company was urging that it be released as a prescription-only product because, said company official Dr. Hazel Hinchley: "We are worried that the drug will be exploited by fringe cosmetic companies on the black market if its use is not restricted to medical conditions only…. We think the drug will have to be sold as a prescription product, not a cosmetic. But it would probably be made available for normal male pattern baldness by private prescription because it is difficult to see why the health service should pay." At that time Upjohn had no tests completed at all, except for the Jackson State Prison results. Nevertheless, the London *Sunday Times* spoke of the company as manufacturers of "a drug which cures baldness."[39]

In Canada the federal government approved the prescription sale of Rogaine on September 5, 1986. After it had been on sale in that country for six months, at a cost of $45 a month in U.S. currency, Dr. Alastair McLeod, secretary-treasurer of the Canadian Dermatological Association, commented: "It is hard to say there has been a hell of a lot of hair growing in Canada. None of the people I have prescribed it for has noticed anything growing yet." He added, "What is turning people off is the fact they have to use this for the rest of their lives." Upjohn declined to disclose Canadian sales figures. Toronto dermatologist Howard Bargman said he had never seen a new drug advertised to doctors so extensively in medical publications.[40]

Belgium became the first European Community country to license the drug for baldness. On February 5, 1987, Regaine Topical Solution was officially launched in Brussels. On hand for the occasion were senior company Belgian and American medical staff with a pile of charts and studies. One was De Villez, who warned the product would not grow hair in every case and said this would leave those users who experienced absolutely no gain with all "the emotional trauma, anxiety, frustration and rage" that apparently accompanied hair loss. Available on prescription only, a one-month supply of Regaine in Belgium was priced at about $52.[41]

Britain finally approved the prescription sale of Regaine in March 1988. The cost was about £30 per month. The approving committee determined the drug had no effect whatsoever on women. Upjohn estimated a market of 8 million balding men in Britain. It was not available through the National Health Service, which meant users had to pay the full cost themselves.[42]

In some countries such as the Bahamas, the drug was available over-the-counter. Advertising was considerably less subtle in such areas. Upjohn signs proclaimed "End Baldness Now" in hotel lobbies in the Bahamas.[43]

Other companies tried desperately to get a drug of their own, seeing all the publicity Upjohn was receiving and the potential profits. Dr. Thomas Nigra began a study with the drug viprostol in the summer of 1985. That drug was produced by American Cyanamid's Lederle Laboratories. In its rush to get it to market, Lederle was looking at ways of avoiding time-consuming back-up studies but getting the drug released OTC while claiming it had growth properties. Early in March 1987, a writer reported that Viprostol had "failed in its initial clinical trial to show a difference from the placebo." Lederle was said to be trying the drug with other test groups. Nothing more was heard from it.[44]

Another large pharmaceutical company was studying the diuretic drug diazoxide, which was used to treat hypertension. A smaller Los Angeles–based firm, Chantal Pharmaceutical Corp., had obtained FDA permission to start human testing of cyoctol in December 1986. Supposedly the drug blocked androgenic hormones. In September 1989, the Squibb unit of Bristol-Myers Squibb Co. acquired the U.S. rights for the drug cyoctol from Chantal. A couple of months later results from a small study done on 32 men with that drug was reported. Supposedly the active group experienced hair growth similar to that found in the early studies of minoxidil. Nothing more was heard from cyoctol.[45]

In 1992, Merck & Co. announced that its drug Proscar, used for shrinking enlarged prostate glands, grew hair on bald men's heads. A year later the company announced it was still testing the drug's supposed hair-growing properties. Around the same time another company announced it had a copper-containing peptide drug called Tricomin which it said could grow hair on bald heads. The company was looking for financial backing to develop the drug. Then there was the naturally occurring enzyme aromatase which was said to "enhance" hair growth.[46]

In the summer of 1987, journalist John Sansing, editor of the *Washingtonian* magazine, wrote of his experience of being one of the 100 people in Upjohn's minoxidil test at Washington Hospital Center in 1983–84. After writing an article on baldness in 1983, he had got a call inviting him to participate in a study. He laughed and declined, but as he explained, "When my wife heard about the opportunity, she didn't laugh, so I decided to try it." Every morning and night he applied the solution; once a month he reported to the center for inspection. When the study was all over one year later, Sansing admitted, "I am an minoxidil failure." During the monthly hair counting, he found a constantly changing array of lab technicians doing the counting. At the end of each inspection, he was asked if he thought he had grown any hair that month. All subjects were informed that after they reached the four-month stage, the placebo group would be switched to a three percent minoxidil solution. This meant that the study was no longer blind after the four months had passed. Every subject then knew he was receiving minoxidil, as did the researchers. That was another serious breach of experimental design principles, which required a control group to the end to be run as a double-blind with neither researchers nor subjects aware of which specific individuals were in the placebo and active groups. Sansing could never see any change in the hair of his waiting-room companions during those monthly visits. Seventy-five men remained in this test when the study ended. Upjohn had promised that after the study each patient could continue to receive minoxidil at no charge until FDA approval was granted. Funding for the physical exams ended after the one year, however, so in order to keep receiving the drug for free, patients had to start paying about $600 a year for medical services. Sansing quit the program.[47]

On August 17, 1988, the FDA approved the sale of Rogaine. Dean Witter Reynolds analyst David Bartash said the product's success would depend on how Upjohn marketed a cosmetic product that still required a doctor's prescription. "It will be make or break depending on how effective the advertising is," he stated. Bartash estimated U.S. sales of Rogaine would be $40 million in 1988, climbing to $125 million in 1989, while worldwide sales would be $60 million in 1988, rising to $200 million in 1989. Merrill Lynch analyst Richard Vietor expected worldwide sales of $80 to $90 million in 1988, $200 million in 1989. He thought sales could reach $600 million worldwide in five years. Upjohn's total sales in 1987 were $2.52 billion. Rogaine was then on the market in 36 other countries and had been approved for marketing in a total of 45 nations. Analysts expected U.S. sales to account for more than half of Rogaine's worldwide sales.[48]

Some observers predicted a slower start. Herman K. Shah of Nomura Securities said, "The takeoff is going to be somewhat slower than many people are predicting." Drexel Burnham Lambert's David B. Lippman noted: "It is an unprecedented type of product, basically a prescription cosmetic. People are not keeling over dying from baldness." Ronald Nordmann of Paine Webber saw a market of 55 million prospective users in the U.S. adding, "The decisive element could well be how much women use Rogaine. Men are not big cosmetic users." To that point the company had not publicly mentioned directing Rogaine to women, but it soon would.[49]

When Rogaine was approved, Robert Stern noted that when Rogaine was used for more than a year, "men gradually continued going bald, although the drug apparently slows the hair loss. Over the long term Nature's effects are probably stronger than Rogaine." Stern also questioned some of the studies because they were not double-blinded: "All the patients were using Rogaine and they knew it. As a result there could be a greater tendency for the researchers to believe that they were witnessing hair growth." One of the original volunteers was Jeff Mulanax, one of 128 male participants at the University of California at San Francisco, where thirty volunteers dropped out. Said Mulanax: "I had eternal hope. Too much hope." He stayed on the drug and had been using it then for over four years. The result, he said, was "a little peach fuzz. No one has mentioned anything." He continued to use it because "frankly, it's the only hope I have." The lead dermatologist of that study, Harry Roth, commented, "This is just a holding drug." He predicted, however, that Rogaine would be popular because "men hate the idea of losing their hair." Another volunteer from the study was disk jockey Rick Shaw, who sprouted some peach fuzz. He continued to use the drug because "you have to look young in this business—think of Dick Clark." Like others, he was afraid that if he stopped using it he would quickly lose what little peach fuzz he gained. He recalled being fired once at the age of 31 for being too old.[50]

The initial strategy for its advertising campaign was for Upjohn to aim at physicians and dermatologists with ads placed in the popular trade journals. Said Upjohn spokesman Terry Reid, "The bottom line is, if physicians aren't prescribing the product, then no one's using it." The company said it had not decided yet whether to advertise directly to consumers. Federal law in the U.S. prohibited manufacturers from advertising prescription drugs by name, as did Canadian law. Upjohn skirted that law in Canada in March 1988 when the company began airing TV ads that showed a bald man on a Florida beach. The ads didn't mention the drug by name but told viewers who were worried about baldness to consult their doctors. At the same time, the company mailed piles of Rogaine promotional material to Canadian doctors and placed saturation ads in Canadian medical journals. Some consumer groups in Canada were angered by the approach, believing it violated at least the spirit of drug advertising legislation, if not the letter. Their complaint to the nongovernmental Canadian Advertising Foundation (a trade association of advertisers) was quickly rebuffed, however, when president Alan Rae commented that maybe Upjohn "did something a little crafty but we really didn't feel they had violated any law." American marketing experts were watching closely to see how Upjohn handled the U.S. introduction of Rogaine. Columbia University marketing professor Joel Steckel noted: "To a certain extent, it is the marketing opportunity of the century. The product, basically, has no competitors. About all they need to do is make the public aware that it exists. The only big no-no is not to upset the doctors. After all, they need doctors to prescribe the drug." Upjohn announced in October 1988 that it expected to sell $100 million worth of Rogaine worldwide that year.[51]

Consumer Reports published an article on baldness in September 1988. Most of it was devoted to minoxidil. Citing Upjohn's well-quoted figures from its studies that 8 percent experienced "dense" new growth of hair, 31 percent moderate growth, and 61 percent no new hair, the magazine said a closer look at the numbers "indicates that those widely publicized odds are greatly overstated." *Consumer Reports* also attacked the way the subjects were selected for the studies. Upjohn used only younger men, those with a small bald area, excluding others such as those with a large amount of baldness and those balding at the temples and front of the head. For unknown reasons, minoxidil had no effect at the temples and front of the head. Even Upjohn admitted that much. Because the subjects were not randomly selected from the balding male population, "the Upjohn study guaranteed a better result than would have been the case if men with all types of baldness had been enrolled at random," said the magazine. Also attacked was the lack of a proper control group. Robert Stern was cited as saying: "I don't think anyone can really tell you what happened at 12 months because of the lack of a placebo. Those are the facts of doing unblinded studies with an agent people think will work."[52]

Consumer Reports also mentioned the *Lancet* article, which concluded that for "90 percent or so" of men with hair loss, minoxidil "does nothing." Additionally, the American magazine looked at the only two studies in the U.S. which had followed up the drug for more than one year, both done independently of Upjohn. Both indicated some regression despite the continued use of the product. Many of the participants lost some hair they had grown during that first year. One study by dermatologist Judith Koperski at the Scripps Clinic and Research Foundation in La Jolla, California, followed 33 patients for 30 months. At the start of the study, the balding patients had an average of 119 hairs in the one-inch circle (about 1,000 hairs would be average in a normal scalp). The hair count peaked at 353 after one year, but after 30 months it had fallen to 250. A second study was done by Elise Olsen at Duke.

Twenty-one men were evaluated for a period extending from 12 months (when they finished an Upjohn study) to 33 months. Initially, at the end of the 12-month Upjohn study, Olsen had rated 15 of the men as having at least moderate regrowth of hair overall. After 33 months that appraisal applied to only one man in the group.[53]

At the end of 1988, a survey of U.S. dermatologists showed broad acceptance of minoxidil as a treatment for hair loss, with 72 percent saying they were prescribing it. The FDA estimated that $100 million was spent annually on fraudulent balding remedies; in 1987 the agency said Americans spent $24 billion on hair care. A month's supply of minoxidil then cost $50 to $85, plus the cost of periodic visits to a dermatologist. Since Rogaine treatment was considered a cosmetic service, most health insurance companies would not reimburse for it. Upjohn by then was running minoxidil tests on women.[54]

Early in 1989, Salomon Bros. analyst Robert Uhl, Jr., downgraded his estimate of 1989 Rogaine sales in the U.S. from $125 million to $80 million and downgraded his estimate for 1990 from $175 million to $110 million. Rogaine's U.S. sales in 1988 were estimated at a very disappointing $30 million. Upjohn introduced an over-the-counter product, Progaine shampoo, in February 1989. Men and women were both targeted in the ad campaign, but the product was marketed mainly to cash in on women's hair loss concerns. Progaine was a hair thickener that Upjohn hoped would benefit from its name, which sounded like Rogaine. According to a survey commissioned by the magazine *Advertising Age*, the total number of balding women was 7.2 million, or 5.6 percent of U.S. women. According to the magazine's findings, 13.3 percent of surveyed women losing their hair had sought treatment, while only 9.9 percent of balding men had done so. Women were believed to have spent most of their $24 billion annual cosmetic outlay on hair care products.[55]

With sales disappointing, Upjohn launched ads directly at U.S. consumers early in 1989. In a thirty-second TV ad, a young man in his 30s was seated on a bench with his dog. Gazing out to sea, he said: "Some things in life are as inevitable as the tide. I always thought there really wasn't anything I could do about my hair loss. Until I talked to my doctor. He diagnosed my problem. We talked about the treatment options. It's good to have the medical facts. And the fact is, there might be some hope for me." A voice-over announcer added, "If you're concerned about hair loss, see your doctor." The Upjohn logo, along with the words "See your doctor," also appeared on the screen.[56]

Turning up the psychological heat as sales stayed flat, Upjohn issued a press release with the headline "Study confirms psychological effects of hair loss." It talked of "genuine worry and distress" caused by baldness. There was also news that baldness "can cause men to be regarded by others in a somewhat less positive light." Upjohn sampled reactions of 108 adults to photos of 36 men, 18 who were balding and 18 who weren't. Those judges "rated the balding men as being less self-assertive, less interpersonally attractive, less likely to be successful in their careers and personal lives, less apt to be liked and less physically active." Intelligence was the only characteristic which wasn't rated as worse for the balding men. Cited in the release was Dr. Thomas F. Cash, who agreed that hair loss was a "genuine concern." Also, the company surveyed a number of balding men to ask them about their feelings when they first started losing their hair. They found 60 percent or so felt self-conscious about it and "wished" they had more hair. Hardly a surprising conclusion.[57]

Upjohn announced plans to step up marketing of Rogaine in May 1989. Sales had averaged only $4 million per month since the product was launched, despite a $20 million annual national advertising budget. *Washington Post* writer Malcolm Gladwell called the new campaign "one of the most aggressive efforts ever undertaken in the United States to market a prescription drug." The Rogaine director of marketing at Upjohn, Keith S. Barton, stated: "We're using unique methods because Rogaine is a unique product. It's clearly a consumer-driven product, and it's causing us to explore some uncharted territory in the area of marketing a prescription drug." New ads featured a toll-free 800 number that men could call to be referred to a physician who would prescribe the treatment. Analysts predicted 1989 sales of Rogaine in the U.S. to be $50 to $70 million at best. Observers felt the typical marketing approach for a prescription drug—educating doctors about the availability and effectiveness of the treatment—would not work with Rogaine. Upjohn spokesman T. R. Reid said, "What we've found is that the men who are most apt to use it and benefit from it don't generally get ill and don't have a physician they see regularly." Marketing surveys showed the main Rogaine target audience, men in the late 20s and 30s, were among the least likely to visit a doctor regularly. Men were also believed to be unlikely to see a doctor just to get treatment for hair loss. Said Wood Gundy Ltd. analyst William Sammon: "The problem is a cultural one. The average guy doesn't want to go in and talk to his doctor about baldness.... It's the ideal over-the-counter product but they can't turn it into one." Experts thought Rogaine could be sold most effectively through a mass marketing campaign like those for shampoos but because of FDA rules, ads for prescription drugs could not mention the trade name of the product.[58]

Rogaine sales for the first half of 1989 were estimated at $25 million in America. By the fall of that year, desperation was setting in as Upjohn increased its yearly advertising budget to an estimated $35 million. Considering the publicity Rogaine had received to that point, Salomon Bros. analyst Robert Uhl observed: "At this point I'm skeptical that even a brand-specific ad for Rogaine will work.... It should have been doing far better by now." In August 1989, Upjohn launched its third major ad campaign. New print ads for the first time mentioned Rogaine by name, emphasizing that Rogaine was the only product the FDA had approved for hair regrowth. TV spots continued not to mention the product by name. To mention the name in print, Upjohn was required to insert a partial page of medical information. In practice that information was often tucked away on a different page so consumers would be less likely to see it and even less likely to read it. First half sales figures for 1989 were listed as $28 million in the U.S. and $51 million worldwide; these figures were expected to rise to $70 million and $130 million, respectively, by the year's end. Observers cited the high cost of the product, difficulty of application, lifetime use, and limited effectiveness as discouraging consumers from using the product. Upjohn was then reportedly researching new formulations of Rogaine. The company had also started a sweepstakes promotion at barbershops and hair salons. A selected group of those businesses were provided with packets of information that could be distributed to customers worried about hair loss. Customers who filled out an information form were entered in the sweepstakes, which would award $100 of free haircare from the participating stylist or barber. Through their toll-free number, Upjohn provided callers with a $10-off certificate for a physician's visit and a rebate coupon worth $20 back on a four-month purchase of Rogaine.[59]

When asked why he thought Rogaine was selling poorly, Michael Mahoney, president of the American Hair Loss Council, replied, "Many people are afraid of ridicule if they even just speak of losing their hair." He thought people were attracted to snake-oil concoctions promoted in the back of magazines and on late-night cable TV because "They can try them in the privacy of their own home, without confronting a doctor."[60]

When journalist Stephen Quickel assessed Rogaine in November 1989 in *Business Month* magazine, he was not optimistic and estimated first-year sales of the product would not top $100 million worldwide. Quickel thought Upjohn's great sin was its refusal to market Rogaine as a consumer cosmetic product. It meant traditional marketing to physicians and pharmacists. As the company panicked, its more aggressive ad campaign ran the risk of further alienating the medical professionals it depended on. "It has been a schizophrenic marketing experience at best, a complete failure at worst," he concluded. Drexel Burnham Lambert's David Lippman remarked, "I always thought minoxidil would be a fad and then fade but it hasn't even done that." Speaking of the ads directed toward consumers, Robert Stern complained, "The new promotional approach directly to patients through the popular press bothers me a great deal." He thought Upjohn was featuring far less complete, and therefore misleading, efficacy statistics in its consumer advertising than in professional journals. What outraged medical people the most was Upjohn's current campaign. A letter from Upjohn to doctors announced that unless doctors returned an enclosed card to Upjohn asking the company not to do so, it would include their names on a list given to men (according to geographic location) who contacted the company for information. It was a negative-option technique mostly used by book or record clubs. Doctors called it "outrageously high-handed." Stern added, "This really makes me quite angry."[61]

Neil Sweig of Prudential-Bache thought worldwide sales could perhaps at some time be pushed to $200 to $250 million per year but at such an exaggerated marketing cost "profits would be nowhere close to what blockbuster drugs earn." In that first year, Upjohn's advertising expenditure on Rogaine was said to be $60 million. Wall Street steadily lowered projections for Upjohn's 1989 and 1990 earnings. Quickel noted that "Rogaine is nowhere near as miraculous as its boosters would have people believe. And these facts were well-known to Upjohn all along." He could think of no reason to pump more money into promoting Rogaine unless Upjohn sold it off to a buyer with more consumer savvy than Upjohn. Summing up his impression of the efficacy of the product, Quickel wrote, "the truth is that Rogaine will grow a small amount of colorless fuzz atop a very limited number of not-very-bald-heads" if the customer used it every day for life.[62]

By early in 1990, Rogaine ads could be found in major magazines and on the sports pages of newspapers. Many of them featured a coupon good for $10 off the cost of a doctor's visit. The product had also started sports sponsorship. Sales remained disappointing, however. Raleigh, North Carolina, hairdresser Dianne Narron said many of the inquiries she received about the drug came from women asking on behalf of husbands too embarrassed to call attention to their baldness. Upjohn was then seeking approval to market the drug to women. One person pleased to see the poor sales was UCLA health researcher Michael Goldstein, who said: "Most of the research on men's health habits tends to make men look bad, because they don't respond to medical symptoms. But hair loss isn't a genuine symptom in the way it's commonly thought about. It's a created symptom and a need that's being artificially created. So if men aren't responding, it's a sign of their mental health, not ill health.[63]

Business Week writer David Woodruff stated that in the first quarter of 1990, Rogaine sales hit $32 million worldwide, up 35 percent from $24 million for the first quarter of 1989. A 50 percent increase to $175 million (up from $117 million) was projected for the full year, with 60 percent of sales in the U.S. Woodruff thought this spurt in sales was due to intensified marketing with a sharper focus. The annual U.S. advertising budget for Rogaine was said to be $50 million in each of 1989 and 1990. Rogaine cost consumers around $700 per year. In February 1990, Upjohn started a test, with FDA approval, in three cities in which fifteen-second TV spots gave the name Rogaine as well as the toll-free number to call for information. Those ads could not describe Rogaine's properties. Nor, of course, could they provide the mound of fine-print detail which the FDA insisted had to accompany the print ads giving the drug's trade name. Woodruff concluded, "Upjohn's growth strategy for Rogaine depends on applying good old-fashioned mass-marketing techniques to this unusual prescription drug."[64]

If Upjohn believed that having Rogaine—the first and only government approved treatment for baldness—was a license to print money the company continued to be disappointed. Worldwide sales for 1991 reportedly were $143 million. In May 1992 the company began a three-city pilot program offering a money-back guarantee to anyone not satisfied with the product after one year's use. "We don't want people going around saying they're not satisfied with Rogaine," explained Upjohn executive Timothy Thieme. "That's not good for the product, and it's not good for the company."[65]

Desperation reached new levels at Upjohn. After Rogaine was approved for women by the FDA in September 1991, Upjohn targeted them in two separate campaigns, apparently with little success. In mid–1993 the company switched advertising agencies, moving its Rogaine account from Klemtner Advertising to Kobs and Draft. Early in 1994 a new TV spot was aired aimed at men, but the thrust of the campaign targeted women. A sixty-second TV spot featuring a woman called "Lois" ran nationally and frequently on MTV, other national cable shows, and in a number of local markets. That ad was aimed at younger women and included the name Rogaine along with the 800 number. "We've tried to advertise to women twice before," said Upjohn executive Amanda Hutchinson. "This time, the ads speak to a younger woman and are more emotional and nurturing than we've been in the past." Print ads led with the line "Lois never thought she'd have thinning hair at 25." Probably because she didn't. To make it even more ludicrous, the TV Lois wore a hat. Not surprising since the number of 25-year-old females with balding crowns, or thinning hair, is just about zero. So convinced was the company that the female market would bail out its product, Upjohn was then reportedly creating the first-year infomercial for a prescription drug. That thirty-minute ad was to target only women. Apparently, Upjohn was relying on the fact that women went to physicians more frequently than men, and the company also hoped to benefit from the fashion for "thick hair." Kobs and Draft general manager David Florence said: "It's acceptable for men to be bald. Men can choose baldness and walk down the street without people turning around to look at them. But women probably do feel more self-conscious about it."[66]

Upjohn continued to search as time ran out on its patent. In 1993 they were experimenting with a five percent solution of minoxidil, experimenting on combining the drug with other agents to increase absorption, and lobbying the FDA to make Rogaine available over-the-counter. Oddest of all was Upjohn's alliance with Boston University School of Medicine urologist Irwin Goldstein. An experiment was slated to begin some time soon in which Goldstein was planning to apply minoxidil to the clitoris to find out if it increased blood flow and led to easier sexual orgasms for women. Upjohn would not admit it was flogging a dead horse.[67]

NOTES

Chapter 1

1. Norman Kuhne, "The Bald Head Is Here to Stay," *Nations Business* 36 (August 1948):66.

2. Condict W. Cutler, "Alopecia," *New York Medical Journal* June 3, 1893, p. 617; Roger Field, "The Big Cover-Up," *Science Digest* 85 (February 1979):85.

3. Gerald Walker, "Baldness Unbared," *New York Times Magazine*, January 4, 1959, p. 62; J. O. Cobb, "Baldness," *New York Medical Journal*, June 26, 1909, p. 1298; Dale Alexander, *Healthy Hair and Common Sense* (West Hartford, Conn.: Witkower, 1974), pp. 50–51.

4. Alexander, *Healthy Hair*, p. 50; Lee Comegys, "Chrome Dome: Keep or Cover It?" *Times-Picayune* (New Orleans), May 11, 1982, sec. 4, p. 1; Penny Ward Moser, "The Bald Truth About Growing Hair," *Discover* 7(June 1986):74; "Julius Caesar," *New York Times Magazine*, April 14, 1957, p. 78; Malcolm W. Browne, "F.D.A. May Issue a Hair-Raising Decision," *New York Times*, March 22, 1987, sec. 4, p. 28; "Baldness," *Fortune* 8 (July 1933):52.

5. John Langone, "Gone Today, Hair Tomorrow," *Time* August 29, 1988, p. 78; Walter Klenhard, *The Bald Book* (Santa Monica, Calif.: Science-Med Press, 1986), pp. 101, 119.

6. Cobb, "Baldness," p. 1298; Comegys, "Chrome Dome"; "Baldness," *Fortune*, p. 52; Dan Carlinsky, "Bald Truths," *Reader's Digest* 122 (June 1983) 99, 102; Richard Selzer, "Bald!" *Esquire* 85 (May 1976) 83; Frank Rossi, "A Growing Problem," *Times-Picayune* (New Orleans), June 7, 1990, p. E1.

7. Cobb, "Baldness," p. 1298; Klenhard, *Bald Book*, pp. 27, 34, 141; Alexander, *Healthy Hair*, p. 50; Selzer, "Bald!" p. 83.

8. Alexander, *Healthy Hair*, p. 51; J. D. Rolleston, "Dermatology and Folk-Lore," *British Journal of Dermatology and Syphilis* 52 (1940): 55.

9. "Bald Is Beautiful," *Time*, January 13, 1975, p. 51; Rolleston, "Dermatology," p. 55.

10. "Music and Bald-Headedness," *Medical Record*, February 22, 1896, p. 275; "Music and Baldness," *Scientific American*, August 29, 1896, p. 185.

11. "Bald-Headed Doctors," *New York Times*, November 17, 1889, p. 16.

12. "The Prevention of Baldness," *Medical Record*, January 23, 1886, p. 101.

13. Virgil G. Eaton, "A Bald and Toothless Future," *Popular Science Monthly* 29 (October 1886): 803–4.

14. "Baldness and Grayness," *Scientific American Supplement*, July 6, 1912, p. 14; "Foot to Head," *Time*, March 2, 1936, p. 32.

15. George De Leon, "The Baldness Experiment," *Psychology Today* 11 (October 1977): 66.

16. "Geography May Influence Baldness in Young Men," *Science News Letter,* April 10, 1948, 233; Sharon Stangenes, "Hot Water Washing May Hasten Hair Loss," *Times-Picayune* (New Orleans), November 24, 1983, sec. 9, p. 29.

17. Allan Carpenter, "They Pull Your Hair to Save It," *Science Digest* 23 (March 1948): 38–39.

18. "Mysterious Germ Makes 300 Bald," *New York Times*, January 17, 1926, p. 10.

19. "Hair Too Thin to Fight," *New York Times*, March 30, 1943, p. 23.

20. "The Prevention of Baldness," *Medical Record*, January 23, 1886, p. 101; Eaton, "Bald and Toothless Future," p. 806; "The Progress and Prevalence of Baldness in America," *Medical Record*, October 2, 1886, p. 380.

21. "Baldness and Its Treatment," *Medical Record*, February 24, 1912, p. 371.

22. "The Cause of Modern Baldness," *Literary Digest*, February 4, 1928, p. 24.

23. "Those Baldness Cures," *Science Digest* 37 (April 1955): back cover.

24. "Bald Men No Lard Heads," *Science Digest* 37 (March 1955): 51.

25. Walker, "Baldness Unbared," p. 62.

26. Miss E. F. Andrews, "Will the Coming Woman Lose Her Hair?" *Popular Science Monthly* 42 (January 1893): 371–72.

27. Woods Hutchinson, "Heads and Hair," *Cosmopolitan* 46 (February 1909): 344; "Hair and Religion," *New York Times*, May 27, 1913, p. 10.

28. Michel Cabanac, "Beards, Baldness, and Sweet Secretion," *European Journal of Applied Physiology and Occupational Physiology*, 58, nos. 1 and 2 (1988): 30, 44.

29. Michel Cabanac, "Beardedness, Baldness, and Northern Climate," *Behavioral and Brain Sciences* 13, no. 2 (June 1990): 351.

30. S. S. Block, "How Food Affects Your Hair," *Science Digest* 15 (May 1944). 15; Selzer, "Bald!" p. 83; "Man's Oldest Fallout Problem: Baldness," *Today's Health* 41 (August 1963): 48; Julio M. Barman, "The Normal Trichogram of the Adult," *Journal of Investigative Dermatology* 44 (1965) 233–35; "Pumping Hair," *Esquire* 108 (September 1987): 231.

31. Sigmund S. Greenbaum, "Are You Losing Your Hair?" *Hygeia* 8 (March 1930): 241; Walker, "Baldness Unbared," p. 62; Sigfrid A. Muller, "Alopecia," *Journal of Investigative Dermatology* 60 (1973): 484.

32. Jane E. Brody, "Hair Loss," *New York Times*, May 3, 1973, p. C12; Lee Smith, "Hair-Raising Happenings at Upjohn," *Fortune*, April 6, 1981, p. 69; Carlinsky, "Bald Truths," p. 100; Edwin Kiester, Jr., "The Bald and the Brave," *50 Plus* 23 (September 1983): 66; "Drug Stimulates New Hair in Tests on Balding Heads," *Times-Picayune* (New Orleans), December 1, 1984, p. 6.

33. Christopher M. Papa and Albert M. Kligman, "Stimulation of Hair Growth by Topical Application of Androgens," *Journal of the American Medical Association*, February 15, 1965, p. 521–22.

34. Walter Pincus, "The Federal Register," *Washington Post*, November 17, 1980, p. A3; Michael Castleman, "Losing It All," *Ms.* 15 (September 1986): 51.

35. Don Wegars, "Hair Grower Gets Mussed," *San Francisco Chronicle*, October 2, 1981, p. 2; John Sansing. "Mirror, Mirror, on the Wall, Please Give Me the Best Head of Hair of All," *Washingtonian* 18 (June 1983): 139; Castleman, "Losing It All," p. 52.

Chapter 2

1. "On the Causes of Alopecia and of Its Greater Frequency in Males Than Females," *American Journal of the Medical Sciences* 55 (April 1868): 416–18.

2. Virgil G. Eaton, "A Bald and Toothless Future," *Popular Science Monthly* 29 (October 1886): 804–6.

3. W. C. Gouinlock, "Hats As a Cause of Baldness," *Popular Science Monthly* 31 (May 1887): 97.

4. Ibid., pp. 98–100.

5. "The Cause of Baldness," *New York Times*, April 24, 1887, p. 8.

6. George Thomas Jackson, "Baldness: What Can We Do for It?" *Medical Record*, May 7, 1887, p. 510.

7. Ibid., p. 534.

8. "The Etiology of Alopecia Praematura Idiopathic," *Medical Record*, July 16, 1887, pp. 75–76.

9. "The Prevention of Baldness," *Medical Record*, January 23, 1886, p. 101; "Treatment of Premature Baldness," *Medical News*, January 21, 1893, p. 81.

10. "The Causes and Treatment of Premature Baldness," *Medical News*, January 21, 1893, p. 81; Ellice M. Alger. "Two Common Forms of Alopecia, with Their Treatment," *Medical Record*, October 27, 1894, p. 536; "The Cause and Cure of Baldness," *Medical Record*, August 8, 1891, p. 157.

11. J. O. Cobb, "Baldness," *New York Medical Journal*, June 26, 1909, pp. 1298–99.

12. Cobb, "Baldness," 1299–1300; "Hats and Baldness," *New York Times*, June 30, 1909, p. 6.

13. Arthur R. Reynolds, "Why Men Are Bald," *American Magazine*, 81 (February 1916): 21, 80–81.

14. "What Causes Baldness?" *New York Times*, May 24, 1913, p. 12; "Symposium on Baldness," *New York Times*, June 27, 1913, p. 8; "Baldness," *New York Times*, April 5, 1914, sec. 3, p. 14.

15. "Dare to Go Hatless!" *New York Times*, September 12, 1925, p. 14; "There's a Risk in Going Bare-headed," *New York Times*, September 15, 1925, p. 18.

16. Benjamin L. Dorsey, *Baldness, Its Causes and Prevention* (Los Angeles: DeVorss, 1939), pp. 66–68, 71, 95.

17. Ibid., pp. 95–96, 98, 100.

18. Ibid., pp. 102, 124, 131–32, 137, 139.

19. "Baldness," *New York Times*, March 10, 1946, sec. 4, p. 9.

20. Irwin I. Lubowe, "Seven Causes of Baldness," *Science Digest* 48 (September 1960): 77–78.

21. "Baldness," *Newsweek*, May 15, 1937, p. 39.

22. "Tense Tops Start Baldness," *Science News Letter*, April 12, 1947, p. 228.

23. "Muscle Heads Don't Get Bald," *Science Digest*, 42 (July 1957): inside cover.

24. "Bald Men No Lard Heads," *Science Digest* 37 (March 1955): 51.

25. "Disprove Theory on Cause of Baldness," *Science News Letter*, October 31, 1959, p. 289.

26. Frederick Hoelzel, "Baldness and Calcification of the Ivory Dome," *Journal of the American Medical Association*, July 18, 1942, p. 968; "Baldness," *New York Times*, August 2, 1942, sec. 4, p. 7; "Baldness Ascribed to Ivory Domes in Men," *Science News Letter*, August 1, 1942, p. 72; "Ivory Dome," *Scientific American* 167 (December 1942): 269.

27. Walter Klenhard, *The Bald Book* (Santa Monica, Calif.: Science-Med Press, 1986), pp. 76–77.

28. Allan Carpenter, "They Pull Your Hair to Save It," *Science Digest* 23 (March 1948): 39.

29. J. M. Blaine, "Etiology of Alopecia Premature," *Journal of the American Medical Association*, March 11, 1899, pp. 524–25.

30. Ibid., p. 525.

31. "The Causes of Baldness," *New York Times*, May 22, 1913, p. 10; "Devitalized Foods," *New York Times*, July 1, 1913, p. 8.

32. "The Causes and Treatment of Premature Baldness," *Medical News*, January 21, 1893, p. 81.

33. Cobb, "Baldness," p. 1299.

34. "Baldness and Grayness," *Scientific American Supplement*, July 6, 1912, p. 15.

35. "Shaving of the Head for Impending Baldness," *New York Medical Journal*, November 3, 1900, p. 767.

36. "Mysterious Germ Makes 300 Bald," *New York Times*, January 17, 1926, p. 10; "Will Women Lose Their Hair?" *Science Digest* 11 (May 1942): 84.

37. "The Bald Man's Bacillus," *Medical News*, April 3, 1897, p. 440; "The Microbe of Baldness," *Medical Record*, May 21, 1898, p. 738; G. Clarke Nuttall, "The Secret of Baldness," *Littell's Living Age*, April 16, 1898, p. 172–76.

38. "The Bacilli of Alopecia," *Medical News*, October 5, 1889, p. 376.

39. "The Microbe That Causes Baldness," *Current Literature* 33 (August 1902): 215.

40. "Dermatitis Seborrhoica and Baldness," *Medical News*, February 4, 1905, p. 223.

41. A. H. Ohmann-Dumesnil, "Some Successful Methods of Treating Alopecia and Alopecia Areata," *Medical News*, August 6, 1892, pp. 146–47.

42. "Treatment of Premature Baldness," *Medical Record*, January 10, 1884, p. 83; "Is Alopecia Premature Contagious?" *Medical News*, November 13, 1886., p. 544.

43. "Seborrhoea and Baldness," *Medical Record*, August 16, 1890, pp. 182–83.

44. Condict Cutler, "Alopecia," *New York Medical Journal*, June 3, 1893, p. 616; George T. Elliot. "A Further Study of Alopecia Praematura or Presenilis," *New York Medical Journal*, October 26, 1895, p. 526; Ellice M. Alger, "Two Common Forms of Alopecia, with Their Treatment," *Medical Record*, October 27, 1894, p. 536; George Thomas Jackson, "Loss of Hair," *Current Literature* 29 (July 1900): 47–78; "Alopecia and Seborrhea," *Medical Record*, October 8, 1910, p. 633.

45. Irwin I. Lubowe, *New Hope for Your Hair* (New York: Dutton, 1960), pp. 60–61.

46. William Brady, "What Can Be Done to Prevent Baldness?" *Illustrated World* 27 (April 1917): 216–17.

47. Isadore Dyer, "Alopecia: Types and Treatment," *New York Medical Journal* June 8, 1912, pp. 1193, 1195.

48. "Baldness and the Race," *Independent*, September 4, 1902, pp. 2152–53.

49. "Baldness and Grayness," *Scientific American Supplement*, July 6, 1912, pp. 14–15.

50. "The Cause and Cure of Baldness," *Medical Record*, August 8, 1891, p. 157; George Thomas Jackson, "Baldness: What Can We Do for It?" *Medical Record*, May 7, 1887, p. 510.

51. "Baldness a Germ Disease?" *New York Times*, June 25, 1913, p. 8.

52. "Antidotes for Baldness," *New York Times*, September 1, 1913, p. 4; "Baldness," *New York Times*, March 28, 1914, p. 12; "Symposium on Baldness," *New York Times*, June 27, 1913, p. 8; "The Germs of Baldness," *New York Times*, June 29, 1913, pt. 3, p. 4.

53. "Baldness and the Race," *Independent*, September 4, 1902, p. 2153.

54. Lester Reynolds, "Science and Your Shining Pate," *Illustrated World* 28 (October 1917): 258.

55. S. Dana Hubbard, "Ways to Keep the 160,000 Hairs on Your Head," *American Magazine* 93 (March 1922): 54.

56. "Women May Get Bald," *Los Angeles Times*, December 19, 1926, p. 1.

57. William P. Cunningham, "Seven Clues to Baldpate," *Medical Record*, August 14, 1915, p. 263.

58. Sigmund S. Greenbaum, "Are You Losing Your Hair?" *Hygeia* 8 (March 1930: 243.

59. Robert P. Little, "That Bald Spot," *Hygeia* 26 (January 1948): 33.

60. "A Plea for the Bald," *New York Times*, May 15, 1948, p. 14.

61. Dan Carlinsky, "Bald Truths," *Reader's Digest* 122 (June 1983): 101.

62. "Blame for Baldness," *Newsweek*, November 12, 1951, p. 94.

Chapter 3

1. "The Causes and Treatment of Premature Baldness," *Medical News*, January 21, 1893, p. 82; "Prophylaxis and Treatment of Baldness," *Medical Record*, July 11, 1903, p. 67; William Brady, "What Can Be Done to Prevent Baldness?" *Illustrated World* 27 (April 1917): 296; "Mysterious Germ Makes 300 Bald," *New York Times*, January 17, 1926, p. 10.

2. "Ultraviolet Light in Alopecia," *New York Medical Journal*, July 27, 1912, p. 192; "The Value of the Cooper Hewitt Quartz Lamp in the Treatment of Alopecia," *Medical Record*, December 2, 1916, p. 1008.

3. William Brady, "What Can Be Done?" p. 217.

4. Sigmund S. Greenbaum, "Are You Losing Your Hair?" *Hygeia* 8 (March 1930): 243; Benjamin Dorsey, *Baldness, Its Causes and Prevention* (Los Angeles: DeVorss, 1939), p. 124.

5. "Exposure to the Sun As an Etiological Factor in Alopecia," *Medical Record*, October 15, 1910, p. 694.

6. "Baldness and Its Treatment," *Medical Record*, February 24, 1912, p. 371.

7. "Twentieth Century Baldness," *Medical Record*, August 20, 1921, p. 343; "The Cause of Modern Baldness," *Literary Digest*, February 4, 1928, p. 24; "There's a Risk in Going Bare-Headed," *New York Times*, September 14, 1925, p. 18.

8. John E. Gibson, "What You Can Do About Your Hair," *Science Digest* 31 (February 1952): 1.

9. George Thomas Jackson, "Baldness: What Can We Do for It?" *Medical Record*, May 7, 1887, p. 510; "The Cause and Treatment of Premature Baldness," *Medical News*, January 21, 1893, p. 82; Condict W. Cutler, "Alopecia," *New York Medical Journal*, June 3, 1893, p. 617; Ellice Alger, "Two Common Forms of Alopecia, with Their Treatment," *Medical Record*, October 27, 1894, p. 536.

10. Lester Reynolds, "Science and Your Shining Pate," *Illustrated World*, 28 (October 1917): 259.

11. William P. Cunningham, "Seven Clues to Baldpate," *Medical Record*, August 14, 1915, p. 263; Brady, "What Can Be Done?", p, 216; "Twentieth Century Baldness," *Medical Record*, p. 343.

12. Greenbaum, "Are You Losing Your Hair," p.243; "Going, Going, Gone," *Literary Digest*, October 17, 1936, p. 21.

13. "The Prevention of Baldness," *Medical Record*, August 4, 1906, 191.

14. Stephen Rae, "Real Men Don't Need Combs," *Newsweek*, February 28, 1983, p. 11; Robert P. Crease, "None But the Bald," *50 Plus* 27 (February 1987): 76.

15. "The Prevention of Baldness," *Medical Record*, January 23, 1886, p. 101; George Thomas Jackson, "Baldness: What Can We Do for It?" *Medical Record*, May 7, 1887, p. 510; George Thomas Jackson, "Loss of Hair," *Current Literature* 29 (July 1900): 47.

16. "The Cause and Cure of Baldness," *Medical Record*, August 8, 1891, p. 157; "The Causes and Treatment of Premature Baldness," *Medical News*, January 21, 1893, p. 81; "Is the Writer a Bald-Head?" *Medical Record*, March 19, 1892, p. 314.

17. "The Causes of Baldness," *New York Medical Journal*, June 16, 1906, p. 1251.

18. Woods Hutchinson, "Heads and Hair," *Cosmopolitan* 46 (February 1909): p. 342; Brady "What Can Be Done?" p. 214; "The Cause of Modern Baldness," *Literary Digest*, February 4, 1928, p. 24.

19. "Baldness," *Fortune* 8 (July 1933): 53; Norman Kuhne, "The Bald Head Is Here to Stay," *Nations Business* 36 (August 1948): 42.

20. "Says Brain's Growth Causes Baldness," *Science Digest* 40 (November 1956): 77; Irwin I. Lubowe, *New Hope for Your Hair* (New York: Dutton, 1960), p. 65; Paige Gold, "The Fallout and What's Behind It," *San Francisco Chronicle*, April 23, 1978, Punch sec., p. 5.

21. "Baldness and Grayness," *Scientific American Supplement*, July 6, 1912, p. 14; "Twentieth Century Baldness," *Medical Record*, p. 343; "Devitalized Foods," *New York Times*, July 1, 1913, p. 8.

22. S. Dana Hubbard, "Ways to Keep the 160,000 Hairs on Your Head," *American Magazine* 93 (March 1922): 50–51; "Says Diet Affects Hair Growth," *New York Times*, April 7, 1939, p. 16; "Nation's Chemists Censure Gov. Bilbo," *New York Times*, September 12, 1930, p. 16.

23. "Indigestion and Baldness," *Medical Record*, November 9, 1895, p. 684.

24. "Relations Between Alopecia and Dental Lesions," *New York Medical Journal*, December 8, 1900, p. 1002; "Alopecia and Earwax," *New York Medical Journal*, January 4, 1919, p. 36; "Alopecia and Dental Abnormalities," *New York Medical Journal*, November 10, 1917, p. 909.

25. Dale Alexander, *Healthy Hair and Common Sense* (West Hartford, Conn.: Witkower, 1974), pp. 14, 18, 19, 27, 29, 39.

26. Ibid., pp. 144, 162.

27. "The Causes and Treatment of Premature Baldness," *Medical News*, January 21, 1893, p. 81; Hubbard, "Ways to Keep the 160,000 Hairs on Your Head," p. 50.

28. "Baldness and Grayness," *Scientific American Supplement*, p. 14.

29. "Alopecia and Earwax," *New York Medical Journal*, p. 36.

30. "Baldness and the Hair Brush," *New York Times*, November 6, 1901, p. 8.

31. "Lays Baldness to Eye Strain," *New York Times*, November 22, 1934, p. 18.

32. "Hair and Religion," *New York Times*, May 27, 1913, p. 10; "Baldness Among Clergymen," *New York Times*, June 5, 1913, p. 10.

33. Jackson, "Baldness," p. 510; "The Cause and Cure of Baldness," *Medical*

Record, August 8, 1891, p. 157; "The Causes and Treatment of Premature Baldness," *Medical News*, January 21, 1893, p. 81; Ellice M. Alger, "Two Common Forms of Alopecia, with Their Treatment," *Medical Record*, October 27, 1894, p. 536.

34. A. H. Ohmann-Dumesnil, "Some Successful Methods of Treating Alopecia and Alopecia Areata," *Medical News*, August 6, 1892, pp. 147–48.

35. George Thomas Jackson, "Loss of Hair," *Current Literature* 29 (July 1900): 47; Brady, "What Can Be Done?" p. 214; "Hair and Religion," *New York Times*, May 27, 1913, p. 10.

36. Hubbard, "Ways to Keep 160,000 Hairs on Your Head," p. 50; "Baldness," *Fortune* 8 (July 1933): 53.

37. "Strain Thins London Hair," *New York Times*, June 14, 1943, p. 20.

38. Thomas S. Szasz and Alan M. Robertson, "A Theory of the Pathogenesis of Ordinary Human Baldness," *Archives of Dermatology and Syphilology* 61 (January 1950): 40; G. B. Lal, "Keep Calm and Keep Your Hair," *Science Digest* 29 (January 1951): 57–58.

39. Szasz and Robertson, "Theory," p. 39.

40. Ibid., p. 47.

41. Szasz and Robertson, "Theory," p. 42; Lal, "Keep Calm," p. 60.

42. John E. Gibson, "What You Can Do About Your Hair," *Science Digest* 31 (February 1952): 4.

43. "Foot to Head," *Time*, March 2, 1936, p. 32; Dan Carlinsky, "Bald Truths," *Reader's Digest* 122 (June 1983): 99.

44. "Nature and Treatment of Alopecia," *New York Medical Record*, November 24, 1900, p. 913; J. O. Cobb, "Baldness," *New York Medical Journal*, June 26, 1909, p. 1298; "Baldness," *Fortune* 8 (July 1933): 53; Louis B. Mount, "The Alopecias," *Medical Record*, May 22, 1915, p. 853.

45. Kuhne, "Bald Head," p. 42; "Bald Men Are More Virile, Brooklyn Doctor Reports," *New York Times*, July 28, 1953, p. 21.

46. William Braden, "Baldness Boosts Virility, Hair Expert Claims," *Times-Picayune* (New Orleans), March 29, 1981, sec. 3, p. 2.

47. John Sansing, "Mirror, Mirror, on the Wall, Please Give Me the Best Head of Hair of All," *Washingtonian* 18 (June 1893): 140; "Cue Balls to Shine at Topless Convention," *Los Angeles Times*, September 1, 1983, sec. 1A, p. 5.

48. Albert Damon, "Baldness of Fathers and Number and Sex Ratio of Children," *Human Biology* 37, no. 4 (December 1965): 366–70.

49. Delos L. Parker, "The Etiology of Alopecia," *Medical Record*, July 13, 1901, p. 45.

50. Ibid., pp. 46–47.

51. Ibid., pp. 49–50.

52. Delos L. Parker, "The Cause of Common Baldness," *Medical Record*, February 7, 1907, pp. 220–21.

53. Ibid., pp. 221, 224.

54. "The Causes and Treatment of Baldness," *Medical Record*, August 12, 1905, p. 273; "Baldness Traced to the Absence of Upper Chest Breathing," *Current Literature* 42 (April 1907): 453; "Baldness and the Race," *Independent*, September 4, 1902, p. 2151.

55. George T. Elliot, "A Further Study of Alopecia Praematura or Praesenilis," *New York Medical Journal*, October 26, 1895, p. 526; Isadore Dyer, "Alopecia: Types and Treatment," *New York Medical Journal*, June 8, 1912, p. 1192; Arthur R. Reynolds, "Why Men Are Bald," *American Magazine* 81 (February 1916): 21.

56. George Thomas Jackson, "Baldness: What Can We Do for It?" *Medical Record,* May 7, 1887, p. 510; Brady, "What Can Be Done?" p. 214.

57. George Thomas Jackson, "Loss of Hair," *Current Literature* 29 (July 1900): 47; "The Causes and Treatment of Premature Baldness," *Medical News,* January 21, 1893, p. 81; "Alopecia and Seborrhea," *Medical Record,* October 8, 1910, p. 633.

58. "Hair," *New York Times,* December 6, 1868, p. 5.

59. Laurence H. Snyder, "The Application of the Gene Frequency Method of Analysis to Sex-Influenced Factors, with Especial Reference to Baldness," *Human Biology,* 7 (1935):608, 611, 613.

60. Harry Harris, "The Inheritance of Premature Baldness in Men," *Annals of Eugenics* 13 (November 1946): 172.

61. James B. Hamilton, "Male Hormone Stimulation Is Prerequisite and an Incident in Common Baldness," *American Journal of Anatomy* 71 (November 1942): 456, 461–65, 477; Harris, "Inheritance of Premature Baldness," p. 172.

62. Harris, "Baldness—He-Man Complaint," *Science Digest* 19 (March 1946): inside cover.

63. Allan Carpenter, "They Pull Your Hair to Save It," *Science Digest* 23 (March 1948): 40; "Baldness Ahead," *Americas* 7 (May 1955): 40.

64. Irwin I. Lubowe, "Seven Causes of Baldness," *Science Digest* 48 (September 1960): 77; Irwin I. Lubowe, *New Hope for Your Hair* (New York: Dutton, 1960), p. 63; "Why It Is—or Isn't," *Newsweek,* May 23, 1960, p. 107A.

65. Irwin I. Lubowe, "Baldness," *Encyclopedia Americana,* international ed., vol. 3 (Danbury, Conn.: Grolier, 1994), pp. 81–82.

66. "Genetic Link Hints at Cure for Baldness," *Vancouver Sun,* March 17, 1994, p. A1.

Chapter 4

1. "The Causes and Treatment of Premature Baldness," *Medical News,* January 21, 1893, p. 82; George Thomas Jackson, "Loss of Hair," *Current Literature* 29 (July 1900): 48.

2. "The Anatomic Factor in Baldness," *Medical News,* April 26, 1902, p. 791; "The Anatomical Factor in the Production of Baldness," *Medical Record,* May 24, 1902, p. 816.

3. J. O. Cobb, "Baldness," *New York Medical Journal,* June 26, 1909, p. 1300.

4. "Baldness of Women," *New York Times,* March 19, 1914, p. 8; "Baldness," *New York Times,* March 28, 1914, p. 12.

5. William Brady. "What Can Be Done to Prevent Baldness?" *Illustrated World* 27 (April 1917): 217; Sigmund S. Greenbaum, "Are You Losing Your Hair?" *Hygeia* 8 (March 1930): 243; "Going, Going, Gone," *Literary Digest* October 17, 1936, p. 21.

6. Van Buren Thorne, "Baldness and Curealls," *New York Times,* January 8, 1922, sec. 7, p. 12.

7. "The Treatment of Baldness," *New York Medical Journal,* November 3, 1883, p. 506.

8. "Alopecia Simplex," *Medical News,* November 2, 1889, p. 488.

9. "Alopecia," *Medical Record,* February 22, 1896, p. 286.

10. "Treatment of Baldness by Simple Aseptic Irritation," *Medical News,* February 4, 1899, p. 144.

11. A. H. Ohmann-Dumesnil, "Some Successful Methods of Treating Alopecia and Alopecia Areata," *Medical News*, August 6, 1892, p. 149.

12. "Lactic Acid As a Remedy for Baldness," *New York Medical Journal*, October 21, 1899, p. 595.

13. Condict Cutler, "Alopecia," *New York Medical Journal*, June 8, 1893, p. 617.

14. "Pneumatic Cure for Baldness," *Medical Record*, December 30, 1899, p. 987.

15. "Machining the Scalp," *Illustrated World* 33 (April 1920): 306–7; Benjamin L. Dorsey, *Baldness, Its Causes and Prevention* (Los Angeles: DeVorss, 1939): p. 124; Frank Rossi, "A Growing Problem," *Times-Picayune* (New Orleans), June 7, 1990, p. E1; Rick Marin, "Kiss It Good-bye," *GQ* 62 (August 1992): 174.

16. "Foot to Head," *Time* March 2, 1936, p. 32; "Going, Going, Gone," *Literary Digest*, October 17, 1936, p. 21.

17. "The Causes and Treatment of Premature Baldness," *Medical News*, January 21, 1893, p. 82.

18. "Alopecia," *Medical Record*, July 4, 1896, p. 31.

19. "Static Electricity As a Cure for Alopecia," *New York Medical Journal*, November 8, 1902, p. 798.

20. George M. MacKee, "The High Frequency Spark in the Treatment of Premature Alopecia," *New York Medical Journal*, July 28, 1906, pp. 181–82.

21. "Potion Makes Bald Men Believers," *San Francisco Chronicle*, January 22, 1979, p. 16.

22. "Hair Sprouts Where Lightning Struck," *Los Angeles Times*, July 5, 1980, p. 2; "Miraculous Lightning Sparks Hair," *Times-Picayune* (New Orleans) July 4, 1980, pp. 1, 6.

23. "Dermatologist Thinks He Can Treat Baldies with Electricity," *Times-Colonist* (Victoria, B.C.), August 5, 1990, p. A12; Alicia Priest, "Electrical Treatment for Baldness Claims Good Results," *Vancouver Sun*, August 4, 1990, p. A5; Geoffrey Rowan, "Treatment Could Be a Real Hair Raiser," *Globe & Mail*, August 18, 1990, pp. B1, B2.

24. Tim Hilchey, "Striving to Get Ahead," *Montreal Gazette*, January 11, 1993, p. B8.

25. S. S. Block, "How Food Affects Your Hair," *Science Digest* 15 (May 1944): 15; Allan Carpenter, "They Pull Your Hair to Save It," *Science Digest* 23 (March 1948): 39.

26. Ena Naunton, "Baldness," *Times-Picayune* (New Orleans), March 19, 1981, sec. 6, p. 4; John Sansing, "Mirror, Mirror, on the Wall, Please Give Me the Best Head of Hair of All," *Washingtonian* 18 (June 1983): 140; Mary-Ellen Siegel, *Reversing Hair Loss* (New York: Simon & Schuster, 1985), p. 22.

27. J. V. Sheppard, "The Myth of the Hairy Male," *Hygeia* 26 (June 1948): 408.

28. Christopher M. Papa and Albert M. Kligman, "Stimulaton of Hair Growth by Topical Application of Androgens," *Journal of the American Medical Association*, February 15, 1965, p. 521; Fred Warshofsky, "Science Tackles the Baldness Problem," *Reader's Digest* 88 (February 1966): 90; "Male Hormone Produces Hair on Bald Heads," *Science News Letter*, March 20, 1965, p. 184.

29. Papa and Kligmann, "Stimulation of Hair Growth," pp. 524–25; "Hormone Cream Restores Lost Hair," *Science Digest* 57 (March 1965): 22.

30. "Hormone Cream Restores Lost Hair," *Science Digest* 57 (March 1965): 22; Walter Sullivan, "A Baldness Cure May Be in Sight," *New York Times*, February 20, 1965, p. 29; "Baldness Breakthrough," *Journal of the American Medical Association*, February 15, 1965, p. 594; "End of Baldness," *New York Times*, February 21, 1965, sec. 4, p. 6.

31. Ronald C. Savin, "The Ineffectiveness of Testosterone in Male Pattern Baldness," *Archives of Dermatology* 98, no. 5 (November 1968): 512–13.

32. Siegel, *Reversing Hair Loss*, p. 60.

33. "Pilocarpine As a Remedy for Baldness," *Medical Record*, September 6, 1879, p. 219; "Influence of Pilocarpine on Baldness," *Medical Record*, April 3, 1880, p. 386; Condict W. Cutler, "Alopecia," *New York Medical Journal*, June 3, 1893, p. 617.

34. "Cure for Skinheads?" *Time*, September 27, 1954, p. 57.

35. "Mirage," *Time*, December 12, 1955, pp. 53–54.

36. Ronald Kotulak, "Hair-Saving Drug Seen in 2 Years," *Chicago Tribune*, May 23, 1973, p. 4.

37. Beth Ann Krier, "Confidence Sprouts in Hair Transplants," *Los Angeles Times*, October 13, 1976, pt. 4, p. 6; Marin, "Kiss It Good-bye," p. 176.

38. "Scientists Find a Key to Bald Heads," *San Francisco Chronicle*, May 2, 1986, p. 26; "Blame It on Your Sebaceous Glands," *Science News*, May 17, 1986, p. 318.

39. "Proteins Point to Roots of Baldness," *Science News*, May 14, 1988, p. 311; Michael McLeod, "Male Strangers Take a Shine to Professor," *Chicago Tribune*, June 20, 1988, sec. 5, p. 1.

40. Linda Wells, "New Hope for Hair Growth May Lie in Drug Study," *New York Times*, December 20, 1986, p. 33.

41. Pearce Wright, "Skin-Deep Key to Curing Baldness," *Times* (London), October 16, 1984, p. 3; "British Quest to Grow Hair in Laboratory," *New York Times*, October 30, 1984, p. C7; "Lab-Grown Hair Could Lead to Baldness Cure," *Chicago Tribune*, November 4, 1984, sec. 6, p. 6.

42. "British Doctor Finds Gland to Restore Hair," *New York Times*, November 13, 1926, p. 6.

43. Bengt Norman Bengstson, "Pituitary Therapy of Alopecia," *Journal of the American Medical Association*, November 7, 1931, pp. 1355–58; "Says Gland Extract Conquers Baldness," *New York Times*, November 4, 1931, p. 28.

44. Bengt Norman Bengtson, "Anterior Pituitary Treatment for Baldness," *Journal of the American Medical Association*, November 28, 1931, p. 1643; "Warning Against New Baldness Cures," *Scientific American* 146 (March 1932): 175.

45. "London Letter," *Medical News*, February 18, 1899, p. 218.

46. "Cures Baldness in Mice," *New York Times*, November 3, 1940, sec. 2, p. 5; S. S. Block, "How Food Affects Your Hair," *Science Digest* 15 (May 1944): 14.

47. "Offers Hope to the Bald," *New York Times*, February 11, 1920, p. 20.

48. "Hair-Raising Development," *Family Health* 8 (July 1976): 25.

49. John Sansing, "Mirror, Mirror, on the Wall, Please Give Me the Best Head of Hair of All," *Washingtonian* 18 (June 1983): 140; Michael Castleman, "Losing It All," *Ms.* 15 (September 1986): 53; Laura Kavesh, "Biotin Gets Hair-Raising Tests in Chicago," *Chicago-Tribune*, July 17, 1983, sec. 15, p. 4.

50. Sansing, "Mirror, Mirror," p. 414; Castleman, "Losing It All," p. 53.

51. Castleman, "Losing It All," p. 53; Siegel, *Reversing Hair Loss*, pp. 57–58; Walter Klenhard, *The Bald Book* (Santa Monica, Calif.: Science-Med Press, 1986), pp. 58–59.

Chapter 5

1. Judy Folkenberg, "Hair Apparent?" *FDA Consumer* 22 (December 1988/January 1989): 9; Condict Cutler, "Alopecia," *New York Medical Journal*, June 3, 1893, p.

617; Malcolm W. Browne, "F.D.A. May Issue a Hair-Raising Decision," *New York Times*, March 22, 1987, sec. 4, p. 28; Penny Ward Moser, "The Bald Truth About Growing Hair," *Discover* 7 (June 1986): 75; Walter Klenhard, *The Bald Book* (Santa Monica, Calif.: Science-Med Press, 1986), p. 66.

2. "Baldness," *Fortune* 8 (July 1933): 54–55.

3. Ibid., pp. 55, 79–80.

4. Ibid., p. 82.

5. "City Prosecutes Baldness Cure Man," *New York Times*, December 17, 1921, p. 13.

6. "Hope for the Bald Held Out by Coué," *New York Times*, January 15, 1924, p. 44.

7. Arthur J. Cramp, "Some Bald Facts," *Hygeia* 5 (October 1927): 497–98.

8. Ibid., pp. 498–99.

9. Charles Nessler, *The Story of Hair* (New York: Boni and Liveright, 1928), pp. 14, 193–94, 198.

10. Ibid., pp. 198, 201, 217.

11. Nessler, *The Story of Hair*, pp. 202, 216; Benjamin L. Dorsey, *Baldness, Its Causes and Prevention* (Los Angeles: DeVorss, 1939): pp. 35–36.

12. "De Wonderkapper," *Time*, June 13, 1949, pp. 20–30.

13. "Bald Claims," *Time*, July 12, 1948, pp. 42–43.

14. "On the Bald," *Newsweek*, April 11, 1949, p. 54.

15. "Hair-Raising Business," *Reader's Digest* 55 (July 1949): 70; "Treatments and Preparations for the Hair and Scalp," *Hygeia* 27 (June 1949): 382.

16. "Hair-Raising Business," *Reader's Digest* pp. 71–72; "Treatments and Preparations for the Hair and Scalp," *Hygeia*, pp. 422, 424.

17. "Scientists Ponder Bald Head Riddle," *New York Times*, February 11, 1950, p. 10; "Baldness Yields to No Scientists," *New York Times*, February 12, 1950, p. 49.

18. "Those Baldness Cures," *Science Digest* 37 (April 1955): back cover.

19. "There's No Known Cure for Baldness, U.S. Rules," *New York Times*, February 2, 1956, p. 54.

20. Gerald Walker, "Baldness Unbared," *New York Times Magazine*, January 4, 1959, p. 62.

21. "Vitamins Won't Put Hair on Bald Head, U.S. Says," *New York Times*, March 27, 1962, pl. 57; "Man's Oldest Fallout Problem: Baldness," *Today's Health* 41 (August 1963): 46.

22. Judy Klemesrud, "Hair Thinning? Don't Flip, Pop," *New York Times*, July 19, 1970, p. 55.

23. "Founder of Zzyzx Spa Convicted on Ad Claims," *New York Times*, July 19, 1970, p. 55.

24. Mike Michaelson, "How Your Man Can Crown Himself with Glory," *Today's Health* 51 (March 1973): 18.

25. Ted Simon, "A Fringe Profession," *Times* (London), May 11, 1970, p. 12; "Betty Has Hairy Theory," *Times-Picayune* (New Orleans), April 1, 1973, sec. 2, p. 7; "Baldness," *Sunday Times* (London), April 13, 1975, p. 42.

26. "Anti-Baldness Vitamins Getting National Ad Drive," *Advertising Age*, February 21, 1977, 22–23.

27. Nat Benezra, "A Hair-Raising Tale," *Family Health* 9 (December 1977): 27.

28. Steve Rubenstein, "How They Grow Hair in Australia," *San Francisco Chronicle*, July 19, 1979, p. 5.

29. Beth Trier, "Jojoba—Snake Oil or Miracle," *San Francisco Chronicle*, August 14, 1979, p. 19.

30. Ena Naunton, "Baldness," *Times-Picayune* (New Orleans), March 19, 1981, sec. 6, p. 4.

31. William Smart, "You: The Bald Facts," *Washington Post*, July 21, 1981, p. D5.

32. John Sansing, "Mirror, Mirror, on the Wall, Please Give Me the Best Head of Hair of All," *Washingtonian* 18 (June 1983): 141.

33. Ibid.

34. Don Wegars, "Hair Grower Gets Mussed," *San Francisco Chronicle*, October 2, 1981, p. 2; Don Wegars, "The Hair Grower's Fans," *San Francisco Chronicle*, October 3, 1981, p. 2.

35. Naunton, "Baldness," sec. b, p. 4; Smart, "You: The Bald Facts," p. D5.

36. Klenhard, *The Bald Book*, pp. 47–48; Mary-Ellen Siegel, *Reversing Hair Loss* (New York: Simon & Schuster, 1985): pp. 52–53.

37. Siegel, *Reversing Hair Loss*, p. 54; Klenhard, *The Bald Book*, pp. 49, 51.

38. Howard D. Groveman, "Lack of Efficacy of Polysorbate 60 in the Treatment of Male Pattern Baldness," *Archives of Internal Medicine* 145 (August 1985): 1454, 1457; Klenhard, *The Bald Book*, pp. 51–52.

39. "The Notebook," *FDA Consumer* 22 (June 1988): 30.

40. Richard C. Thompson, "Balding Is Forever, Experts Say," *FDA Consumer* 15 (February 1981): 10.

41. Thompson, "Balding Is Forever," pp. 10, 12; "Agency Proposes a Ban on Sales of Products to Prevent Baldness," *New York Times*, November 9, 1980, p. 43.

42. Irvin Molotsky, "Baldness Potions Don't Work, F.D.A. Warns," *New York Times*, January 15, 1985, pp. A1, A12; Otto Friedrich, "Hope Sprouts Eternal," *Time*, January 28, 1985, p. 92.

43. Nancy Giges, "Upjohn Covers Bald Spot in Haircare Market," *Advertising Age*, February 28, 1985, p. 40.

44. "Treatment for Baldness," *Which?* (August 1973): 229–31.

45. "Baldness in Men. Is There an Answer?" *Which?* (September 1983): 391–92.

46. Dan Dorfman, "Another Product that Claims It Can Cover Bald Pates," *San Francisco Chronicle*, January 11, 1986, p. 47.

47. Ibid.

48. Dan Dorfman, "A Hair-Raising Tale," *New York*, January 20, 1986, pp. 11, 14; Dorfman, "Another Product," p. 47.

49. Moser, "Bald Truth," p. 75.

50. Ibid.

51. Pat Sloan, "Hair-Restorer Drugs Brush with the FDA," *Advertising Age*, September 15, 1986, p. 82.

52. Yue Haitao, "Japan Buys Hair Treatment," *Beijing Review*, August 4, 1986, p. 29.

53. Yao Jianguo, "Chinese Trichogen Cure Finds Market," *Beijing Review*, November 3, 1986, p. 29.

54. Edward A. Gargan, "In Baldness War, Rumors of Advance for Hairline," *New York Times*, January 26, 1988, p. 4; Zhao Xuejun, "Zhao Zhangguang—Inventor of '1o1' Hair Tonic," *Beijing Review*, October 17, 1988, pp. 27–28.

55. Gargan, "Baldness War," p. 4; "Side-Effects Normal for Baldness Cure," *Beijing Review*, October 17, 1988, p. 40.

56. "Baldy Sufferers: Despair and Joy," *Beijing Review*, January 18–31, 1993, p. 38; "101 Creates a Furore [sic] in Greece," *Beijing Review*, March 15, 1993, p. 32.

57. Benezra, "Hair-Raising Tale," p. 27.

58. "Brother, Can You Spare a Dome?" *People*, June 4, 1984, p. 61; "Primrose," *Times* (London), December 15, 1986, p. 3.

59. Al Morch, "A Hair-Raising Solution," *San Francisco Chronicle*, February 26, 1989, pp. El; "Bald-Faced Hair Scam," *FDA Consumer* 23 (March 1989): 35.

60. Sloan, "Hair-Restorer Drugs," p. 82; Andrea Adelson, "Hope in a Bottle," *New York Times*, March 13, 1988, sec. 3, p. 5.

61. Gretchen Busch, "Hair Care Producers Betting on Niches," *Chemical Marketing Reporter*, July 24, 1989, SR14.

62. "Government Bans Most Baldness Treatments," *New York Times*, July 8, 1989, p. 6; "Baldness Lotions to Be Limited Under Order Planned by FDA," *Chemical Marketing Reporter*, July 10, 1989, p. 4.

63. "Baldness Lotions," *Chemical Marketing Reporter*, p. 27.

64. Folkenberg, "Hair Apparent," p. 9.

65. Laurie Freeman, "Rogaine Sprouts Haircare Products," *Advertising Age*, September 26, 1988, p. 38; "Pumping Hair," *Esquire* 108 (September 1987): 232; John Sansing, "Bald Truths," *Washingtonian* 22 (July 1987): 105.

66. Malcolm Brown, "Heading for Baldness Cure," *Sunday Times* (London), October 9, 1988, p. D20.

67. Michael Segell, "The Bald Truth About Hair," *Esquire* 121 (May 1994): 111, 117.

Chapter 6

1. Clif Garboden, "Periwigs," *Boston Globe Magazine*, March 12, 1989, p. 14.

2. "Baldness," *Fortune* 8 (July 1933): 82.

3. Fred Sparks, "I'm Glad I Bought a Toupee," *Saturday Evening Post*, December 15, 1956, pp. 33, 64–65.

4. Gerald Walker, "Baldness Unbared," *New York Times Magazine*, January 4, 1959, p. 62; "Baldness Is a Sign of Normality," *Times* (London), September 15, 1969, p. 3.

5. Beth Ann Krier, "Hair-Raising Tales of Male Baldness," *Los Angeles Times*, October 12, 1976, pp. 1, 4; Chris Robbins, "Bald Is Best," *Sunday Times* (London), January 5, 1975, p. 32.

6. Hugh Thomson, "Why Men Won't Own Up to Wigs," *Sunday Times* (London), June 5, 1977, p. 43.

7. Nat Benezra, "A Hair-Raising Tale," *Family Health* 9 (December 1977): 26.

8. Terry Brown, "Hair Apparently Is Growth Field," *Chicago Tribune*, March 10, 1983, sec. 3, p. 3.

9. Dan Carlinsky, "Bald Truths," *Reader's Digest* 122 (June 1983): 102.

10. "Baldness in Men. Is There an Answer?" *Which?* (September 1983): 392.

11. Paddy Calistro, "Top Secret," *Los Angeles Times*, June 28, 1987, p. 34.

12. Clifford Pugh, "The Bald Truth," *Houston Post Magazine*, September 27, 1987, p. 6.

13. Al Morch, "New Drug Stimulates Sales of Hairpieces," *San Francisco Chronicle*, February 26, 1990, p. E4.

14. William G. Glanagan, "The Bald Truth," *Forbes* July 22, 1991, pp. 309–10.

15. Matthew Franklin, "Japanese Hair-Care Affair," *Herald-Sun* (Melbourne), November 26, 1990, p. 13.

16. Sachiko Sakamaki, "Hair-Raising Sales Pitch," *Far Eastern Economic Review*, February 3, 1994, p. 48.

17. Judy Klemesrud, "Tired of a Toupee? Try Hair-Weaving," *New York Times*, April 15, 1968, p. 38.

18. Ibid.

19. Ibid.

20. Charles D. Bennett, "City Plans to Look into Hair-Weaving Complaints," *New York Times*, November 23, 1968, p. 36.

21. Robbins, "Bald Is Best," p. 32; "Baldness in Men," *Which?*, p. 392.

22. Krier, "Hair-Raising Tales," p. 5.

23. Benezra, "Hair-Raising Tale, p. 29.

24. Pugh, "Bald Truth," p. 6.

Chapter 7

1. "The Operative Treatment of Baldness," *Medical Record*, May 13, 1899, p. 696.

2. "Plants Human Hair," *New York Times*, July 31, 1914, p. 8.

3. "Plants Hair on Bald Heads," *New York Times*, March 5, 1914, p. 3; "A Cloak for Baldness," *Times* (London), April 28, 1914, p. 6; "Plants Human Hair," *New York Times*, p. 8; "Hope for the Bald," *Literary Digest*, April 25, 1914, p. 983.

4. "Hair Implants Devised," *New York Times*, August 7, 1971, p. 38.

5. Mike Michaelson, "How Your Man Can Crown Himself with Glory," *Today's Health* 51 (March 1973): 18.

6. Beth Ann Krier, "Hair-Raising Tales of Male Baldness," *Los Angeles Times*, October 12, 1976, p. 1.

7. Ibid., p. 4.

8. Ibid.

9. Nat Benezra, "A Hair-Raising Tale," *Family Health* 9 (December 1977): 29.

10. Charles Petit, "A Controversy Over Baldness Clinics," *San Francisco Chronicle*, February 3, 1979, p. 2.

11. Matt Clark, "Bald Men Beware," *Newsweek*, February 16, 1979, p. 54; Lawrence Galton, "The Bald Truth: Avoid Fiber Implants," *Washington Post*, April 1, 1979, Parade sec., pp. 7–8.

12. Petit, "Controversy," p. 2.

13. Peter Kuchl, "The Bald Truth About a Sales Pitch," *San Francisco Chronicle*, February 3, 1979, p. 2.

14. Petit, "Controversy," p. 2.

15. Clark, "Bald Men Beware," p. 54; Ralph Blumenthal, "A Baldness Remedy Is Assailed," *New York Times*, March 14, 1979, pp. C1, C10; "The Scalpers," *Time*, September 3, 1979, p. 49.

16. Blumenthal, "Baldness Remedy," pp. C1, C10.

17. Ibid.

18. Ibid.

19. Ibid.

20. Roger Field, "The Big Cover Up," *Science Digest* 85 (February 1979): 86.

21. "Hair Today Hurts Tomorrow," *Chicago Tribune*, March 28, 1979, p. 6.

22. James Green, "Artificial Hair Transplants Pose Real Danger," *Chicago Tribune*, December 1, 1979, pp. 13–14; "The Scalpers," *Time*, September 3, 1979, p. 49.

23. "Judge Puts Crimp in Hair Clinic," *San Francisco Chronicle*, July 28, 1979, p. 4.

24. "FDA Bans Implants of Hair Fibers," *Chicago Tribune*, June 4, 1983, p. 3; "Hair Fibers Banned," *FDA Consumer* 17 (September 1983): 26–27.

25. Earl Ubell, "Is Baldness Reversible?" *Washington Post*, July 19, 1987, Parade sec., p. 15.

Chapter 8

1. "Hope for Bald Heads," *Medical Record*, October 25, 1890, p. 468.

2. "Doctor Says Scalp Graft Can Eliminate Baldness," *New York Times*, December 7, 1961, p. 46; "Reforested Pates," *Newsweek*, December 18, 1961, 60.

3. Fred Warshofsky, "Science Tackles the Baldness Problem," *Reader's Digest* 88 (February 1966): 87–89.

4. Ibid., p. 89.

5. "Baldness Cured by Grafting Hair," *New York Times*, March 15, 1967, p. 49.

6. Richard D. Lyons, "Patching Bald Spots," *New York Times*, March 26, 1967, sec. 4, p. 7.

7. "Bald Men: Be Careful of Hair-Grafters," *Washington Post*, July 23, 1972, Parade sec., pp. 10–11; Mike Michaelson, "How Your Man Can Crown Himself with Glory," *Today's Health* 51 (March 1973): 16, 18, 25.

8. "Patients Satisfied with Hair," *Times-Picayune* (New Orleans), January 9, 1972, sec. 4, p. 16; Michaelson, "How Your Man Can Crown Himself," p. 17.

9. "Bald Men: Be Careful of Hair-Grafters," *Washington Post*, Parade sec., pp. 10–11; Michaelson, "How Your Man Can Crown Himself," p. 19.

10. Timothy S. Robinson, "Clinic Pair Guilty of Fraud for Promises of More Hair," *Washington Post*, July 2, 1975, pp. C1, C2.

11. Claudia Cuther, "State Files Suit on Hair Transplant Ads," *Los Angeles Times*, August 24, 1977, pt. 2, p. 5.

12. Ridgely Hunt, "Turning Heads from Deserts to Meadows," *Chicago Tribune*, April 10, 1975, pp. 1, 4.

13. Ibid., p. 4.

14. Beth Ann Krier, "Confidence Sprouts in Hair Transplants," *Los Angeles Times*, October 13, 1976, p. 4, p. 1.

15. "Elton Shows His New Hair," *San Francisco Chronicle*, October 27, 1978, p. 5.

16. Chris Robbins, "Bald Is Best," *Sunday Times* (London), January 5, 1975, p. 32.

17. "Top Secret," *Times* (London), January 15, 1976, p. 14.

18. "Head Planter," *Sunday Times* (London), May 8, 1977, p. 72.

19. "Baldness in Men. Is There an Answer?" *Which?* (September 1983): 392; "No Cure for Baldness, Magazine Survey Says," *Times* (London), September 8, 1983, p. 3.

20. Sharon Litwin, "Bald Facts," *Times-Picayune* (New Orleans), February 10, 1984, sec. 5, p. 1; Greg Kemmis, "Hair-Raising Operation Hailed in Baldness Battle," *Times-Picayune* (New Orleans), June 23, 1984, p. 19.

21. Deborah K. Mann, "Transplants Boast Hair-Raising Results," *Houston Post*, December 18, 1988, p. F12.

22. Kathleen Maxa, "Take a Little Off the Top," *Washingtonian* 22 (July 1987): 109; Clifford Pugh, "The Bald Truth," *Houston Post Magazine*, September 27, 1987, p. 6.

23. "Baldness, Is There Hope?" *Consumer Reports* 53 (September 1988): 547.

24. William G. Flanagan, "The Bald Truth," *Forbes*, July 22, 1991, p. 310; Bud Robertson, "Let the Buyer Beware When Purchase Is Hair," *Winnipeg Free Press*, March 21, 1993, p. A1.

25. Tim Hilchey, "Striving to Get Ahead," *Montreal Gazette*, January 11, 1993, p. B8.

26. Fred Warshofsky, "Science Tackles the Baldness Problem," *Reader's Digest* 83 (February 1966): 89–90.

27. Krier, "Confidence Sprouts," p. 5.

28. Roger Field, "The Big Cover-Up," *Science Digest* 85 (February 1979): 85–86.

29. Joseph C. Carey, "Taking to the Bottle Won't Help Man Who's Losing Hair," *Times-Picayune* (New Orleans), July 7, 1981, sec. 4, p. 4; John Sansing, "Mirror, Mirror, on the Wall, Please Give Me the Best Head of Hair of All," *Washingtonian* 18 (June 1983): 143; Walter Sullivan, "Hair-Loss Experts Cite Innovations," *New York Times*, June 17, 1984, p. 21.

30. Pugh, "Bald Truth," p. 6; "Baldness, Is There Hope?" *Consumer Reports*, p. 547; Hilchey, "Striving to Get Ahead," p.B8.

31. John Pope, "Surgeon Scalps His Patients to Cure Baldness," *Times-Picayune* (New Orleans), March 22, 1981, p. 6.

32. "£3,902 Damages for Hair Graft Blunder," *Times* (London), February 16, 1983, p. 3.

33. Walter Sullivan, "Hair Loss Experts," p. 21.

34. David Perlman, "Tissue Expander May Help Bald Men," *San Francisco Chronicle*, July 11, 1986, p. 10.

35. Sheldon S. Kabaker, "Tissue Expansion in the Treatment of Alopecia," *Archives of Otolaryngol Head & Neck Surgery* 112 (July 1986): 725; Larry Doyle, "Surgeons Splitting Hairs Over Baldness," *Houston Post*, August 28, 1986, p. 8C.

36. Thomas Maugh III, "Swelled Head First Step in Surgical Baldness Cure," *Los Angeles Times*, March 12, 1990, p. B3; Pugh, "Bald Truth," p. 6.

Chapter 9

1. Fred Sparks, "I'm Glad I Bought a Toupee," *Saturday Evening Post*, December 15, 1956, pp. 64–65.

2. Chris Robbins, "Bald Is Best," *Sunday Times* (London), January 5, 1975, p. 32.

3. Martha Smilgis, "If Bald Isn't Beautiful," *People*, June 23, 1980, p. 96.

4. Beth Ann Krier, "Hair-Raising Tales of Male Baldness," *Los Angeles Times*, October 12, 1976, p. 4; Jimmy Thornton, "Baldness No Joke—It's a Glaring Problem," *Times-Picayune* (New Orleans), March 29, 1981, sec. 3, p. 2; John H. Corcoran, Jr., "A Bald-Faced Almanac," *San Francisco Chronicle*, April 23, 1978, Punch sec., p. 4.

5. Frank White III, "How Young Men Cope with Baldness," *Ebony* 38 (June 1983: 54, 56.

6. John Sansing, "Mirror, Mirror on the Wall, Please Give Me the Best Head of Hair of All," *Washingtonian* 18 (June 1983): 139.

7. Mike Royko, "Splitting Hairs Over Heady Issue," *Chicago Tribune*, October 12, 1984, p. 3.

8. Walter Klenhard, *The Bald Book* (Santa Monica, Calif.: Science-Med Press, 1986), p. 30; Karen Heller, "Thinning Hair: A Star Is Shorn," *Chicago Tribune*, August 27, 1986, sec. 7, p. 9; Gaile Robinson, "Losing It," *Los Angeles Times*, June 21, 1991, p. E1.

9. Jane Woolridge, "20 Million American Men Are Facing the Bare Facts," *Times-Picayune* (New Orleans), November 17, 1985, p. B9; Tamara Jones, "Gimme Some Skin," *Houston Post*, April 9, 1987, p. 10C.

10. Jones, "Gimme Some Skin," p. 10C.

11. "Bald Is Beautiful," *Time*, January 13, 1975, pp. 51–52; Vera Glaser, "Coverups on Capitol Hill," *San Francisco Chronicle*, June 8, 1987, p. 42; John Sansing, "Mirror, Mirror," p. 140.

12. Martha Smilgis, "If Bald Isn't Beautiful," p. 96; Kathleen Maxa, "Take a Little Off the Top," *Washingtonian* 22 (July 1987): 109.

13. Matthew V. Storin, "Facing Up to a Bald Spot," *Boston Globe*, April 9, 1989, p. 77; Vera Glaser, "Coverups," p. 42; Iris Krasnow, "The Men Who Grin and Bare Their Baldness," *Los Angeles Times*, December 6, 1987, sec. 6, p. 10.

14. Vera Glaser, "Coverups," pp. 40, 42.

15. Ibid., p. 42.

16. "Can a Bald Man Be Elected President," *Washingtonian* 13 (April 1978): 105.

17. Ibid., pp. 105–6.

18. T. Gerald Aldhizer, *The Doctor's Book on Hair Loss* (Englewood Cliffs, N.J.: Prentice-Hall, 1983), pp. 23–24; Albert Vorspan, "America's Hair Apparent," *New York Times*, April 30, 1983, p. 23; Stephen Chapman, "We Should Vote for Candidates Not for Their Combs," *Chicago Tribune*, August 4, 1988, p. 25.

19. Lee Sigelman, "Hair Loss and Electability: The Bald Truth," *Journal of Nonverbal Behavior* 14, no. 4 (Winter 1990): 272–75.

20. Ibid., pp. 276–82.

21. Vladimire Voinovich, "The Bald and the Hairy," *Encounter* 72 (February 1989): 41.

22. Philip Purser, "Baldness Be My Friend," *Sunday Times* (London), April 22, 1979, p. 13.

23. "Light on the Baldness," *Economist* June 8, 1991, p. 88.

Chapter 10

1. Woods Hutchinson, "Heads and Hair," *Cosmopolitan* 46 (February 1909): 341; Christopher M. Papa and Albert Kligman, "Stimulation of Hair Growth by Topical Application of Androgens," *Journal of the American Medical Association*, February 15, 1965, p. 524.

2. J. V. Sheppard, "The Myth of the Hairy Male," *Hygeia* 26 (June 1948): 409.

3. Condict W. Cutler, "Alopecia," *New York Medical Journal*, June 3, 1893, p. 616; "Pneumatic Cure for Baldness," *Medical Record*, December 30, 1899, p. 987; "Baldness and the Race," *Independent*, September 4, 1902, p. 2152; William P. Cunningham, "Seven Clues to Baldpate," *Medical Record*, August 14, 1915, p. 262; Lester Reynolds, "Science and Your Shining Pate," *Illustrated World* 28 (October 1917): 257.

4. Albert Griffin, "Are Bald Heads Advantageous?" *The New Statesman and Nation* December 22, 1934, p. 937.

5. Frank White III, "How Young Men Cope with Baldness," *Ebony* 38 (June 1983): 56.

6. "Hair," *New York Times*, December 6, 1868, p. 5.

7. Kathleen Maxa, "Take a Little Off the Top," *Washingtonian* 22 (July 1987): 108.

8. Cunningham, "Seven Clues to Baldpate," p. 261; Griffin, "Are Bald Heads Advantageous?", p. 937; Dan Carlinsky, "Bald Truths," *Reader's Digest* 122 (June 1983): 101.

9. Jon Carroll, "The Calpurnia of Comb-Overs," *San Francisco Chronicle*, December 13, 1990, p. E10; Preston Lerner, "The Will O' the Wisp," *Los Angeles Times Magazine*, February 3, 1991, p. 30.

10. "Their Loss, His Gain," *New York Times*, August 31, 1891, p. 3.

11. Douglas Martin, "Mirror, Mirror: Dream Factory for the Hairless," *New York Times*, October 21, 1987, p. B1.

12. Jane Leahy, "Going Bald," *Washington Post Magazine*, November 23, 1986, p. 32.

13. Steve Harvey, "Baldness Is No Joke," *Los Angeles Times*, April 4, 1983, pt. 2, p. 5; Michael Castleman, "Losing It All," *Ms.* 15 (September 1986): 51.

14. "Grow Bald Gracefully," *Science Digest* 35 (March 1954): 48.

15. "Baldness Is a Sign of Normality," *Times* (London), September 15, 1969, p. 3.

16. Matthew V. Storin, "Facing Up to a Bald Spot," *Boston Globe*, April 9, 1989, p. 77; Fred Sparks, "I'm Glad I Bought a Toupee," *Saturday Evening Post* December 15, 1956, p. 65; "Baldness in Men. Is There an Answer?" *Which?* (September 1983): 390.

17. Thomas Stuttaford, "Restoration of Self-Respect," *Times* (London), May 4, 1989, p. 12.

18. William Smart, "You: The Bald Facts," *Washington Post*, July 21, 1981, p. D5; Sharon Litwin, "Bald Facts," *Times-Picayune* (New Orleans), February 10, 1984, sec. 5, p. 1.

19. "Curran Defends Bald-Headed Man," *New York Times*, December 15, 1938, p. 8.

20. Jane Woolridge, "20 Million American Men Are Facing the Bare Facts," *Times-Picayune* (New Orleans), November 17, 1985, p. B9; Iris Krasnow, "The Men Who Grin and Bare Their Baldness," *Los Angeles Times*, December 6, 1987, sec. 6, p. 11; Walter Klenhard, *The Bald Book* (Santa Monica, Calif.: Science-Med Press, 1986), p. 27; "Going Bald Gracefully," *New York Times Magazine*, March 3, 1985, p. 66.

21. Norman Kuhne, "The Bald Head Is Here to Stay," *Nations Business* 36 (August 1948): 66; Gerald Walker, "Baldness Unbared," *New York Times Magazine*, January 4, 1959, p. 62.

22. Walker, "Baldness Unbared," p. 62; Mike Michaelson, "How Your Man Can Crown Himself with Glory," *Today's Health* 51 (March 1978): 25.

23. Clarence Patersen, "And Now for the Baldfaced Truth," *Chicago Tribune*, April 8, 1988, sec. 5, p. 1.

24. John Sansing, "Mirror, Mirror, on the Wall, Please Give Me the Best Head of Hair of All," *Washingtonian* 18 (June 1983): 138.

25. Ruth Boyer Scott, "Stop Worrying About Baldness," *Today's Health* 36 (April 1958): 59; "Baldness Is Not a Loss of Hair," *Science Digest* 49 (March 1961): 48.

26. "Bald Is Beautiful," *Time*, January 13, 1975, p. 51; Charles Leerhsen, "The Bald

Truth: This Is In," *Newsweek*, September 29, 1986, p. 61; Elizabeth Snead, "Toss That Toupee—Thinning Hair Is In," *USA Today*, int'l ed., November 28, 1990, p. 9A.

27. Eric Zorn, "Some Men Take a Shine to Baldness in Women," *Chicago Tribune*, August 17, 1980, p. 3.

28. Dave Kansas, "This Campaign May Give Politicos a New Reason to Steer Clear of '92," *Wall Street Journal*, September 6, 1991, p. B1.

29. Karen Heller, "Thinning Hair: A Star Is Shorn," *Chicago Tribune*, August 27, 1986, sec. 7, p. 12.

30. "The Bald Facts," *Chicago Tribune*, March 15, 1983, p. 18.

31. "Pessimistic, Irritable?" *Montreal Gazette*, November 19, 1992, p. B1.

32. Samuel Roll, "Stereotypes of Scalp and Facial Hair As Measured by the Semantic Differential," *Psychological Reports* 28 (June 1971): 976–79.

33. Paul Chance, "That Bald Feeling," *Psychology Today* 22 (July/August 1988): 16.

34. Thomas F. Cash, "Losing Hair, Losing Points? The Effects of Male Pattern Baldness on Social Impression Formation," *Journal of Applied Social Psychology* 20, no. 2, pt. 1 (February 1990): 162–65.

35. J. Passchier, "Why Men with Hair Loss Go to the Doctor," *Psychological Reports* 65 (August 1989): 325–26.

36. E.B.G. de Koning, "Psychological Problems with Hair Loss in General Practice and the Treatment Policies of General Practitioners," *Psychological Reports* 67 (December 1990): 775–76.

37. Stephen L. Franzoi, "Individual Differences in Men's Perceptions of and Reactions to Thinning Hair," *Journal of Social Psychology* 130, no. 2 (April 1990): 214–15.

38. "Balding Men Do Suffer, Studies Find," *Winnipeg Free Press*, December 30, 1991, p. C21.

39. "Fit Bits," *Bicycling* 35 (July 1994): 22.

40. Bertil Persson, "The Kockum Study: Twenty-two-year Follow Up," *Acta Medica Scandinavia* 216, no. 5 (1984): 485, 488.

41. "Baldness Seen as a Link to Risk Factors in Heart Disease," *New York Times*, March 31, 1990, p. B8.

42. Carlos A. Herrera, "Is Baldness a Risk Factor for Coronary Artery Disease?" *Journal of Clinical Epidemiology* 43, no. 11 (1990): 1255.

43. Lawrence K. Altman, "A Bald Spot on Top May Predict Heart Risk," *New York Times*, February 24, 1993, pp. A1, A7.

44. Ken Walker, "Baldness Linked to Heart Disease," *Times-Colonist* (Victoria, B.C.), October 24, 1993, p. A9.

45. "Bald Head Club on Parade," *New York Times*, February 8, 1896, p. 9.

46. "Bald Head Club Organizer," *New York Times*, August 21, 1920, p. 5; "Baldheads Would Expand," *New York Times*, January 18, 1921, p. 32; "Aid Bald Head Club," *New York Times*, May 27, 1921, p. 15; "Legislators Merry Over Baldheads," *New York Times*, April 7, 1921, p. 19.

47. "Annual Hair Census at Bald Head Club," *New York Times*, May 10, 1921, p. 9.

48. "Bald Headed Club Opposes Hair Culture College Move," *New York Times*, January 26, 1926, p. 29.

49. "Baldness," *Fortune* 8 (July 1933): 52.

50. "Bald Truth Unites Leaders," *New York Times*, June 5, 1956, p. 36; "World Rally of Bald Men Held," *Times* (London), May 24, 1960, p. 12; "Bald Men Decline

Cure Offer," *Times* (London), September 2, 1968, p. 3; Guy Martin, "Thoughts on the Top of My Head," *Esquire* 98 (October 1982): 89.

51. "A Time to Shine," *Sports Illustrated*, May 22, 1989, p. 11; Douglas Martin, "Mirror, Mirror: Dream Factory for the Hairless," *New York Times*, October 21, 1987, p. B1.

52. "Bald Is Beautiful," *Time*, January 13, 1975, p. 51; Al Morch, "Capping All Baldies with Pride," *San Francisco Chronicle*, February 26, 1989, p. E1; Town Hosts Convention to Help Bald Men Celebrate Lack of Roots," *Houston Post*, September 11, 1982, p. 4A; Andrea Higbie, "A Group Where Less Is More," *New York Times*, November 9, 1988, p. C4.

53. Richard C. Thompson, "Balding Is Forever, Experts Say," *FDA Consumer* 15 (February 1981): 10; "Laughter Can Be Good Medicine for Bald-Headed," *Times-Picayune* (New Orleans), July 7, 1981, sec. 4, p. 4.

54. "Join the Club," *Washington Post*, July 21, 1981, p. D5.

55. "Town Hosts Convention," *Houston Post*, p. 4A; "Judges Appreciate His Sexy Bald Pate," *Houston Post*, September 12, 1982, p. 3A.

56. Robert P. Crease, "None But the Bald," *50 Plus* 27 (February 1987): 76; Morch, "Capping All Baldines," p. E1.

57. Andrea Higbie, "A Group Where Less Is More," p. C4.

58. Richard Sandomir, "Hail! The Bald and the Beautiful," *Los Angeles Times*, September 14, 1989, sec. 5, pp. 1, 5, 7.

Chapter 11

1. Malcolm W. Browne, "F.D.A. May Issue a Hair-Raising Decision," *New York Times*, March 22, 1987, sec. 4, p. 28; Adam Smith, "Upjohn's Bald Ambitions," *Esquire* 106 (October 1986): 73; Lee Smith, "Hair-Raising Happenings at Upjohn," *Fortune* April 6, 1981, p. 68; Renee Peck, "Some Hair-Raising Experiments by a Tulane Researcher," *Times-Picayune* (New Orleans), February 10, 1984, sec. 5, p. 1.

2. Ronald Kotulak, "Drug Aids Growth of Hair," *Chicago Tribune*, May 22, 1973, p. 1A; John Sansing, "Mirror, Mirror, on the Wall, Please Give Me the Best Head of Hair of All," *Washingtonian* 18 (June 1983): 142; Stephen W. Quickel, "Bald Spot," *Business Month* 134 (November 1989): 40.

3. Lee Smith, "Hair-Raising Happenings," p. 67.

4. Anthony R. Zappacosta, "Reversal of Baldness in Patient Receiving Minoxidil for Hypertension," *New England Journal of Medicine*, December 18, 1980, p. 1480; Stanley N. Wellborn, "Searching for Their Roots," *U.S. News & World Report*, October 27, 1986, p. 66; Lee Smith, "Hair-Raising Happenings," pp. 68–69.

5. Smith, "Hair-Raising Happenings," p. 68.

6. "Bare Today, Hair Tomorrow?" *Washington Post*, July 2, 1981, p. D5; Sansing, "Mirror, Mirror," p. 142.

7. Edwin Kiester, Jr., "The Bald and the Brave," *50 Plus* 23 (September 1983): 65–67.

8. Peck, "Hair-Raising Experiments," p. 5.

9. "Drug Stimulates New Hair in Tests on Balding Heads," *Times-Picayune* (New Orleans), December 1, 1984, p. 6; "Bare Today, Hair Tomorrow?" *Washington Post*, July 2, 1981, p. D5; "Drug May Prevent Baldness," *Chicago Tribune*, December 1, 1984, p. 8; Janice Hopkins Tanne, "Gone Today, Hair Tomorrow," *New York*, December 10, 1984, p. 70.

10. Nancy Giges, "Upjohn Covers Bald Spot in Haircare Market," *Advertising Age*, February 28, 1985, p. 40; John Crudele, "Hair Growth Drug Seen As a Wonder for Upjohn," *New York Times*, May 28, 1985, p. D5.

11. "Baldness Drug Gains Support," *Chicago Tribune*, June 21, 1985, sec. 3, p. 3.

12. Walter Sullivan, "Hair-Loss Experts Cite Innovations," *New York Times*, June 17, 1984, p. 21; Tanne, "Gone Today," pp. 72–73; Crudele, "Hair Growth Drug," p. D1.

13. Crudele, "Hair Growth Drug," pp. D1, D11.

14. Robert S. Stern, "Topical Minoxidil," *Archives of Dermatology*, 123 (July 1986): 62–63.

15. "Warning on Experimental Baldness Drug," *FDA Consumer* 19 (November 1985): 4–5; "Upjohn Draws U.S. Scrutiny," *New York Times*, May 10, 1986, p. 36.

16. "Me Too Copiers Ape Upjohn Baldness Cure," *Drug & Cosmetic Industry* 139 (July 1986): 40.

17. "Hair-Growth Found As a Side-Effect," *Chicago Tribune*, August 18, 1985, sec. 2, p. 13; Elise A. Olsen, "Topical Minoxidil in Early Male Pattern Baldness," *Journal of the American Academy of Dermatology* 13 (August 1985): 185–92.

18. "Baldness Drug," *Chicago Tribune*, sec. 3, p. 3; "Upjohn in Filing on Baldness Cure," *New York Times*, December 20, 1985, p. D4.

19. Pamela Sherrod, "Hair-Growth Drug Works, Upjohn Says," *Chicago Tribune*, April 30, 1986, sec. 3, p. 3; "Me Too Copiers," *Drug & Cosmetic Industry*, p. 40; "Dangers of a Baldness Cure," *New York Times*, May 6, 1986, p. C3.

20. "Upjohn Draws U.S. Scrutiny," *New York Times*, p. 36; Irwin Arieff, "FDA: Upjohn Exaggerating Claims for Baldness Cure," *Washington Post*, June 18, 1986, p. G2.

21. Stern, "Topical Minoxidil," pp. 64–65.

22. Anastasia Teufexis, "Some Bald Facts about Minoxidil," *Time*, July 14, 1986, p. 43.

23. Michael Castleman, "Losing It All," *Ms.* 15 (September 1986): 51; Penny Ward Moser, "The Bald Truth about Growing Hair," *Discover* 7 (June 1986): 74.

24. Castleman, "Losing It All," pp. 53, 55.

25. Charles Leerhsen, "The Bald Truth: Thin Is In," *Newsweek*, September 29, 1986, p. 61; Smith, "Upjohn's Bald Ambitions," pp. 73–74; Wellborn, "Searching for Their Roots," p. 66.

26. Wellborn, "Searching for Their Roots," p. 66; Quickel, "Bald Spots," p. 41.

27. "Bald Facts," *Economist*, February 7, 1987, p. 19.

28. Irwin Molotsky, "Arguing the Case for Hair," *New York Times*, March 14, 1987, p. 56.

29. Michael Abramowitz, "Panel Approves Hair-Growth Drug," *Washington Post*, March 17, 1987, pp. A1, A25; Irwin Molotsky, "Baldness Drug Gains Support," *New York Times*, March 17, 1987, p. A26.

30. Molotsky, "Baldness Drug," p. A26; "Upjohn Offers Hope for Those Balding Blues," *Chemical Week*, March 25, 1987, p. 13.

31. Rhein, "Upjohn Offers Hope," p. 13; "Panel Approves Hair-Growth Drug," p. A25.

32. "Prescription for a Scalping," *New York Times*, March 19, 1987, p. 26.

33. Anton C. DeGroot, "Hope for the Bald?" *Lancet*, May 2, 1987, pp. 1020–21.

34. Ibid., p. 1021.

35. "Upjohn Co. Moves to Protect Sole Rights to Baldness Drug," *Washington Post*, April 9, 1987, p. E12.

36. "A Hairy Problem," *FDA Consumer* 21 (April 1987): 37–38.

37. "Putting the Brakes on the Baldness-Cure Bandwagon," *FDA Consumer* 21 (September 1987): 34–35.

38. John Sansing, "Bald Truths," *Washingtonian* 22 (July 1987): 105.

39. Oliver Gillie, "Battling for the Bald Man's Scalp," *Sunday Times* (London), November 6, 1983, p. 72.

40. Leerhsen, "Bald Truth," p. 61; Howard Witt, "Drug Less Than Hair-Raising in Canada," *Chicago Tribune*, March 19, 1987, sec. 3, pp. 1, 6.

41. Richard Owen, "Belgians Tackle Baldness," *Times* (London), February 6, 1987, p. 7.

42. Alan Hamilton, "A Small Step for Cranial Moonscapes," *Times* (London), March 26, 1988, p. 2.

43. Rick Marin, "Kiss It Good-Bye," *GQ* 62 (August 1992): 175.

44. "Hello, Baldness," *New York Times*, August 18, 1985, p. 48; Pat Sloan, "Hair-Restorer Drugs Brush with the FDA," *Advertising Age*, September 15, 1986, p. 82; Rhein, "Upjohn Offers Hope," p. 13.

45. John Sansing, "Bald Truths," *Washingtonian* 22 (July 1987): 105; "Experimental Drug Cyoctol Can Produce Hair in Some Balding Men, Study Finds," *Wall Street Journal*, December 5, 1989, p.. B4; Linda Roach Monroe, "Study Suggests Drug May Reverse Balding in Men," *Los Angeles Times*, December 5, 1989, p. A3.

46. Michael Waldholz, "Merck Says Experimental Prostate Drug Might Grow Hair on Bald Men's Heads," *Wall Street Journal*, April 29, 1992, p. B6; "ProCyte Study May Lead to New Drug for Baldness," *Wall Street Journal*, July 29, 1992, p. B4; Jeff Stevenson, "Making Headway," *Men's Health* 8 (May 1993): 25.

47. Sansing, "Bald Truths," pp. 103–4.

48. "Ads Key to Future of Antibaldness Drug," *Chicago Tribune*, August 14, 1988, sec. 7, p. 10.

49. Gina Kolata, "Hair-Growth Drug Approved, the First Cleared in the U.S." *New York Times*, August 18, 1988, p. B13; Milt Freudenheim, "Upjohn Awaiting Rogaine Results," *New York Times*, August 19, 1988, p. D4.

50. Kolata, "Hair-Growth Drug," p. B13; Tony Bizjak, "Hair Drug Users Face the Bald Truth," *San Francisco Chronicle*, August 20, 1988, p. 3.

51. Bruce Horovitz, "Doctors at Head of Upjohn's List of Targets for Baldness-Drug Ads," *Washington Post*, August 21, 1988, p. H3; "Upjohn Files Suit," *New York Times*, October 14, 1988, p. D3.

52. "Baldness, Is There Hope?" *Consumer Reports* 53 (September 1988): 543–45.

53. Ibid., p. 546.

54. "Minoxidil vs. Baldness," *Washington Post*, November 16, 1988, p. D5; Judy Folkenberg, "Hair Apparent?" *FDA Consumer* 22 (December 1988/January 1989): D5.

55. Laurie Freeman, "Upjohn Takes a Shine to Balding Women," *Advertising Age* February 27, 1989, p. 51.

56. Al Morch, "A Hair-Raising Solution," *San Francisco Chronicle*, February 26, 1989, p. E4.

57. Matthew V. Storin, "Facing Up to a Bald Spot," *Boston Globe*, April 9, 1989, p. 77.

58. Malcolm Gladwell, "Upjohn's New Ads Bid Baldies to Comb Again," *Washington Post*, May 18, 1989, pp. E1, E4.

59. Joan Beck, "Unfounded Hopes for Restoring Hair Are Receding Rapidly,"

Chicago Tribune, July 10, 1989, p. 11; Laurie Freeman, "Can Rogaine Make Gains Via Ads?" *Advertising Age* September 11, 1989, p. 12.

60. Bernice Kanner, "Hair Today," *New York*, October 30, 1989, p. 20.

61. Quickel, "Bald Spot," pp. 36, 40, 42.

62. Ibid., pp. 40, 42–43.

63. Linda Roach Monroe, "The Rub in a Hair Remedy," *Los Angeles Times*, March 13, 1990, pp. E1, E3.

64. David Woodruff, "For Rogaine No Miracle Cure—Yet," *Business Week*, June 4, 1990, p. 100.

65. Christopher Byron, "Drug Problems," *New York*, June 15, 1992, p. 18.

66. Emily DeNitto, "Rogaine Raises Women's Interest," *Advertising Age*, February 28, 1994, p. 12.

67. Linda Roach Monroe, "Baldness Remedy an Orgasm Aid?" *Toronto Star*, July 27, 1993, p. B3.

BIBLIOGRAPHY

Abramovitz, Michael. "Panel Approves Hair-Growth Drug." *Washington Post*, March 17, 1987, pp. A1, A25.

Adelson, Andrea. "Hope in a Bottle." *New York Times*, March 13, 1988, sec. 3, p. 5.

"Ads Key to Future of Antibaldness Drug." *Chicago Tribune*, August 14, 1988, sec. 7, p. 10.

"Agency Proposes a Ban on Sales of Products to Prevent Baldness." *New York Times*, November 9, 1980, p. 43.

Aldhizer, T. Gerald. *The Doctor's Book on Hair Loss*. Englewood Cliffs, N.J.: Prentice-Hall, 1983.

Alexander, Dale. *Healthy Hair and Common Sense*. West Harford, Conn.: Witkower Press, 1974.

Alger, Ellice M. "Two Common Forms of Alopecia, with Their Treatment." *Medical Record*, October 27, 1984, pp. 536–37.

"Alopecia." *Medical Record*, February 22, 1896, p. 286.

"Alopecia." *Medical Record*, July 4, 1896, p. 31.

"Alopecia and Dental Abnormalities." *New York Medical Journal*, November 10, 1917, p. 909.

"Alopecia and Earwax." *New York Medical Journal*, January 4, 1919, p. 36.

"Alopecia and Seborrhea." *Medical Record*, October 8, 1910, p. 611.

Altman, Lawrence K. "A Bald Spot on Top May Predict Heart Risk." *New York Times*, February 24, 1993, pp. A1, A7.

"The Anatomic Factor in Baldness." *Medical News*, April 26, 1902, p. 791.

"The Anatomical Factor in the Production of Baldness." *Medical Record*, May 24, 1902, p. 816.

Andrews, Miss E. F. "Will the Coming Woman Lose Her Hair?" *Popular Science Monthly* 42 (January 1893): 370–72.

"Anti-Baldness Vitamins Getting National Ad Drive." *Advertising Age*, February 21, 1977, pp. 22–23.

"Antidotes for Baldness." *New York Times*, September 1, 1913, p. 4.

Arieff, Irwin. "FDA: Upjohn Exaggerating Claims for Baldness Cure." *Washington Post*, June 18, 1986, p. G2.

"Bald Claims." *Time*, July 12, 1948, pp. 42–43.

"Bald-Faced Hair Scam." *FDA Consumer* 23 (March 1989): 34–35.

"The Bald Facts." *Chicago Tribune*, March 15, 1983, p. 18.

"Bald Facts." *Economist*, February 7, 1987, p. 19.

"Bald Is Beautiful," *Time*, January 13, 1975, 51–52.

"The Bald Man's Bacillus." *Medical News*, April 3, 1897, p. 440.

"Bald Men Are More Virile, Brooklyn Doctor Reports." *New York Times*, July 28, 1953, p. 21.

"Bald Men Are No Lard Heads." *Science Digest* 37 (March 1955): 51.

"Bald Men: Be Careful of Hair-Grafters." *Washington Post*, July 23, 1972, Parade sec., p. 10–11.

"Bald Men Decline Cure Offer." *Times* (London), September 2, 1968, p. 3.

"Bald Truth Unites Leaders." *New York Times*, June 5, 1956, p. 36.

"Balding Men Do Suffer, Studies Find." *Winnipeg Free Press*, December 30, 1991, p. C21.

"Baldness." *New York Times*, March 28, 1914, p. 12

"Baldness." *New York Times*, April 5, 1914, pt. 3, p. 14.

"Baldness." *Fortune* 8 (July 1933): 52–55+.

"Baldness." *Newsweek*, May 15, 1937, p. 39.

"Baldness." *Sunday Times* (London), April 13, 1975, p. 42.

"Baldness a Germ Disease?" *New York Times*, June 25, 1913, p. 8.

"Baldness Ahead." *Americas* 7 (May 1955): 40.

"Baldness Among Clergymen." *New York Times*, June 5, 1913, p. 10.

"Baldness and Grayness." *Scientific American Supplement*, July 6, 1912, pp. 14–15.

"Baldness and Its Treatment." *Medical Record*, February 24, 1912, p. 371.

"Baldness and the Hair Brush." *New York Times*, Novemer 6, 1901, p. 8.

"Baldness and the Race." *Independent*, September 4, 1902, pp. 2152–53.

"Baldness Breakthrough." *Journal of the American Medical Association*, February 15, 1965, p. 594.

"Baldness Cured by Grafting Hair." *New York Times*, March 15, 1967, p. 49.

"Baldness Drug Gains Support." *Chicago Tribune*, June 21, 1985, sec. 3, p. 3.

"Baldness—He-Man Complaint." *Science Digest* 19 (March 1946): inside cover.

"Baldness in Men. Is There an Answer?" *Which?* (September 1983): 390–92.

"Baldness Is a Sign of Normality." *Times* (London), September 15, 1969, p. 3.

"Baldness, Is There Hope?" *Consumer Reports* 53 (September 1988): 543–47.

"Baldness Is Not a Loss of Hair." *Science Digest* 49 (March 1961): 48.

"Baldness Lotions to Be Limited Under Order Planned by FDA." *Chemical Marketing Reporter*, July 10, 1989, pp. 4, 27.

"Baldness of Women." *New York Times*, March 19, 1914, p. 8.

"Baldness Seen As a Link to Risk Factors in Heart Disease." *New York Times*, March 31, 1990, p. B8.

"Baldness Traced to the Absence of Upper Chest Breathing." *Current Literature* 42 (April 1907): 453.

"Baldness Yields to No Scientists." *New York Times*, February 12, 1950, p. 49.

"Baldy Sufferers: Despair and Joy." *Beijing Review*, January 18–31, 1993, p. 38.

"Bare Today, Hair Tomorrow?" *Washington Post*, July 2, 1981, p. D5.

Barman, Julio M. "The Normal Trichogram of the Adult." *Journal of Investigative Dermatology* 44 (1965): 233–36.

Beck, Joan. "Unfounded Hopes for Restoring Hair Are Receding Rapidly." *Chicago Tribune*, July 10, 1989, p. 11.

Benezra, Nat. "A Hair-Raising Tale." *Family Health* 9 (December 1977): 25–29.

Bengtson, Bengt Norman. "Anterior Pituitary Treatment for Baldness." *Journal of the American Medical Association*, November 28, 1931, p. 1643.

_____ "Pituitary Therapy of Alopecia." *Journal of the American Medical Association*, November 7, 1931, pp. 1355–58.

Bennett, Charles G. "City Plans to Look into Hair-Weaving Complaints." *New York Times*, November 23, 1968, p. 36.

"Betty Has Hairy Theory." *Times-Picayune* (New Orleans), April 1, 1973, sec. 2, p. 7.

Bizjak, Tony. "Hair Drug Users Face the Bald Truth." *San Francisco Chronicle*, August 20, 1988, p. 3.

Blaine, J. M. "Etiology of Alopecia Prematura." *Journal of the American Medical Association*, March 11, 1899, pp. 524–25.

"Blame for Baldness." *Newsweek*, November 12, 1951, p. 94.

"Blame It on Your Sebaceous Glands." *Science News*, May 17, 1986, p. 318.

Block, S. S. "How Food Affects Your Hair." *Science Digest* 15 (May 1944): 13–17.

Blumenthal, Ralph. "A Baldness Remedy Is Assailed." *New York Times*, March 14, 1979, pp. C1, C10.

Braden, William. "Baldness Boosts Virility, Hair Expert Claims." *Times-Picayune* (New Orleans), March 29, 1981, sec. 3, p. 2.

Brady, William. "What Can Be Done to Prevent Baldness." *Illustrated World*, 27 (April 1917): 213–17.

"British Doctor Finds Gland to Restore Hair." *New York Times*, November 13, 1926, p. 6.

"British Quest to Grow Hair in Laboratory." *New York Times*, October 30, 1984, p. C7.

Brody, Jane E. "Hair Loss." *New York Times*, May 3, 1978, pp. C1, C12.

"Brother, Can You Spare a Dome?" *People*, June 4, 1984, p. 61.

Brown, Malcolm. "Heading for Baldness Cure." *Sunday Times* (London), October 9, 1988, p. D20.

Brown, Terry. "Hair Apparently Is Growth Field." *Chicago Tribune*, March 10, 1982, sec. 3, p. 3.

Browne, Malcolm W. "F.D.A. May Issue a Hair-Raising Decision." *New York Times*, March 22, 1987, sec. 4, p. 28.

Bush, Gretchen. "Hair Care Producers Betting on Niches." *Chemical Marketing Reporter*, July 24, 1989, pp. SR13-SR14.

Byron, Christopher. "Drug Problems." *New York*, June 15, 1992, pp. 18–19.

Cabanac, Michel. "Beardedness, Baldness, and Northern Climate." *Behavioral and Brain Sciences* 13, no. 2 (June 1990): 351.

_____"Beards, Baldness, and Sweat Secretion." *European Journal of Applied Psychology and Occupational Physiology* 58, nos. 1–2 (1988): 39–46.

Calistro, Paddy. "Top Secret." *Los Angeles Times Magazine*, June 28, 1987, p. 34.

"Can a Bald Man Be Elected President?" *Washingtonian* 13 (April 1978): 104–6.

Carey, Joseph C. "Taking to the Bottle Won't Help Man Who's Losing Hair." *Times-Picayune* (New Orleans), July 7, 1981, sec. 4, p. 4.

Carlinsky, Dan. "Bald Truths." *Reader's Digest* 122 (June 1983): pp. 99–102.

Carpenter, Allan. "They Pull Your Hair to Save It." *Science Digest*, 23 (March 1948): 38–40.

Carroll, Jon. "The Calpurnia of Comb-Overs." *San Francisco Chronicle*, December 13, 1990, p. E10.

Cash, Thomas F. "Losing Hair, Losing Points? The Effects of Male Pattern Baldness on Social Impression Formation." *Journal of Applied Social Psychology* 20 (February 1990); 154–67.

Castleman, Michael. "Losing It All." *Ms.* 15 (September 1986): 51–53+.

"The Cause of Modern Baldness." *Literary Digest*, February 4, 1928, p. 24.

"The Causes and Treatment of Baldness." *Medical Record*, August 12, 1905, p. 273.

"The Causes of Baldness." *New York Times*, May 22, 1913, p. 10.

Chance, Paul. "That Bald Feeling." *Psychology Today* 22 (July/August 1988): 16.

Chapman, Stephen. "We Should Vote for Candidates, Not for Their Combs." *Chicago Tribune*, August 4, 1988, p. 25.

"City Prosecutes Baldness Cure Man." *New York Times*, December 17, 1921, p. 13.

Clark, Matt. "Bald Men Beware." *Newsweek*, February 16, 1979, p. 54.

Cobb. J. O. "Baldness." *New York Medical Journal*, (1909): 1298–1300.

Comegys, Lee. "Chrome Dome: Keep or Cover It?" *Times-Picayune* (New Orleans) May 11, 1982, sec. 4, p. 1.

Corcoran, John H., Jr. "A Bald-Faced Almanac." *San Francisco Chronicle*, April 23, 1978, Punch sec., p. 4.

Cramp, Arthur J. "Some Bald Facts," *Hygeia* 5 (October 1927): 497–99.

Crease, Robert P. "None But the Bald." *50 Plus* 27 (February 1987): 74+.

Crudele, John. "Hair Growth Drug Seen As a Wonder for Upjohn." *New York Times*, May 28, 1985, pp. D1, D11.

"Cue Balls to Shine at Topless Convention." *Los Angeles Times*, September 1, 1983, sec. 1A, p. 5.

Cunningham, William P. "Seven Clues to Baldpate." *Medical Record*, August 14, 1915, pp. 262–67.

"Cure for Skinheads?" *Time*, September 27, 1954, p. 57.

"Cures Baldness in Mice." *New York Times*, November 3, 1949, sec. 2, p. 5.

"Curran Defends Bald-Headed Man." *New York Times*, December 15, 1938, p. 8.

Cutler, Condict W. "Alopecia." *New York Medical Journal*, June 3, 1893, pp. 616–17.

Damon, Albert. "Baldness of Fathers and Number of Sex Ratio of Children." *Human Biology*, 37, no. 4 (December 1965): 366–70.

"Dangers of a Baldness Cure." *New York times*, May 6, 1986, p. C3.

"Dare to Go Hatless!" *New York Times*, September 12, 1925, p. 14.

de Koning, E.B.G. "Psychological Problems with Hair Loss in General Practice and the Treatment Policies of General Practitioners." *Psychological Reports* 67 (December 1990): 775–78.

De Leon, George. "The Baldness Experiment." *Psychology Today* 11 (October 1977): 62–63, 66.

"De Wonderkapper." *Time*, June 13, 1949, pp. 29–30.

DeGroot, Anton C. "Minoxidil: Hope for the Bald?" *Lancet*, May 2, 1987, pp. 1019–22.

DeNitto, Emily. "Rogaine Raises Women's Interest." *Advertising Age*, February 28, 1994, p. 12.

"Dermatitis Seborrhoria and Baldness." *Medical News*, February 4, 1905, p. 223.

"Dermatologist Thinks He Can Test Baldies with Electricity." *Times-Colonist* (Victoria, B.C.), August 5, 1990, p. A12.

"Devitalized Foods." *New York Times*, July 1, 1913, p. 8.

"Disprove Theory on Cause of Baldness." *Science News Letter*, October 31, 1959, p. 289.

"Doctor Says Scalp Graft Can Eliminate Baldness." *New York Times*, December 7, 1961, p. 46.

Dorfman, Dan. "A Hair-Raising Tale." *New York*, January 20, 1986, pp. 11, 14.

_____"Another Product That Claims It Can Cover Bald Pates." *San Francisco Chronicle*, January 11, 1986, p. 47.

Dorsey, Benjamin L. *Baldness, Its Causes and Prevention.* Los Angeles: DeVorss, 1939.

Doyle, Larry. "Surgeons Splitting Hairs Over Baldness." *Houston Post*, August 28, 1986, p. 8C.

"Drug May Prevent Baldness." *Chicago Tribune,* December 1, 1984, p. 8.

"Drug Stimulates New Hair in Tests on Balding Heads." *Times-Picayune* (New Orleans), December 1, 1984, p. 6.

Dyer, Isadore. "Alopecia; Types and Treatment." *New York Medical Journal,* June 8, 1912, 1192–95.

Elliot, George T. "A Further Study of Alopecia Praematura or Praesenilis." *New York Medical Journal,* October 26, 1895, pp. 525–28.

Ellis, Susan Gottenberg. *Make Sense of Your Dreams.* Largo, Fla.: Sudavel, 1988.

"Elton Shows His New Hair." *San Francisco Chronicle,* October 27, 1978, p. 5.

The Encyclopedia Americana. Int'l ed. vol. 3. Danbury, Conn.: Grolier, 1994, pp. 81–82.

"End of Baldness." *New York Times,* February 21, 1965, sec. 4, p. 6.

"Experimental Drug Cyoctol Can Produce Hair in Some Balding Men, Study Finds." *Wall Street Journal,* December 5, 1989, p. B4.

"Exposure to the Sun As an Etiological Factor in Alopecia." *Medical Record,* October 15, 1910, p. 694.

"FDA Band Implants of Hair Fibers." *Chicago Tribune,* June 4, 1983, p. 3.

Field, Roger. "The Big Cover-Up." *Science Digest* 85 (February 1979): pp. 85–86.

"Fit Bit." *Bicycling* 35 (July 1994): 22.

Flanagan, William G. "The Bald Truth." *Forbes,* July 22, 1991, pp. 309–10.

Folkenberg, Judy. "Hair Apparent?" *FDA Consumer* 22 (December 1988/January 1989): 8–11.

"Foot to Head." *Time,* March 2, 1936, p. 32.

"Founder of Zzyzx Spa Convicted on Ad Claims." *New York Times,* July 19, 1970, p. 55.

Franklin, Matthew. "Japanese Hair-Care Affair." *Herald-Sun* (Melbourne), November 26, 1990, p. 13.

Franzoi, Stephen L. "Individual Differences in Men's Perception of and Reactions to Thinning Hair." *The Journal of Social Psychology,* 130, no. 2 (April 1990): 209–18.

Freeman, Laurie. "Can Rogaine Make Gains Via Ads?" *Advertising Age,* September 26, 1988, p. 38.

_____"Upjohn Takes a Shine to Balding Women." *Advertising Age,* February 27, 1989, p. 51.

Freudenheim, Milt. "Upjohn Awaiting Rogaine Results." *New York Times,* August 19, 1988, p. D4.

Friedrich, Otto. "Hope Sprouts Eternal." *Time,* January 28, 1985, p. 92.

Gallagher, T. F. "The Daily Urinary Excretion of Estrogenic and Androgenic Substances of Normal Men and Women." *Journal of Clinical Investigation* 16 (1937): 695–703.

Galton, Lawrence. "The Bald Truths: Avoid Fiber Implants." *Washington Post,* April 1, 1979, Parade sec., pp. 7–8.

Garboden, Clif. "Periwigs." *Boston Globe Magazine,* March 12, 1989, p. 14.

Gargan, Edward A. "In Baldness War, Rumors of Advance for Hairline." *New York Times,* January 26, 1988, p. 4.

"Genetic Link Hints at Cure for Baldness." *Vancouver Sun,* March 17, 1994, p. A1.

"Geography May Influence Baldness in Young Men." *Science News Letter,* April 10, 1948, p. 233.

"The Germs of Baldness." *New York Times,* June 29, 1913, pt. 3, p. 4.

Gibson, John E. "What You Can Do About Your Hair." *Science Digest* 31 (February 1952): 1–4.

Giges, Nancy. "Upjohn Covers Bald Spot in Haircare Market." *Advertising Age*, February 28, 1985, p. 40.

Gillie, Oliver. "Battling for the Bald Man's Scalp." *Sunday Times* (London), November 6, 1983, p. 72.

Gladwell, Malcolm. "Upjohn's New Ads Bid Baldies to Comb Again." *Washington Post*, May 18, 1989, pp. E1, E4.

Glaser, Vera. "Coverups on Capitol Hill." *San Francisco Chronicle*, June 8, 1987, pp. 40, 42.

"Going Bald Gracelessly." *New York Times Magazine*, March 3, 1985, p. 66.

"Going, Going, Gone." *Literary Digest*, October 17, 1936, p. 21.

Gold, Paige. "The Fallout and What's Behind It." *San Francisco Chronicle*, April 23, 1978, Punch sec., p. 5.

Gonzalez-Wippler, Migene. *Dreams and What They Mean to You*. St. Paul, Minn.: Llewellyn, 1989.

"Government Bans Most Baldness Treatments." *New York Times*, July 8, 1989, p. 6.

Greenbaum, Sigmund S. "Are You Losing Your Hair?" *Hygeia* 8 (March 1930): 241–45.

Greene, James. "Artificial Hair Transplants Pose Real Danger." *Chicago Tribune*, December 1, 1979, pp. 13–14.

Griffin, Albert. "Are Bald Heads Advantageous?" *New Statesman and Nation*, December 22, 1934, p. 937.

Groveman, Howard D. "Lack of Efficacy of Polysorbate 60 in the Treatment of Male Pattern Baldness." *Archives of Internal Medicine* 145 (August 1985): 1451–58.

"Grow Bald Gracefully." *Science Digest* 35 (March 1954): 48.

"Hair." *New York Times*, December 6, 1868, p. 5.

"Hair and Religion." *New York Times*, May 27, 1913, p. 10.

"Hair Fibers Banned." *FDA Consumer* 17 (September 1983): 26–27.

"Hair Growth Found As a Side-Effect." *Chicago Tribune*, August 18, 1985, sec. 2, p. 13.

"Hair Implants Devised." *New York Times*, August 7, 1971, p. 33.

"Hair-Raising Business." *Reader's Digest* 55 (July 1949): 70–72.

"Hair-Raising Development." *Family Health* 8 (July 1976): 25.

"Hair Sprouts Where Lightning Struck." *Los Angeles Times*, July 5, 1980, p. 2.

"Hair Today Hurts Tomorrow: U.S." *Chicago Tribune*, March 28, 1979, p. 6.

"Hair Too Thin to Fight." *New York Times*, March 30, 1943, p. 23.

"The Hairlessness of Man." *Science*, October 16, 1931, sup. 12.

"A Hairy Problem." *FDA Consumer* 21 (April 1987): 37–38.

Haitao, Yue. "Japan Buys Hair Treatment." *Beijing Review*, August 4, 1986, p. 29.

Hamilton, Alan. "A Small Step for Cranial Moonscapes." *Times* (London), March 26, 1988, p. 2.

Hamilton, James B. "Male Hormone Stimulation Is Prerequisite and an Incident in Common Baldness." *American Journal of Anatomy* 71 (November 1942): 451–8.

Harris, Harry. "The Inheritance of Premature Baldness in Men." *Annals of Eugenics* 13 (November 1946): 172–81.

Harvey, Steve. "Baldness Is No Joke." *Los Angeles Times*, April 4, 1983, pt. 2, p. 5.

"Hats and Baldness." *New York Times*, June 30, 1909, p. 6.

"Head Planter." *Sunday Times* (London), May 8, 1977, p. 72.

Heller, Karen. "Thinning Hair: A Star Is Shorn." *Chicago Tribune*, August 27, 1986, sec. 7, pp. 9, 12.

"Hello, Baldness." *New York Times*, August 18, 1985, p. 48.

"Here's Hope for Hair." *Newsweek*, February 16, 1959, p. 92.

Herrera, Carlos R. "Is Baldness a Risk Factor for Coronary Artery Disease? *Journal of Clinical Epidemiology* 43, no. 11 (1990): 1255–60.

Higbie, Andrea. "A Group Where Less Is More." *New York Times*, November 9, 1988, p. C4.

Hilchey, Tim. "Striving to Get Ahead." *Montreal Gazette*, January 11, 1993, p. B8.

Hoelzel, Frederick. "Baldness and Calcification of the Ivory Dome." *Journal of the American Medical Association*, July 18, 1942, p. 968.

The Home Book of Humorous Quotations. New York: Dodd, Mead, 1969.

The Home Book of Quotations. 8th ed. New York: Dodd, Mead, 1956.

"Hope for the Bald Held Out by Coué." *New York Times*, January 15, 1924, p. 44.

"Hormone Cream Restores Lost Hair." *Science Digest* 57 (March 1965): 22–23.

Horovitz, Bruce. "Doctors at Head of Upjohn's List of Targets for Baldness-Drug Ads." *Washington Post*, August 21, 1988, p. H3.

Hubbard, S. Dana. "Ways to Keep the 160,000 Hairs on Your Head." *American Magazine* 93 (March 1922): 50–51+.

Hunt, Ridgely. "Turning Heads from Deserts to Meadows." *Chicago Tribune*, April 10, 1975, pp. 1, 4.

Hutchinson, Woods. "Heads and Hair." *Cosmospolitan* 46 (February 1909): 340–46.

"Indigestion and Baldness." *Medical Record*, November 9, 1895, p. 684.

Jackson, George Thomas. "Los of Hair." *Current Literature* 29 (July 1900): 46–48.

"Join the Club." *Washington Post*, July 21, 1981, p. D5.

Jones, Tamara. "Gimme Some Skin." *Houston Post*, April 9, 1987, p. 10C.

"Judge Puts Crimp in Hair Clinic." *San Francisco Chronicle*, July 28, 1979, p. 4.

"Judges Appreciate His Sexy Bald Pate." *Houston Post*, September 12, 1982, p. 3A.

"Julius Caesar." *New York Times Magazine*, April 14, 1957, p. 78.

Kabaker, Sheldon S. "Tissue Expansion in the Treatment of Alopecia." *Archives of Otolaryngol Head & Neck Surgery*, 112 (July 1986): 725.

Kanner, Bernice. "Hair Today." *New York*, October 30, 1989, pp. 20, 22.

Kansas, Dave. "This Campaign May Give Politicos a New Reason to Steer Clear of '92." *Wall Street Journal*, September 6, 1991, p. B1.

Kavesh, Laura. "Biotin Gets Hair-Raising Tests in Chicago." *Chicago Tribune*, June 17, 1983, sec. 15, p. 4.

Kemmis, Greg. "Hair-Raising Operation Hailed in Baldness Battle." *Times-Picayune* (New Orleans), June 23, 1984, p. 19.

Kiester, Edwin, Jr. "The Bald and the Brave." *50 Plus* 23 (September 1983): 64–67.

Klemesrud, Judy. "Hair Thinning? Don't Flip, Pop." *New York Times*, February 24, 1968, p. 18.

_____"Tired of a Toupee? Try Hair-Weaving." *New York Times*, April 15, 1968, p. 38.

Klenhard, Walter. *The Bald Book.* Santa Monica, Calif.: Science-Med Press, 1986.

Kolata, Gina. "Hair-Growth Drug Approved, the First Cleared in the U.S." *New York Times*, August 18, 1988, pp. A1, B13.

Kotulak, Ronald. "Drug Aids Growth of Hair." *Chicago Tribune*, May 22, 1973, p. 7.

_____"Hair-Saving Drug Seen in 2 Years." *Chicago Tribune*, May 23, 1973, p. 4.

Krasnow, Iris. "The Men Who Grin and Bare Their Baldness." *Los Angeles Times*, December 6, 1987, sec. 6, pp. 10–11.

Krier, Beth Ann. "Confidence Sprouts in Hair Transplants." *Los Angeles Times*, October 13, 1976, pt. 4, p. 1, 4–6.

_____"Hair-Raising Tales of Male Baldness." *Los Angeles Times*, October 12, 1976, pp. 1, 4–5.

Kuchl, Peter. "The Bald Truth About a Sales Pitch." *San Francisco Chronicle*, February 3, 1979, p. 2.

Kuhne, Norman. "The Bald Head Is Here to Stay." *Nations Business* 36 (August 1948): 41–42+.

"Lab-Grown Hair Could Lead to Baldness Cure." *Chicago Tribune*, November 4, 1984, sec. 6, p. 6.

"Lactic Acid As a Remedy for Baldness." *New York Medical Journal*, October 21, 1899, p. 595.

Lal, G. B., "Keep Calm and Keep Your Hair." *Science Digest* 29 (January 1951): 57–60.

Langone, John. "Gone Today, Hair Tomorrow." *Time*, August 29, 1988, p. 78.

"Laughter Can Be Good Medicine for Bald-Headed." *Times-Picayune* (New Orleans), July 7, 1981, sec. 4, p. 4.

"Lays Baldness to Eye Strain." *New York Times*, November 22, 1934, p. 18.

Leahy, Jane. "Going Bald." *Washington Post Magazine*, November 23, 1986, pp. 30–32.

Leerhsen, Charles. "The Bald Truth: Thin Is In." *Newsweek*, September 29, 1986, p. 61.

Lerner, Preston. "The Will O' the Wisp." *Los Angeles Times Magazine*, February 3, 1991, p. 30.

"Light on the Baldness." *Economist*, June 8, 1991, p. 88.

Little, Robert P. "That Bald Spot." *Hygeia* 26 (January 1948): 32–33.

Litwin, Sharon. "Bald Facts." *Times-Picayune* (New Orleans), February 10, 1984, sec. 5, p. 1.

"London Letter." *Medical News*, February 18, 1899, p. 218.

Lubowe, Irwin I. *New Hope for Your Hair*. New York: Dutton, 1960.

_____ "Seven Causes of Baldness." *Science Digest* 48 (September 1960): 74–80.

Luther, Claudia. "State Files Suit on Hair Treatment Ads." *Los Angeles Times*, August 24, 1977, pt. 2, p. 5.

Lyons, Richard D. "Patching Bald Spots." *New York Times*, March 26, 1967, sec. 4, p. 7.

"Machining the Scalp." *Illustrated World* 33 (April 1920): 306–7.

McLeod, Michael. "Male Strangers Take a Shine to Professor." *Chicago Tribune*, June 20, 1988, sec. 5, p. 1.

MacKee, George M. "The High Frequency Spark in the Treatment of Premature Alopecia." *New York Medical Journal*, July 28, 1906, pp. 180–84.

"Male Hormone Produces Hair on Bald Heads." *Science News Letter*, March 20, 1965, p. 184.

Mann, Deborah K. "Transplants Boast Hair-Raising Results." *Houston Post*, December 18, 1988, p. F12.

"Man's Oldest Fallout Problem: Baldness." *Today's Health* 41 (August 1963): 46–50.

Marin, Rick. "Kiss It Good-bye." *GQ* 62 (August 1992): 172–77.

Martin, Douglas. "Mirror, Mirror: Dream Factory for the Hairless." *New York Times*, October 21, 1987, p. B1.

Martin, Guy. "Thoughts on the Top of My Head." *Esquire* 98 (October 1985):89.

Maugh, Thomas H. II. "Swelled Head First Step in Surgical Baldness Cure." *Los Angeles Times*, March 12, 1990, p. B3.

Maxa, Kathleen. "Take a Little Off the Top." *Washingtonian*, 22 (July 1987): 106–11.

"Me Too Copiers Are Upjohn Baldness Cure." *Drug & Cosmetic Industry* 139 (July 1986): 40.

Michaelson, Mike. "How Your Man Can Crown Himself with Glory." *Today's Health* 51 (March 1973): 16–19+.

"The Microbe of Baldness." *Medical Record*, May 21, 1898, p. 738.

"The Microbe That Causes Baldness." *Current Literature* 33 (August 1902): 215.

Miller, Gustavus Hindman. *10,000 Dreams Interpreted.* New York: Bell, 1988.

"Minoxidil Vs. Baldness." *Washington Post*, November 16, 1988, p. D5.

"Miraculous Lightning Sparks Hair." *Times-Picayune* (New Orleans), July 4, 1980, pp. 1, 6.

"Mirage." *Time*, December 12, 1955, pp. 53–54.

Molotsky, Irvin. "Arguing the Case for Hair." *New York Times*, March 14, 1987, p. 56.

_____"Baldness Drug Gains Support." *New York Times*, March 17, 1987, pp. A1, A26.

_____"Baldness Potions Don't Work, F.D.A. Warns." *New York Times*, January 15, 1985, pp. A1, A12.

Monroe, Linda Roach. "Baldness Remedy on Orgasm Aid?" *Toronto Star*, July 27, 1993, p. B3.

_____"The Rub in a Hair Remedy." *Los Angeles Times*, March 13, 190, pp. E1, E3.

_____"Study Suggests Drug May Reverse Balding in Men." *Los Angeles Times*, December 5, 1989, pp. A3, A36.

Morch, Al. "Capping All Baldies with Pride." *San Francisco Chronicle*, February 26, 1989, p. E1.

_____"A Hair-Raising Solution." *San Francisco Chronicle*, February 26, 1989, pp. E1, E4.

_____"New Drug Stimulates Sales of Hairpieces." *San Francisco Chronicle*, February 26, 1989, p. E4.

Moser, Penny Ward. "The Bald Truth About Growing Hair." *Discover* 7 (June 1986): 72–81.

Mount, Louis B. "The Alopecias." *Medical Record* May 22, 1915, pp. 852–54.

Muller, Sigfrid A. "Alopecia." *Journal of Investigative Dermatology* 60 (1973): 475–92.

"Muscle Heads Don't Get Bald." *Science Digest* 42 (July 1957): inside cover.

"Mysterious Germ Makes 300 Bald." *New York Times*, January 17, 1926, p. 10.

"Nation's Chemists Censure Gov. Bilbo." *New York Times*, September 12, 1930, p. 16.

"Nature and Treatment of Alopecia." *New York Medical Journal*, November 24, 1900, p. 913.

Naunton, Ena. "Baldness." *Times-Picayune* (New Orleans), March 19, 1981, sec. 6, p. 4.

Nessler, Charles. *The Story of Hair.* New York: Boni and Liveright, 1928.

"No Cure for Baldness, Magazine Survey Says." *Times* (London), September 1983, p. 3.

"The Notebook." *FDA Consumer* 22 (June 1988): 30.

Nuttall, G. Clarke. "The Secret of Baldness." *Littell's Living Age*, April 16, 1898, 172–76.

"Offers Hope to the Bald." *New York Times*, February 11, 1920, p. 20.

Ohmann-Demesnil, A. H. "Some Successful Methods of Treating Alopecia and Alopecia Areata." *Medical News* August 6, 1892, 146–49.

Olsen, Elise A. "Topical Minoxidil in Early Male Pattern Baldness." *Journal of the American Academy of Dermatology* 13 (August 1985): 185–92.

"On the Bald." *Newsweek*, April 11, 1949, p. 54.

"On the Causes of Alopecia and of Its Greater Frequency in Males than Females." *American Journal of the Medical Sciences* 55 (April 1868): 416–18.

"101 Creates a Furore [*sic*] in Greece." *Beijing Review*, March 15, 1993, p. 32.

Owen, Richard. "Belgians Tackle Baldness." *Times* (London), February 6, 1987, p. 7.

Papa, Christopher M., and Albert Kligman. "Stimulation of Hair Growth by Topical Application of Androgens." *Journal of the American Medical Association*, February 15, 1965, pp. 521–25.

Parker, Delos L. "The Cause of Common Baldness." *Medical Record*, February 9, 1907, pp. 220–26.

_____ "The Etiology of Alopecia." *Medical Record*, July 13, 1901, pp. 45–51.

Passchier, J. "Why Men with Hair Loss Go to the Doctor." *Psychological Reports* 65 (August 1989): 323–30.

"Patients Satisfied with Hair." *Times-Picayune* (New Orleans), January 9, 1972, sec. 4, p. 16.

Peck, Renee. "Some Hair-Raising Experiments by a Tulane Researcher." *Times-Picayune* (New Orleans), February 10, 1984, sec. 5, pp. 1, 3.

Perlman, David. "Tissue Expander May Help Bald Men." *San Francisco Chronicle*, July 11, 1986, p. 10.

Perry, James A. "Shaving (Almost) Hair-Raising Experiences." *Times-Picayune* (New Orleans), June 7, 1990, pp. E1, E8.

Persson, Bertil. "The Kockum Study: Twenty-Two-Year Follow Up." *Acta Medica Scandinavia* 216, no. 5 (1984): 485–93.

"Pessimistic, Irritable?" *Montreal Gazette*, November 19, 1992, p. A11.

Petersen, Clarence. "And Now for the Baldfaced Truth." *Chicago Tribune*, April 8, 1988, sec. 5, p. 1.

Petit, Charles. "A Controversy Over Baldness Clinics." *San Francisco Chronicle*, February 3, 1979, p. 2.

Pincus, Walter. "The Federal Register." *Washington Post*, November 17, 1980, p. A3.

"Planting Hair on Bald Heads," *Scientific American*, August 1, 1914, pp. 83, 91.

"A Plea for the Bald." *New York Times*, May 15, 1948, p. 14.

"Pneumatic Cure for Baldness." *Medical Record*, December 30, 1899, p. 987.

"Poisoned by Hair Dye." *New York Times*, August 21, 1869, p. 6.

Pope, John. "Surgeon Scalps His Patient to Cure Baldness." *Times-Picayune* (New Orleans), March 22, 1981, p. 6.

"Potion Makes Bald Men Believers." *San Francisco Chronicle*, January 22, 1979, pp. 1, 16.

"Prescription for a Scalping." *New York Times*, March 19, 1987, p. 26.

"The Prevention of Baldness." *Medical Record*, August 4, 1906, p. 191.

Priest, Alicia. "Electrical Treatment for Baldness Claims Good Results." *Vancouver Sun*, August 4, 1990, p. A5.

"Primrose." *Times* (London), December 15, 1986, p. 3.

"ProCyte Study May Lead to New Drug for Baldness." *Wall Street Journal*, July 29, 1992, p. B4.

"Prophylaxis and Treatment of Baldness." *Medical Record*, July 11, 1903, p. 67.

"Proteins Point to Roots of Baldness." *Science News*, May 14, 1988, p. 311.

Pugh, Clifford. "The Bald Truth." *Houston Post Magazine*, September 27, 1987, p. 6.

"Pumping Air." *Esquire* 108 (September 1987): 231–32.

Purser, Philip. "Baldness Be My Friend." *Sunday Times* (London), April 22, 1979, p. 13.

"Putting the Brakes on the Baldness-Cure Bandwagon." *FDA Consumer* 21 (September 1987): 34–35.

Quickel, Stephen W. "Bald Spot." *Business Month* 134 (November 1989): 36–37+.

Rae, Stephen. "Real Men Don't Need Combs." *Newsweek*, February 28, 1983, p. 11.

"Reforested Pates." *Newsweek*, December 18, 1961, 60.

"Relations Between Alopecia and Dental Lesions." *New York Medical Journal*, December 8, 1900, p. 1002.

"Researchers Grow Hair in Test Tube." *Chicago Tribune*, October 26, 1990, sec. 1, p. 5.

Reynolds, Arthur R. "Why Men Are Bald." *American Magazine* 81 (February 1916): 21, 80–81.

Reynolds, Lester. "Science and Your Shining Pate," *Illustrated World* 28 (October 1917): 257–59.

Rhein, Reginald. "Upjohn Offers Hope for Those Balding Blues." *Chemical Week*, March 25, 1987, pp. 11, 13.

Robbins, Chris. "Bald Is Best." *Sunday Times* (London), January 5, 1975, p. 32.

Robertson, Bud. "Let the Buyer Beware When the Purchase Is Hair." *Winnipeg Free Press*, March 21, 1993, pp. A1, A8.

Robinson, Gaile. "Losing It." *Los Angeles Times*, June 2, 1991, pp. E1, E9.

Robinson, Timothy S. "Clinic Pair Guilty of Fraud for Promises of More Hair." *Washington Post*, July 2, 1975, pp. C1, C2.

Roll, Samuel. "Stereotypes of Scalp and Facial Hair As Measured by the Semantic Differential." *Psychological Reports* 28 (June 1971): 975–80.

Rolleston, J. D. "Dermatology and Folk-Lore." *The British Journal of Dermatology and Syphilis* 52 (1940): 43–57.

Roper, John. "Money Spent on Lost Hair Is Thrown Away *Which?* Says." *Times* (London), August 23, 1973, p. 16.

Rossi, Frank. "A Growing Problem." *Times-Picayune* (New Orleans), June 7, 1990, pp. E1, E8.

Rowan, Geoffrey. "Treatment Could Be a Real Hair Raiser." *Globe & Mail*, August 18, 1990, pp. B1, B2.

Royko, Mike. "Splitting Hairs Over Heady Issue." *Chicago Tribune*, October 12, 1984, p. 3.

Rubenstein, Steve. "How They Grow Hair in Australia." *San Francisco Chronicle*, July 19, 1979, p. 5.

Sakamaki, Sachiko. "Hair-Raising Sales Pitch." *Far Eastern Economic Review*, February 3, 1994, 48.

Sandomir, Richard. "Hail! The Bald and the Beautiful." *Los Angeles Times*, September 14, 1989, sec. 5, pp. 1, 5–7.

Sansing, John. "Bald Truths." *Washingtonian* 22 (July 1987): 103–5.

____"Mirror, Mirror, on the Wall, Please Give Me the Best Head of Hair of All." *Washingtonian* 18 (Jun3 1983): 138–43.

Savin, Ronald C. "The Ineffectiveness of Testosterone in Male Pattern Baldness." *Archives of Dermatology*, 98, no. 5 (November 1968): 512–14.

____"Minoxidil; Upjohn on Its Clinical Role." *Dermatologic Clinics*, 11, no. 1 (January 1993): 55–64.

"Says Brain's Growth Causes Baldness," *Science Digest* 40 (November 1956): 77.

"Says Diet Affects Hair Growth." *New York Times*, April 7, 1939, p. 16.

"Says Gland Extract Conquers Baldness." *New York Times*, November 4, 1931, p. 28.

"The Scalpers." *Time*, September 3, 1979, p. 49.

"Scientists Find a Key to Bald Heads." *San Francisco Chronicle*, May 2, 1986, p. 26.

"Scientists Ponder Bald Head Riddle." *New York Times*, February 11, 1950, p. 10.

Scott, Ruth Boyer. "Stop Worrying About Baldness." *Today's Health*, 36 (April 1958): 43+.

Segell, Michael. "The Bald Truth About Hair," *Esquire*, 121 (May 1994): 111–17.

Selzer, Richard. "Bald!" *Esquire* 85 (May 1976): 82–83.

"Shaving of the Head for Impending Baldness." *New York Medical Journal*, November 3, 1900, p. 767.

Sheppard, J. V. "The Myth of the Hairy Male." *Hygeia* 26 (June 1948): 408–9+.

Sherrod, Pamela. "Hair-Growth Drug Works, Upjohn Says." *Chicago Tribune*, April 30, 1986, sec. 3, p. 3.

"Side-Effects Normal for Baldness Cure." *Beijing Review*, October 17, 1988, p. 40.

Siegel, Mary-Ellen. *Reversing Hair Loss*. New York: Simon & Schuster, 1985.

Sigelman, Lee. "Hair Loss and Electability: The Bald Truth." *Journal of Nonverbal Behavior* 14, no. 4 (Winter 1990): 269–83.

Simon, Ted. "A Fringe Professor." *Times* (London), May 11, 1970, p. 12.

Sloan, Pat. "Hair-Restorer Drugs Brush with the FDA." *Advertising Age*, September 15, 1986, p. 82.

Smart, William. "You: The Bald Facts." *Washington Post*, July 21, 1981, p. D5.

Smilgis, Martha. "If Bald Isn't Beautiful." *People*, June 23, 1980, pp. 94, 96.

Smith, Adam. "Upjohn's Bald Ambitions." *Esquire* 106 (October 1986): 73–74.

Smith, Lee. "Hair-Raising Happenings at Upjohn." *Fortune*, April 6, 1981, pp. 67–69.

Snead, Elizabeth. "Toss That Toupee—Thinning Hair Is In." *USA Today*, int'l ed., November 28, 1990, p. 9A.

Snyder, Laurence H. "The Application of the Gene Frequency Method of Analysis to Sex-Influenced Factors, with Especial Reference to Baldness." *Human Biology* 7 (1935): 608–15.

Sparks, Fred. "I'm Glad I Bought a Toupee." *Saturday Evening Post*, December 15, 1956, pp. 32–33+.

Strangenes, Sharon. "Hot Water Washing May Hasten Hair Loss." *Times-Picayune* (New Orleans), November 24, 1983, sec. 9, p. 29.

"Static Electricity As a Cure for Alopecia." *New York Medical Journal*, November 8, 1902, p. 798.

Stern, Robert S. "Topical Minoxidil." *Archives of Dermatology* 123 (July 1986): 62–65.

Stevenson, Jeff. "Making Headway." *Men's Health* 8 (May 1993): 25.

Storin, Matthew V. "Facing Up to a Bald Spot." *Boston Globe*, April 9, 1989, p. 77.

"Strain Thins London Hair." *New York Times*, June 14, 1943, p. 20.

Stuttaford, Thomas. "Restoration of Self-Respect." *Times* (London), May 4, 1989, p. 12.

Sullivan, Walter. "A Baldness Cure May Be in Sight." *New York Times*, February 20, 1965, pp. 27, 29.

_____ "Hair-Loss Experts Cite Innovations." *New York Times*, June 17, 1983, p. 21.

"Symposium on Baldness." *New York Times*, June 27, 1913, p. 8.

Szasz, Thomas S. "A Theory of the Pathogenesis of Ordinary Human Baldness." *Archives of Dermatology and Syphilology* 61 (January 1950): 34–48.

Tanne, Janice Hopkins. "Gone Today, Hair Tomorrow." *New York*, December 10, 1984, pp. 70+.

Tanner, Wilda B. *The Mystical, Magical, Marvelous World of Dreams*. Tahlequah, Okla.: Sparrow Hawk, 1988.

"Tense Tops Start Baldness." *Science News Letter*, April 12, 1947, p. 228.

"Test Tube Hair Prompts Hope on Baldness." *New York Times*, October 27, 1990, p. 24.

Teufexis, Anastasia. "Some Bald Facts About Minoxidil." *Time*, July 14, 1986, p. 43.

"Their Loss, His Gain." *New York Times*, August 31, 1891, p. 3.

"There's No Known Cure for Baldness, U.S. Rules." *New York Times*, February 2, 1956, p. 54.

"There's a Risk in Going Bare-Headed." *New York Times*, September 14, 1925, p. 18.

Thompson, Richard C. "Balding Is Forever, Experts Say." *FDA Consumer* 15 (February 1981): 10–12.

Thomson, Hugh. "Why Men Won't Own Up to Wigs." *Sunday Times* (London), June 5, 1977, p. 43.

Thorne, Van Buren. "Baldness and Curealls." *New York Times*, January 8, 1922, sec. 7, p. 12.

Thornton, Jimmy. "Baldness No Joke—It's a Glaring Problem." *Times-Picayune* (New Orleans), March 29k, 1981, sec. 3, p. 2.

"Those Baldness Cures." *Science Digest* 37 (April 1955): back cover.

"£3,902 Damages for Hair Graft Blunder." *Times* (London), February 16, 1983, p. 3.

"Time Himself Is Bald." *New York Times Magazine*, April 9, 1967, pp. 126–27.

"A Time to Shine." *Sports Illustrated*, May 22, 1989, p. 11.

"Top Secret." *Times* (London), January 15, 1976, p. 14.

"Town Hosts Convention to Help Bald Men Celebrate Lack of Roots." *Houston Post*, September 11, 1982, p. 4A.

"Treatment for Baldness." *Which?* (August 1973):228–31.

"Treatment of Baldness by Simple Aseptic Irritation." *Medical News*, February 4, 1899, p. 144.

"Treatments and Preparations for the Hair and Scalp." *Hygeia* 27 (June 1949): 382–83+.

Trier, Beth. "Jojoba—Snake Oil or Miracle." *San Francisco Chronicle*, August 14, 1979, p. 19.

"Twentieth Century Baldness." *Medical Record*, August 20, 1921, p. 343.

Ubell, Earl. "Is Baldness Reversible?" *Washington Post*, July 19, 1987, Parade sec., pp. 14–15.

"Ultraviolet Light in Alopecia." *New York Medical Journal*, July 27, 1912, p. 192.

"Upjohn Co. Moves to Protect Sole Rights to Baldness Drug." *Washington Post*, April 9, 1987, p. E12.

"Upjohn Draws U.S. Scrutiny." *New York Times*, May 10, 1986, p. 36.

"Upjohn Files Suit." *New York Times*, October 14, 1988, p. D3.

"Upjohn in Filing on Baldness Cure." *New York Times*, December 20, 1985, p. D4.

"Upjohn Plant." *New York Times*, August 8, 1985, p. D5.

"The Value of the Cooper Hewitt Quartz Lamp in the Treatment of Alopecia." *Medical Record*, December 2, 1916, p. 1008.

"Vitamins Won't Put Hair on Bald Head, U.S. Says." *New York Times*, March 27, 1962, p. 57.

Voinovich, Vladimir. "The Bald and the Hairy." *Economist* 72 (February 1989): 41–42.

Vorspan, Albert. "America's Hair Apparent." *New York Times*, April 30, 1983, p. 23.

Waldholz, Michael. "Merck Says Experimental Prostate Drug Might Grow Hair on Bald Men's Heads." *Wall Street Journal*, April 20, 1992, p. B6.

Walker, Gerald. "Baldness Unbared." *New York Times Magazine*, January 4, 1959, p. 62.

Walker, Ken. "Baldness Linked to Heart Disease." *Times-Colonist* (Victoria, B.C.), October 24, 1993, p. A9.

"Warning Against New Baldness Cures." *Scientific American* 146 (March 1932): 175, 179.

"Warning on Experimental Baldness Drug." *FDA Consumer* 19 (November 1985): 4–5.

Warshofsky, Fred. "Science Tackles the Baldness Problem." *Reader's Digest* 88 (February 1966): 87–91.

Wegars, Don. "Hair Grower Gets Mussed." *San Francisco Chronicle*, October 2, 1981, p. 2.

_____ "The Hair Grower's Fans." *San Francisco Chronicle*, October 3, 1981, p. 2.

Wellborn, Stanley N. "Searching for Their Roots." *U.S. News & World Report*, October 27, 1986, p. 66.

Wells, Linda. "New Hope for Hair Growth May Lie in Drug Study." *New York Times*, December 20, 1986, p. 33.

"What Causes Baldness?" *New York Times*, May 24, 1913, p. 12.

White, Frank III. "How Young Men Cope with Baldness." *Ebony* 38 (June 1983): 54+.

"Why It Is—Or Isn't." *Newsweek*, May 23, 1960, pp. 107A–107B.

"Will Women Lose Their Hair?" *Science Digest* 11 (May 1942): 84.

Witt, Howard. "Drug Less Than Hair-Raising in Canada." *Chicago Tribune*, March 19, 1987, sec. 3, pp. 1, 6.

"Women May Get Bald." *Los Angeles Times*, December 19, 1926, p. 1.

Woodruff, David. "For Rogaine No Miracle Cure—Yet." *Business Week*, June 4, 1990, p. 100.

Woolridge, Jane. "20 Million American Men Are Facing the Bare Facts." *Times-Picayune* (New Orleans), November 17, 1985, p. B9.

"World Rally of Bald Men Held." *Times* (London), May 24, 1960, p. 12.

Wright, Pearce. "Skin-Deep Key to Curing Baldness." *Times* (London), October 16, 1984, p. 3.

Yao Jianguo. "Chinese Trichogen Cure Finds Market." *Beijing Review*, November 3, 1986, p. 29.

Zappacosta, Anthony R. "Reversal of Baldness in One Patient Receiving Minoxidil for Hypertension." *New England Journal of Medicine*, December 18, 1980, p. 1480.

Zhao Xuejun. "Zhao Zhangguang—Inventor of 101 Hair Tonic." *Beijing Review*, October 17, 1988, pp. 26–29.

Zorn, Eric. "Some Men Take a Shine to Baldness in Women." *Chicago Tribune*, August 17, 1980, p. 3.

INDEX

209